TIME
ANNUAL
1992: The Year In Review

Published by TIME Books
Time Inc.
1271 Avenue of the Americas
New York, NY 10020

ISBN: 0-8487-1156-4
EAN: 978-08487-1156-6
Printed in the United States of America
First edition

TIME

1992: The Year in Review

TIME
ANNUAL

1992: THE YEAR IN REVIEW

Election of the year?

The struggle to fix America's economy

"No justice, no peace!" In Los Angeles, rage bursts from the shadows

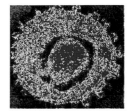

EDITOR-IN-CHIEF: Jason McManus
EDITORIAL DIRECTOR: Richard B. Stolley
CORPORATE EDITOR: Gilbert Rogin
DIRECTOR OF NEW MEDIA: John Papanek

TIME INC.
CHAIRMAN, CEO: Reginald K. Brack Jr.
PRESIDENT: Don Logan
EXECUTIVE VICE PRESIDENTS: Donald J. Barr, Donald M. Elliman Jr., Robert L. Miller

TIME

Founders: Briton Hadden 1898-1929   Henry R. Luce 1898-1967

MANAGING EDITOR: Henry Muller
DEPUTY MANAGING EDITOR: John F. Stacks
EXECUTIVE EDITORS: Richard Duncan, Ronald Kriss
ASSISTANT MANAGING EDITORS: Walter Isaacson, James Kelly
EDITOR AT LARGE: Strobe Talbott
EDITORIAL OPERATIONS DIRECTOR: Oliver Knowlton
SENIOR EDITORS: Charles P. Alexander, Joelle Attinger, Nancy R. Gibbs, S.C. Gwynne, Stephen Koepp, Johanna McGeary, Christopher Porterfield, Barrett Seaman, Claudia Wallis, Paul A. Witteman
ART DIRECTOR: Rudolph C. Hoglund
GRAPHICS DIRECTOR: Nigel Holmes   **DESIGN DIRECTOR:** Arthur Hochstein
CHIEF OF RESEARCH: Betty Satterwhite Sutter
PICTURE EDITOR: Michele Stephenson
COPY CHIEF: Susan L. Blair   **PRODUCTION MANAGER:** Gail Music
SENIOR WRITERS: George J. Church, Richard Corliss, Martha Duffy, Paul Gray, John Greenwald, William A. Henry III, Robert Hughes, Richard Lacayo, Eugene Linden, Lance Morrow, Bruce W. Nelan, Priscilla Painton, Walter Shapiro, Richard Zoglin
ASSOCIATE EDITORS: Richard Behar, Janice Castro, Philip Elmer-DeWitt, Christine Gorman, Sophfronia Scott Gregory, Michael D. Lemonick, Thomas McCarroll, Richard N. Ostling, Janice C. Simpson, Jill Smolowe, Anastasia Toufexis
CONTRIBUTORS: Kurt Andersen, Bonnie Angelo, Laurence I. Barrett, Jesse Birnbaum, Jay Cocks, Barbara Ehrenreich, John Elson, Otto Friedrich, Pico Iyer, Edward L. Jamieson (Consulting Editor), Leon Jaroff, Stefan Kanfer, Michael Kinsley, Charles Krauthammer, Dennis Overbye, Richard Schickel, R.Z. Sheppard, John Skow, Martha Smilgis, Richard Stengel, George M. Taber, Andrew Tobias
ASSISTANT EDITORS: Ursula Nadasdy de Gallo, Andrea Dorfman, Brigid O'Hara-Forster, William Tynan, Sidney Urquhart, Jane Van Tassel (Department Heads); Bernard Baumohl, David Bjerklie, Val Castronovo, Mary McC. Fernandez, Georgia Harbison, Ratu Kamlani, Sue Raffety, Susan M. Reed, Elizabeth Rudulph, Susanne Washburn, Linda Young
REPORTERS: Ginia Bellafante, Elizabeth L. Bland, Ketanji O. Brown, Barbara Burke, Wendy Cole, Tom Curry, Kathryn Jackson Fallon, Janice M. Horowitz, Jeanette Isaac, Daniel S. Levy, Michael Quinn, Andrea Sachs, Alain L. Sanders, David Seidman, David E. Thigpen
COPY DESK: Judith Anne Paul, Shirley Barden Zimmerman (Deputies); Barbara Dudley Davis, Evelyn Hannon, Jill Ward (Copy Coordinators); Minda Bikman, Doug Bradley, Robert Braine, Bruce Christopher Carr, Barbara Collier, Julia Van Buren Dickey, Dora Fairchild, Judith Kales, Sharon Kapnick, Claire Knopf, Melinda J. McAdams, M.M. Merwin, Anna F. Monardo, Maria A. Paul, Jane Rigney, Elyse Segelken, Terry Stoller, Amelia Weiss (Copy Editors)
BUREAUS: Suzanne Davis (Director of Administration) **Chief Political Correspondent:** Michael Kramer **Washington Contributing Editor:** Hugh Sidey **Senior Correspondents:** David Aikman, Jonathan Beaty, Sandra Burton, Barry Hillenbrand, J. Madeleine Nash, Frederick Ungeheuer, Bruce van Voorst
Washington: Stanley W. Cloud, Ann Blackman, Margaret Carlson, Michael Duffy, Dan Goodgame, Ted Gup, Julie Johnson, J.F.O. McAllister, Jay Peterzell, Elaine Shannon, Dick Thompson, Nancy Traver, Adam Zagorin **Boston:** Sam Allis **Chicago:** Jon D. Hull, Elizabeth Taylor **Detroit:** William McWhirter **Atlanta:** Michael Riley **Houston:** Richard Woodbury **Miami:** Cathy Booth **Los Angeles:** Jordan Bonfante, Sally B. Donnelly, Jeanne McDowell, Sylvester Monroe, James Willwerth, Patrick E. Cole **San Francisco:** David S. Jackson
London: William Mader **Paris:** Thomas A. Sancton, Margot Hornblower **Brussels:** Jay Branegan **Bonn:** James O. Jackson **Central Europe:** James L. Graff **Moscow:** John Kohan, James Carney, Ann M. Simmons **Rome:** John Moody **Istanbul:** James Wilde **Jerusalem:** Lisa Beyer **Cairo:** Dean Fischer, William Dowell **Beirut:** Lara Marlowe **Nairobi:** Marguerite Michaels, Andrew Purvis **Johannesburg:** Scott MacLeod **New Delhi:** Jefferson Penberthy **Beijing:** Jaime A. FlorCruz **Southeast Asia:** Richard Hornik **Tokyo:** Edward W. Desmond, Kumiko Makihara **Ottawa:** Gavin Scott **Latin America:** Laura López
Administration: Susan Lynd, David Richardson, Hope Almash, Melissa August, Breena Clarke, Donald N. Collins, Joan A. Connelly, Ann V. King, Linda Lofaro, Anne D. Moffett, Judith R. Stoler **News Desks:** Brian Doyle, Waits L. May III, Susanna M. Schrobsdorff, Pamela H. Thompson, Diana Tollerson, Ann Drury Wellford, Mary Wormley
ART: Betsy Brecht, Robert C. Raines (Senior Associate Directors); Linda Louise Freeman (Covers); Steve Conley, Thomas M. Miller, Billy Powers, Ina Saltz (Associate Art Directors); Joseph Aslaender, Kenneth B. Smith (Assistant Art Directors); David Drapkin, Leah M. Purcell (Designers); John P. Dowd (Traffic) **Maps and Charts:** Joe Lertola (Associate Graphics Director); Paul J. Pugliese (Chief of Cartography); Leslie Dickstein, Steven D. Hart, Deborah L. Wells **Administration:** Marilyn Rudnick-Salinger
PHOTOGRAPHY: Richard L. Booth, MaryAnne Golon, Rose Keyser, Robert B. Stevens (Associate Editors); Kevin J. McVea (Operations); Renee Mancini (Syndication); Arnold H. Drapkin (Consultant); Dorothy Affa Ames, Sarah Buffum, Gary Roberts, Nancy Smith-Alam (Assistant Editors); Cristina T. Scalet, Marie Tobias, Mary Worrell-Bousquette (Researchers) **Bureaus:** Martha Bardach, Sahm Doherty, Leny Heinen, Stanley Kayne, Glenn Mack, Barbara Nagelsmith, Anni Rubinger, Melanie Stephens, Simonetta Toraldo **Photographers:** Terry Ashe, P.F. Bentley, William Campbell, Greg Davis, Rudi Frey, Dirck Halstead, Kenneth Jarecke, Cynthia Johnson, Shelly Katz, David Hume Kennerly, Steve Liss, Christopher Morris, Robin Moyer, Carl Mydans, James Nachtwey, Matthew Naythons, Robert Nickelsberg, Chris Niedenthal, David Rubinger, Anthony Suau, Ted Thai, Diana Walker
MAKEUP: Charlotte J. Quiggle (Chief)
TECHNOLOGY: Ken Baierlein (Manager); Nora Jupiter, Kevin Kelly, George Mendel, Peter K. Niceberg, Michael M. Sheehan, Lamarr Tsufura
IMAGING: Mark Stelzner (Manager); Gerard Abrahamsen, Lois Rubenstein (Supervisors); Steven Cadicamo, Charlotte Coco, John Dragonetti, Raphael Joa, Kin Wah Lam, Carl Leidig, Linda Parker, Robert Pfleger, Mark P. Polomski, Richard Shaffer, David Spatz, Lorri Stenton, Paul White
PRODUCTION: Joseph J. Scafidi (Deputy); Trang Ba Chuong, Theresa Kelliher, L. Rufino-Armstrong (Supervisors); Robert L. Becker, Silvia Castañeda Contreras, Michael Dohne, Osmar Escalona, Garry Hearne, Agustin Lamboy, Jeannine Laverty, Janet L. Lugo, Peter J. McGullam, Sandra Maupin, Michael Skinner
ADMINISTRATION: Rafael Soto, Alan J. Abrams, Catherine M. Barnes, Denise Brown, Tresa Chambers, Anne M. Considine, Tosca LaBoy, Marilyn V.S. McClenahan, Katharine K. McNevin, Elliot Ravetz, Teresa D. Sedlak, Deborah R. Slater, Marianne Sussman, Raymond Violini
EDITORIAL FINANCE: Genevieve Christy (Manager); Patricia Hermes, Esther Cedeño, Morgan Krug, Katherine Young (Domestic); Camille Sanabria, Carl Harmon, Sheila Charney, Aston Wright (News Service); Linda D. Vartoogian, Wayne Chun, Edward Nana Osei-Bonsu (Pictures)
LETTERS: Amy Musher (Chief); Gloria J. Hammond (Deputy); Marian Powers (Administration)
EDITORIAL SERVICES: Christiana Walford (Director); Jennie Chien, Hanns Kohl, Benjamin Lightman, Beth Bencini Zarcone

TIME INTERNATIONAL
MANAGING EDITOR: Karsten Prager
Assistant Managing Editor: José M. Ferrer III
Senior Editors: Christopher Redman, George Russell
Senior Writer: James Walsh
Associate Editors: William R. Doerner, Barbara Rudolph, Michael S. Serrill
Contributors: Robert Ball, Marguerite Johnson, Dominique Moïsi, Christopher Ogden, Frederick Painton, Michael Walsh
Assistant Editors: Tam Martinides Gray (Research Chief), Ariadna Victoria Rainert (Administration), Oscar Chiang, Lois Gilman, Valerie Johanna Marchant, Adrianne Jucius Navon
Reporters: Kevin Fedarko, Sinting Lai, Emily Mitchell, Lawrence Mondi, Jeffery C. Rubin, Megan Rutherford, Sribala Subramanian
Art: Jane Frey (Senior Associate Director); James Elsis (Associate Director); Nomi Silverman (Assistant Art Director); Victoria Nightingale (Designer)
Photography: Julia Richer (Associate Editor); Eleanor Taylor, Karen Zakrison (Assistant Editors)
Makeup: Eugene F. Coyle (Chief); Alison E. Ruffley, Leonard Schulman
Administration: Helga Halaki, Barbara Milberg

PUBLISHER: Elizabeth P. Valk
Associate Publisher/Advertising: Edward R. McCarrick
General Manager: Gregory J. Zorthian
Consumer Marketing Director: Kenneth Godshall
Production Director: Brian F. O'Leary
Business Manager: A.P. Duffy
Marketing Director: Linda McCutcheon Conneally
Public Affairs Director: Robert Pondiscio

TIME
ANNUAL

1992: The Year In Review

Editor
Edward Jamieson

Managing Editor
Kelly Knauer

Art Director
Janet Waegel

Picture Editor
Mary Worrell Bousquette

Research Director
Leah Gordon

Editorial Production
Michael Skinner

Essays
George J. Church, Richard Corliss, Paul Gray, John Greenwald, Michael Kramer, Lance Morrow, J. Madeleine Nash, Hugh Sidey

Information Design
Nigel Holmes, Joe Lertola, Steve Hart, Deborah Wells

Research Associates
Beth Bland, Ketanji Brown, Wendy Cole, Lois Gilman

Assistant Picture Editor
Jay Colton

Design Associates
Leah Purcell, Carl Ferrero

Special thanks to:
Susan Blair, Richard Duncan, Linda Freeman, Arthur Hochstein, Rudy Hoglund, Kevin Kelly, Oliver Knowlton, Bob Marshall, Gail Music, Paul Pugliese, Betty Satterwhite, Michele Stephenson, Mark Stelzner, Lamarr Tsufura

---

NEW BUSINESS DEVELOPMENT
Director
David Gitow

Assistant Director
Mary Warner McGrade

Senior Manager
Frederica Wald

Operations Director
Deborah Heilig

Production Director
John Calvano

The work of the following TIME writers and editors is represented in this volume:

Charles P. Alexander, Sam Allis, Laurence I. Barrett, Margaret Carlson, James Carney, Janice Castro, George J. Church, Jay Cocks, Richard Corliss, Martha Duffy, Michael Duffy, David Ellis, Philip Elmer-Dewitt, Kevin Fedarko, Nancy Gibbs, Dan Goodgame, Christine Gorman, Paul Gray, John Greenwald, Sophfronia Scott Gregory, S. C. Gwynne, William A. Henry III, Margot Hornblower, Jon D. Hull, Robert Hughes, Walter Isaacson, Pico Iyer, James O. Jackson, Marguerite Johnson, John Kohan, Michael Kramer, Richard Lacayo, Scott MacLeod, Thomas McCarroll, Jeanne McDowell, Lance Morrow, Bruce Nelan, Richard N. Ostling, Priscilla Painton, Michael Riley, Richard Schickel, Walter Shapiro, Hugh Sidey, Janice C. Simpson, Jill Smolowe, Strobe Talbott, Anastasia Toufexis, Michael Walsh, John Wyles, Richard Zoglin

Foreword

THIS 1992 TIME *ANNUAL* CAN perhaps most easily be defined by what it is not. It is not a picture book or a coffee-table book, though it features many of the year's most remarkable photographs and lends itself, we hope, to repeated revisiting and page turning. It is not an almanac of 1992, though it does provide many valuable statistics about the year. Nor is it the weekly TIME magazine on steroids, a compilation of readers' favorite stories of 1992—although it does contain a generous helping of those. Instead, the TIME *Annual* draws something from the impulse behind each of these ideas in its effort to involve the reader in the great—and a few not-so-great—events of 1992.

The *Annual* employs all the journalistic tools at TIME magazine's command. But here the reporting, writing, illustration and photographs are designed to outline and illuminate an entire year rather than a single week. The book's greater length and freer format allow for longer stories than the weekly, for a more lavish display of pictures, for the creation of graphics on a larger scale, for essays whose reach encompasses "this year" rather than "this week."

Much of the material in the volume is created specifically for its pages. Taking a leaf from TIME's new design, introduced in April 1992, the book leads off with the Year in Review, a month-by-month overview of the major news events of the year. Eight TIME writers have contributed new essays to introduce the major sections of the book; a new picture gallery showcases the most memorable images from the Olympic Games; and TIME's graphics department has created new charts for the volume. All the news stories in the book have been re-edited, redesigned and updated; some draw material from more than 20 separate TIME stories to provide a single running narrative.

The book reflects the tone of a year in which the capitals of the world's mental map were Sarajevo, Mogadishu and South Central Los Angeles, a year in which people around the globe expressed the hope for a "new world order." This volume cannot truthfully report that those dreams were realized; instead, its editors hope it provides an orderly presentation of 12 exciting but most unruly months.

TIME
ANNUAL

THE YEAR IN REVIEW

By PAUL GRAY

O N NEW YEAR'S MORNING 1992, THE EARTH awoke—for the first time in more than two millenniums—without a governing empire. The final collapse of the Soviet Union in December 1991 had slapped shut, at least for the time being, history's book on the imperium. Once voracious powers were no longer expanding through force; they were pulling themselves apart by choice. As a result, the old specter of the cold war, of a bipolar world spinning under the threat of nuclear annihilation, was dwindling into memories.

As it happened, there would be little time for remembering during the year that followed. The cold war left behind a jumbled worldscape, in many respects a clean slate. Mapmakers worked overtime trying to keep pace with the proliferation of new nations splintering off the communist bloc. Binding alliances and allegiances vaporized almost overnight. Something was bound to take their place—people cannot live together without rules and loyalties—and the new ways were also bound to break sharply with the recent past.

Surprises were to be expected, and they came. At the beginning of the year, hardly anyone thought George Bush could lose the 1992 presidential election; certainly not such prominent Democrats as Mario Cuomo, Lloyd Bentsen, Bill Bradley and Sam Nunn, who all found reasons not to contest a popular incumbent. That chore fell to a little-known Arkansas Governor who, running against 12 years of Republican White House entrenchment, naturally made "change" his campaign mantra. The invocation worked magic because the electorate, no longer concerned with an overseas Soviet threat, looked homeward and did not like what it saw.

Spirits were low, moods ugly. The April Los Angeles riot—the costliest and most lethal civil disorder in U.S. history—traced in flames the image of a society at war with itself. Tensions were triggered not only by race but also by money: too little of it to go around and not enough hope that times would get better. THE ECONOMY, STUPID, read a hortatory sign at Clinton campaign headquarters; somehow George Bush did not get the message. His international achievements struck many voters as irrelevant. The world may have been made safer under his watch, but the nation seemed to be growing poorer and more dangerous.

One of Bush's last major foreign policy acts—dispatching U.S. troops to aid food distribution in Somalia—was thus poignant and ironic. Both the U.S. President and the Somalis had been caught up in post–cold war confusions. The stick-thin women and children who began appearing in the news in midsummer were starving not because there was no food to give them but because of anarchy caused by warring clans. Somalia had quite recently been a strategic cold war location on the Indian Ocean, with a cooperative dictator in place, accepting aid and arms from the Soviets first and after 1977 from the U.S. When superpower interest waned and the dictator was toppled, ancient feuds re-emerged, the antagonists bearing modern weapons.

Operation Restore Hope displayed a familiar strain in the U.S. character: a willingness to help, to take on faraway problems that poorer or more prudent nations avoid. In the geopolitical past, critics could always claim that American benevolence only masked self-interest. That was not so in Somalia, where the sole purpose was to enable starving people to eat. But if humanitarian aid had become a U.S. military objective, why limit it to one country? What about Bosnia and Herzegovina?

It grew obvious during the year that something wicked was happening in what had once been Yugoslavia. Again, news pictures provoked disbelief: a prison enclosure and emaciated figures peering with hopeless eyes through a snarl of barbed wire. The term for this barbarism, Serbs blandly suggested, was "ethnic cleansing," meaning that Muslims and Croats were being driven, by any means necessary, out of territories the Serbs were trying to control. Among those means were siege, starvation, massacre and systematic rape. Relief workers spoke of fierce fighting with no clear front lines, of neighbor brutalizing neighbor, of a bewildering crossfire of bullets and hatreds.

The new Balkan mess added to an already increasing testiness within and between the nations of Europe. The long delicate progress toward economic and political unity hit some bumps. Danish voters rejected a treaty that would have taken the unification process a step further. Squabbles broke out over currency exchange rates. In reunified Germany, a neo-Nazi fringe reacted violently to the presence of immigrants and foreign workers. Some wondered aloud whether the ideal of a single Europe was still worth working for. Why unify, why submit to some central authority when so much of the rest of the world was dividing?

For all their surface variety, the changes of 1992 moved in the pattern of an old debate, one that was frozen in place rather than solved by the cold war. Empires beg this question by dictating the answer: On what basis should people live together and govern themselves? Last year, free to think for themselves, millions decided that separatism was the best answer. It is easy to understand the appeal. Separatism originates in the closest, most intimate human ties, in the family, on the common ground of shared history, race, culture or religious belief. First impressions of the outside world are shaped by such influences. Identity, solace, understanding, purpose, pride—all can be found in the company of the familiar, within the circle of People Like Us.

There is nothing inherently wrong with the clan or the tribe. But separatism has an unfortunate side effect, as 1992 proved: it can turn ugly and dangerous when it breeds intolerance of the unfamiliar, of People Like Them.

Separatism originates in the most intimate human ties . . . but it can turn dangerous when it breeds intolerance of the unfamiliar, of People Like Them

To those unversed in the former Yugoslavia, there is little visible evidence to distinguish a Serb from a Croat from a Muslim. The same is true of Somalia, where virtually all the citizens share the same ethnic and tribal backgrounds and a devotion to Islam as well. Yet the dissimilarities these people, in Yugoslavia, in Somalia, saw among themselves led to unimaginable cruelties and slaughter.

The year ended with a sweeping new disarmament treaty between the U.S. and Russia. Compared with the old possibility of nuclear apocalypse, 1992's outbreaks of violence can be seen as regrettable but mercifully limited, confined to a few pockets of unusual volatility. That is an accurate but shortsighted view. If 1992 taught anything, it was the self-perpetuating and contagious nature of small hatreds. They feed on themselves. They spread not only through actual offenses but through the suspicion that offenses are being planned by the other side. Hitting first seems a better plan than hitting back. How to halt this escalation of private quarrels without resorting to the iron fist or the jailer's lash? 1993 arrived with no good answer in sight.   ■

JANUARY

"I was just trying to get some attention," Bush quipped after fainting

NATION

Bush's Bad Trip

Pushing trade in Japan, the President gets promises—and a bug

WITH THE U.S. ECONOMY AND HIS APPROVAL ratings slumping, George Bush turned hunter-gatherer, trekking through four Pacific nations with an entourage of corporate chiefs on a quest to relax trade barriers and return home laden with "jobs, jobs, jobs." The mission was impossible. Bush was derided at home for belittling his office, publicly lectured by Japan's Prime Minister—even denounced by his fellow travelers from Detroit, who found the visit's trade deals scanty.

But the nadir came at a state dinner in Tokyo, when the fatigued President vomited on Kiichi Miyazawa's trousers and briefly passed out on the floor. Though Bush recovered quickly, the spectacle of Miyazawa cradling the fallen leader of the free world in his lap sent shudders around the globe and became an easy metaphor for the American economy: flat on its back, seeking succor from a resurgent Japan.

> ❝ This 15th of January will be inscribed in golden letters in 14 centuries of Croatian existence. ❞
>
> –President Franco **Tudjman** *of newly independent Croatia*

Clinton's Crisis

A tabloid tale of adultery derails the issues in New Hampshire

AS FEBRUARY'S PRIMARY APPROACHED, THE Democratic presidential pack began to thin out in the snows of New Hampshire. First to go was Governor Douglas Wilder of Virginia. Then Governor Mario Cuomo—the Hamlet of Albany—refused to get in, after a long tease. But the spotlight fell most harshly on the promising campaign of national newcomer and Arkansas Governor Bill Clinton. The supermarket tabloid *Star* paid for and printed allegations by state employee and sometime cabaret singer Gennifer Flowers that she and Clinton had a 12-year affair. The candidate and wife Hillary took their case to the nation on *60 Minutes* following the SuperBowl. Clinton denied all of Flowers' allegations, while refusing to discuss whether he had ever committed adultery.

WORLD

Chaos in Georgia

Gamsakhurdia flees as Tbilisi burns

IN 1991 HE BECAME the first person to win the presidency of a Soviet republic by popular vote. But now anticommunist leader Zviad Gamsakhurdia of Georgia made history of a different sort: he became the first elected President of a former Soviet republic to be ousted in a paramilitary coup. Following two weeks of fighting

A victorious rebel in burning Tbilisi

in the capital of Tbilisi, Gamsakhurdia and his followers took to the hills, fleeing to Armenia.

Elsewhere:

- **Cuba** Air Force Lieutenant Jerman Pompa Gonzales commandeered a troop transport helicopter and flew to asylum in Florida with 33 friends and relatives.
- **Russia** Boris Yeltsin freed prices, which soared overnight, further devaluing the ruble.
- **Korea** North and South Korea signed a six-point "expression of principle" restricting nuclear weapons on the Korean peninsula.
- **Algeria** The army forced the resignation of President Chadli Benjedid and canceled elections that had promised to hand power to Muslim fundamentalists.
- **Haiti** Record numbers of Haitians fled by sea to the U.S., which refused asylum and interned them at Guantánamo Bay naval base.

Setting Their Sights On the Rising Sun

Sport of the month: Japan bashing

ON THE HEELS OF GEORGE BUSH'S ILL-FATED trade trip to Japan, a wave of anti-Japanese sentiment swept America. Writer Michael Crichton made hay from the frenzy with his potboiler-cum-tirade *Rising Sun*, which charged the Japanese with conspiring to subvert America's economy from within. The Los Angeles County transportation commission yanked a contract for railcars from Japan's Sumitomo and claimed it would build the cars in L.A. By year's end the fever had passed, and the commission quietly gave Sumitomo a smaller contract for new cars.

Elsewhere:
- **R.H. Macy,** the 134-year-old New York City retailer, filed for bankruptcy.

Stopping Silicone

The FDA clamps down on breast implants for women

IN A DECISION THAT STUNNED MILLIONS OF women around the world, FDA chief David Kessler declared a moratorium on silicone

breast implants. Citing new evidence of health risks from leakage, Dr. Kessler urged surgeons to stop inserting the implants in women. In Spain and Australia health officials quickly followed suit; Canada, Britain and France promised to review their policies.

The FDA decision to halt silicone implants struck a drug industry already reeling from investigations and lawsuits involving such widely used nostrums as the sleeping pill Halcion and the antidepressant Prozac

LET IT SNOW, LET IT SNOW, LET IT SNOW

Heralding an unpredictable weather year throughout the world, a 16-in. snowfall surprised Jerusalem—and led to some highly unorthodox pastimes

Shake, Seattle, and Roll

Nirvana tops the charts, and America takes the plunge for grunge

WHO *ARE* THESE GUYS? IN A MOVE THAT STUNNED the record industry, upstart Seattle rockers Nirvana rode their independent release *Nevermind* to the top of *Billboard*'s hit list. Initially derided as a freak blip on the music scene, Nirvana's success actually heralded the emergence of a full-blown Seattle "grunge rock" scene. By year's end fellow Washington State bands Pearl Jam, Soundgarden and Alice in Chains were also high on the charts, and the scene had been Hollywoodized in the movie *Singles*.

Nirvana's *Nevermind:* the album cover

- **Hospitalized** Mother Theresa, 81, apostle to Calcutta's poor and afflicted, was treated for pneumonia and congestive heart failure in La Jolla, Calif.
- **Silenced** Howard Cosell, 73, retired from his two shows for ABC radio. His 14 years on ABC-TV's *Monday Night Football* had made Cosell one of the most liked—and disliked—sports journalists in America.

FEBRUARY

Take that! G.O.P. maverick Pat Buchanan was giving the White House fits in New Hampshire.

> **❝ I know society will never be able to forgive me. I know the families of the victims will never be able to forgive me for what I have done. ❞**
>
> –*Milwaukee serial killer* **Jeffrey Dahmer,** *on being sentenced to 15 consecutive life terms*

NATION

Mad as Hell, Voters Turn to New Faces

New Hampshire likes Pat Buchanan and Paul Tsongas

ENRAGED BY HARD TIMES, NEW HAMPSHIRE'S Republican primary voters registered a primal scream of discontent, giving incumbent George Bush only 53% of their vote while lavishing 37% on upstart right-wing commentator Pat Buchanan. The warning was clear.

Next-door neighbor Paul Tsongas won the Democratic race with 33% of the vote. But Bill Clinton claimed that his second-place finish at 25% made him the "Comeback Kid," as he survived withering assaults on his character. Following the Gennifer Flowers brouhaha, Clinton's campaign was rocked by a second charge: that he had used influence to dodge the draft while a Rhodes scholar at Oxford. The losers: Vietnam vet Senator Bob Kerrcy of Nebraska (11%), Iowa's old-line liberal Senator Tom Harkin (10%) and quixotic 800-number warrior Jerry Brown (8%).

Perot Is Willing

Call-ins create a controversy

AT THE MOMENT IT WAS LITTLE NOTED, BUT ITS implications were extraordinary. Appearing on Larry King's talk show on CNN, Texas electron-

ics billionaire Ross Perot announced he would run for the presidency—if the public were to show its support by placing his name on the ballot in all 50 states. A telephone blitz from cheering Perot admirers created a boomlet. And before you could say "Ross is my hoss," a campaign was born.

WORLD

Israel's Revenge

Hizballah is hit hard, but peace talks stay on track in Washington

THE VIOLENCE BEGAN FEB. 14, WHEN ARAB guerrillas infiltrated an Israeli army camp and hacked three soldiers to death. Two days later, Israeli Apache helicopters fired three missiles at the motorcade of Sheik Abbas Musawi, leader of the Iranian-backed Hizballah, killing Musawi and his wife and son. When Hizballah retaliated with rockets, the Jewish state sent a column of armored vehicles into two Hizballah strongholds; eight U.N. peacekeepers were wounded. Surprisingly, the dismal spiral of violence had no impact on the Middle East peace process. Lebanon, Syria and even Palestine—after threatening to boycott—attended the third round of talks in the U.S.

Elsewhere:

● **Ireland** The Irish Supreme Court overturned a High Court ruling that had prevented a pregnant 14-year-old from traveling to Britain to circumvent Ireland's near absolute prohibition of abortion. The girl had allegedly been raped by a friend's father.

● **Moscow** In the first violent demonstration under Boris Yeltsin's rule, 5,000 communists and ultranationalists clashed with police.

BUSINESS

United Way Chief Resigns Under Fire

He took at the office

AS PRESIDENT OF UNITED WAY OF AMERICA FOR the past 21 years, William Aramony was credited with boosting receipts and recognition for the charity. But Aramony resigned under widespread criticism of his life-style after the Washington *Post* disclosed he was earning $463,000 in salary and other benefits and enjoyed the use of a condominium in Manhattan and an apartment in Coral Gables, Florida, financed by local United Way chapters.

Elsewhere:

● **Time Warner** In a surprise shake-up, Nicholas J. Nicholas was ousted as chief executive officer at the world's largest media company. Gerald Levin, an old rival, was named to replace him and share power at the top of the company with former Warner Communications chief Steve Ross.

SCIENCE

Space-Age Explorers Find a Lost City

Ubar unearthed by unearthly means

FOR CENTURIES THE LEGENDARY CITY OF UBAR lay hidden beneath the desert, eluding explorers. "The Atlantis of the Sands," T.E. Lawrence called this fabled trading city of ancient Arabia, from whose jewel-encrusted walls the Queen of Sheba set out bearing frankincense for King Solomon. Ubar was Islam's Sodom: the Koran

Ptolemy's ancient map helped in the search for Ubar, called Iram in the Koran.

evoked the grandeur of its lofty pillars, but claimed God had destroyed the great trade center as punishment for its luxurious ways.

Centuries later, the lost city was found—from space. Urged on by documentary filmmaker Nicholas Clapp, scientists used the space shuttle's imaging radar and satellite infrared optical systems to trace trade routes long vanished on the ground. Some of the faint trails lay under sand dunes over 600 feet high. The ancient routes converged on a spot in present-day Oman. There, after weeks of digging, archaeologists unearthed an octagonal castle with high walls and pillars. Although the cautious scientists would not claim with certainty to have found Ubar, they had discovered something entirely new: a space-age tool for exploration.

Hockey on stilts? Athletes gathered in Albertville, France, where the Winter Olympics opened in a ceremony aglow with Gallic whimsy.

ARTS

Request Granted

Arts Endowment head John Frohnmayer is forced from office

FOR TWO YEARS, HE HAD BEEN THE MAN IN THE middle: National Endowment for the Arts chairman John Frohnmayer was attacked by conservatives for funding offensive works of art and vilified by the arts establishment for suspending grants to controversial artists. Finally Frohnmayer resigned, forced from office by the Bush Administration. He was replaced by his conservative deputy, Anee-Imelda Radice.

PEOPLE

● **Resigned** Barry Diller, Hollywood's "Miracle Mogul," left 20th Century Fox, claiming he wanted to go into business for himself.

● **Convicted** Mike Tyson, former heavyweight champion, was found guilty of rape by an Indianapolis, Indiana, jury.

● **Indicted** Jack Kevorkian, suicide-machine inventor, was charged with murder in the death of two women north of Detroit. The charges were later dismissed.

MARDI GRAS BROUHAHA

The New Orleans city council threatened the Big Easy's big time with an ordinance requiring the parade's racially and sexually homogeneous private "krewes" to stop discriminating—or stop marching. A diverse majority of irate citizens fought the krewe-cut. "The city's falling apart, and they go after one of the few things that still work," said one parader.

MARCH

NATION
Clinton Prevails; Bush Holds On

Tsongas surrenders, but Buchanan keeps chasing the President

> 66 We're not disorganized. We just have a kind of organization that transcends understanding. 99
>
> –Jacques Barzahi, *campaign guru to Jerry Brown*

IN THE SECOND ROUND OF DEMOCRATIC PRIMARIES, Paul Tsongas captured Utah, Maryland and Washington; Bill Clinton won in Georgia; and Jerry Brown took Colorado. Clinton went on to sweep seven Southern- and border-state contests on Super Tuesday, then battled off a Brown surge in Michigan and took Illinois as well. With funds and energy dwindling, Paul Tsongas suspended his campaign, leaving only Brown to challenge Clinton.

Meanwhile, feisty Pat Buchanan continued to bedevil the White House, losing every primary but keeping the focus on voters' deep disenchantment with Bush. Relishing his role as gadfly—and perhaps thinking of 1996—Buchanan stayed in the race.

WORLD
Beginning of the End For Apartheid?

A strong majority of white South Africans agrees to share power

White South Africans said yes to the hopes of the black majority.

IN A SURPRISINGLY LARGE MANDATE FOR RE-form, white South Africans—including a majority of the Afrikaans-speaking descendants of the original Dutch settlers—voted resoundingly for continuing negotiations with their black compatriots on a new constitution. At least 85% of the registered voters turned out; 69% of them said yes to the talks, aimed at creating a new political system in which the black majority would participate fully. Surprised and delighted by the overwhelming vote, President F.W. de Klerk exclaimed, "Today we have closed the book on apartheid."

Elsewhere:

● **Georgia** Former Soviet diplomat Eduard Shevardnadze was appointed to chair the new State Council, effectively giving him stewardship of his mountainous homeland.

● **France** In elections for regional councils, voters rejected Mitterrand's Socialist Party, but also turned their back on conservatives as well. Environmental parties doubled their previous share, and the National Front, led by extreme-right-winger Jean-Marie le Pen, established itself as a force in every region of the country.

● **Bosnia and Herzegovina** Led by Muslims and Croats, citizens voted to follow Slovenia, Croatia and Macedonia into independence, triggering a war with Serbia that would devastate the nation.

BUSINESS
New Era At Chrysler

Automaker shops for a leader—at GM!

FOR CHRYSLER CORP., THE AGE OF A.I.—AFTER Iacocca—was finally dawning. In 11 years at the wheel, Lee Iacocca produced one federal bailout, two best-selling autobiographies, one Statue of Liberty renovation and countless television commercials. But he had never found a successor. Finally Chrysler's board of directors stepped in, easing Lee out and finding a replacement—at General Motors! The new boss: Robert Eaton, 52, president of GM's profitable European business, who was to take over in January.

Elsewhere:

● **Colt** The firearms company—synonymous with the Wild West—declared bankruptcy. Officers said a $10 million line of credit from the Connecticut Development Authority and an Austrian bank would help them reload and reorganize.

● **CEO Pay** Stockholder gripes about executive greed began to make dents in armor of the some of the nation's top brass. Both Westinghouse Electric and IBM slashed the compensation of their top officers.

Michelangelo Sows March Madness

A dreaded global computer virus creates more hype than havoc

MICHELANGELO WAS RUMORED TO BE THE BIG-gest, baddest, most contagious computer virus ever. It spawned a week-long frenzy of hype and handholding that led to fears that comput-ers everywhere would be afflicted by a memo-ry-erasing virus on March 6, the artist's birth-day. But the bug's bark exceeded its byte; only a few isolated computers were affected. Though most computer buffs felt a bit let down, the vendors of antivirus software seemed to be enjoying themselves.

SOCIETY

Nameless, Homeless And Sexless

Faces in the crowd bring social issues to life

A TRIO OF UNRELATED MARCH NEWS STORIES put names and faces on some of the most per-plexing social problems in the U.S.

- **Aging** An elderly Alzheimer's patient was found abandoned in a wheelchair at a dog track in Idaho, with no identification. Later, his daughter was charged with kidnapping him.
- **The homeless** A federal appeals court over-turned street person Richard Kreimer's vic-tory over a public library in Morristown, New Jersey, that had denied him admission because of his poor personal hygiene.
- **Crime** Steven Allen Butler, an accused rap-ist, asked a Texas District Judge to castrate him, then let him go free. He withdrew the offer after a change of heart—following an outcry from legal experts.

PEOPLE

- **Separated** Buckingham Palace announced that Britain's Duke and Duchess of York, a.k.a. Andy and Fergie, were formally sepa-rating, with the option of divorce in two years. According to scornful palace officials, the woman mocked by the press as Freebie Fergie and Duchess Do-Little was "unsuit-able for royal life."
- **Sentenced** Self-anointed hotel queen Leo-na Helmsley was sentenced to four years in a federal medical prison for underpayment of income taxes.
- **Indebted** Police found checks signed by N.B.A. superstar Michael Jordan—adding up to $108,000 in alleged gambling debts—in the briefcase of a murdered North Caroli-na bail bondsman.

SAVED BY A NOSE

Calumet Farm was the Old Kentucky Home of thoroughbred racing's finest: two Triple Crown horses and nine Kentucky Der-by champions, in addition to the great Alydar, who stole hearts while winning neither. But now the farm was buried in debt, and all 850 acres of bluegrass, bales and barns were on the auction block. Would the spread be split up? No! At the last minute avia-tion magnate Henryk de Kwiatkowski arrived—sans white horse—with a winning bid of $17 million. He told more than 3,000 cheering spectators, "Not a whisker of this farm will be changed."

APRIL

Years of anger exploded when rioters and police squared off in L.A.

NATION

L.A.'s Days of Rage
A jarring verdict unleashes anarchy

A SUPERIOR COURT JURY IN SIMI VALLEY, AN overwhelmingly white suburb of Los Angeles, acquitted on all but one count the four white L.A. policemen on trial for beating black motorist Rodney King. The April 29 verdict prompted disbelief, since the beating had been captured on a widely seen videotape. Outraged, L.A.'s black community rioted in protest, spreading fearsome anarchy throughout the city for the next three days. Wholesale looting went unchecked; fires raged out of control; entire blocks were leveled. Smaller demonstrations and outbursts occurred across the country, as Americans came to grips with the still unhealed wounds of the inner cities.

Fearing an overturn of the Supreme Court's 1973 *Roe v. Wade* decision, hundreds of thousands of pro-choice demonstrators marched in Washington; it was the largest rally in the capital's history

Chicago's $800 Million-Dollar Flood
Goldfish invade Marshall Field's

RIVERS GENERALLY FLOOD BY OVERFLOWING. But the Great Chicago Flood of 1992 began when the Chicago River *underflowed* on Monday, April 13. After a small leak enlarged to become a car-size hole in the riverbed, more than 250 million gallons of water whirlpooled down into a network of tunnels that run beneath it, and ultimately into the basements of dozens of downtown Chicago buildings. Ele-

vators stopped, computer systems crashed, workers cleared out, and the Chicago Board of Trade and the Mercantile Exchange closed down. Even the IRS took pity, offering taxpayers a week's extension. The monstrous mess took weeks to clear up; damage was estimated to top $800 million.

Clinton Takes the New York Primary
Protest vote awards second place to noncandidate Tsongas

THE NEW YORK DEMOCRATIC PRIMARY WAS A classic street fight, with the candidates playing to ethnic voting blocs, but it produced neither a knockout for Bill Clinton nor an upset for Jerry Brown. Only Paul Tsongas emerged smiling; he came in second by staying away. When it was over, Clinton had 41% of the vote against 26% for Brown and a stunning 29% for Tsongas, who had suspended his candidacy in March. "Tsongas is Greek for 'none of the above,'" said one analyst.

WORLD

A Major Victory
Britain's Tories survive—narrowly

BUCKING AN ANTI-INCUMBENT TREND ACROSS Europe, voters defied pollsters' predictions and stuck with the Conservative Party of Prime Minister John Major, giving him a majority of 21 seats in the 651-seat House of Commons.
Elsewhere:
●**Peru** President Fujimori closed down Congress and said he would rule by decree.

HOW TO MAKE A BIG SPLASH

Kinzie Bridge

Sub-basement

Chicago River

Leak

Tunnel

The disaster occurred when the Chicago River began leaking into the roof of a tunnel system 40 ft. (12 m) below street level that was built around the turn of the century. The tunnels were used to deliver coal and freight until the 1950s, and are now used by telephone, cable and utility companies. Many downtown buildings have access to these tunnels through their sub-basements and were flooded. Workers plugged the hole with sandbags, gravel and cement. It took weeks to clean up the swampy situation.

TIME Graphic by Joe Lertola

After 14 years, Afghanistan's *mujahedin* moved into Kabul in triumph

BUSINESS

Air Fare Warfare

American Airlines shakes up the industry, and travelers rejoice

AMERICAN AIRLINES LAUNCHED A STREAMLINED new fare structure, to the applause of the public. The reforms jettisoned a maddening maze of rates and restrictions, replacing them with simplified fares offering savings of 40% to 50%. Competitors hit the afterburners to join the cut-and-simplify frenzy, and vacation plans changed overnight as reservations surged.

Elsewhere:
- **General Motors** in a sudden move, GM's board demoted chairman Robert Stempel and two key lieutenants, signaling it would take a more active role in company affairs.

SCIENCE

Humongous Fungus

World's largest being dwells underground in Midwest

THE SCIENTISTS WHO FOUND IT CLAIMED IT was the largest organic object ever discovered—and for the moment, no one argued. The organism was both gigantic and venerable: estimated to be 1,500 years old, it may weigh as much as 1,000 tons. It has taken over a whopping 37 acres along the Wisconsin-Michigan border—and it's still growing. "It" was a humongous fungus: a mass of cytoplasm tangled into stringlike tendrils that spread below the surface of the ground. To reproduce, it sends spore-bearing appendages—better known as mushrooms—above ground.

Big Bang Backing

Forget the details; this God is in the very large picture

SCIENTISTS ANNOUNCED THAT NASA'S COSMIC Background Explorer satellite had found something astronomers have been seeking for nearly 30 years: an almost imperceptible pattern of warm and cool patches in the cosmic microwave background radiation, the oldest light in the cosmos. The temperature variations offered strong support for the Big Bang theory, the foundation of modern astrophysics. "If you're religious, it's like looking at God," said George Smoot, astronomer at the University of California, Berkeley.

SOCIETY

Shame of the Navy

Reports confirm sexual harassment at flyers' convention

TRIGGERING A CONTROVERSY THAT WOULD roil its waters for the rest of the year, two U.S. Navy reports on a September 1991 convention of aviators in Las Vegas confirmed accounts that junior officers had harassed and groped female officers and civilians in a hotel corridor. The scandal's toll: one officer fired, two retired, one reassigned and three censured.

PEOPLE
- **Guilty** Manuel Noriega, former Panamanian dictator, was convicted of eight of 10 counts of narcotics trafficking.
- **Survived** Yasser Arafat was rescued 12 hours after his plane crashed in Libya.

" Study hard and you might grow up to be President. But let's face it, even then you'll never make as much money as your dog. **"**

–**George Bush,** *speaking to students after learning his dog Millie earned more than $800,000 in book royalties in 1991.*

French intellectuals called it a "cultural Chernobyl." But the folks at Disney had high hopes for their latest amusement park, Euro Disneyland. By year's end, though, it seemed to be more a cash Chernobyl, with attendance running below estimates.

MAY

NATION

Dan Quayle vs. Murphy Brown

Unreal! VP tangles with fictional character, wrestles her to a draw

IN THIS CORNER, VICE PRESIDENT DAN QUAYLE. In the other—a fictional TV character? Speaking in San Francisco, Quayle argued that the Los Angeles riots were caused in part by a "poverty of values" that included the acceptance of unwed motherhood, as celebrated by the hit CBS sitcom *Murphy Brown*. The divorced title character, played by Candice Bergen, became pregnant and chose to have a baby boy; his "birth" was watched by 38 million Americans. Quayle's gambit to stir debate on the issue of "family values" was successful, as the odd mix of fiction and politics both provoked and amused the nation.

Canadians voted to create a new territory, Nunavut, as a home for the Inuit—or Eskimo—of the country's eastern Arctic region

Perot Tops the Polls

Texan's surge stuns Washington

THREE MONTHS EARLIER, BILLIONAIRE ROSS Perot had been just another talk-show guest; now, suddenly, he led the polls for President and was attracting volunteers nationwide. In a mid-May TIME poll, Perot's 33% topped Bush's 28% and Clinton's 24%—even though the Texan was still officially undeclared.

Perot's posse of supporters—many of whom claimed to be deeply disaffected with national politics—rallied, passed out flyers and collected signatures to get his name on the ballot.

DON'T GIVE ME YOUR POOR
Boat people had been fleeing Haiti in droves since President Jean-Bertrand Aristide was overthrown in September of 1991, and the Bush Administration had been quarantining them at the U.S. Naval Base in Guantánamo, Cuba. Now the White House said it would force refugees found on the seas to return home and would shut down the Guantánamo refugee camp.

WORLD

Revolt in Thailand

The army fires on civilians, and the King brokers a truce

IT WAS CLOSE TO CIVIL WAR IN THE "LAND OF smiles." Middle-class Thais who increasingly resented the authoritarian rule of unelected Prime Minister General Suchinda Kraprayoon took to the streets to protest. The Thai press described the upscale demonstrators as "the mobile-phone mob." Led by Chamlong Srimuang, the ascetic former governor of Bangkok, they met stiff resistance from the army, which repeatedly fired into the crowd, killing more than 50. Soldiers also arrested the popular Chamlong. Finally, revered King

Bhumibol Adulyadej brought the two factions together. General Suchinda released Chamlong and resigned; the next day Parliament passed an amendment requiring future Prime Ministers to be members of the legislature.

BUSINESS

A Big Builder Is Broke

Olympia & York files for bankruptcy

IT WAS A MIGHTY COMEDOWN FROM THE DAYS when Olympia & York's spectacular and widely acclaimed World Financial Center in Manhattan and Canary Wharf complex in London were changing the face of city planning. Now the world's biggest builder sought the shelter of bankruptcy courts in Toronto and New York. Headed by Canada's secretive Reichmann brothers, the company struggled vainly for months to restructure $12 billion in debt. The bankruptcy filing drove down bank stocks and sent shock waves reverberating through world financial markets.

SCIENCE

Gotcha! How to Snag A Balky Satellite

The space-walking Endeavor crew improvises a great catch

THE ASSIGNMENT: GRAB A 4.5-TON, 17-FT.-LONG telecommunications satellite from its useless orbit 230 miles above earth, then attach a rocket booster that would send it into its higher, correct orbit. Two nerve-racking attempts by Endeavor's crew to reel in the satellite with a spring-loaded capture bar failed. So the astronauts improvised, concocting a dangerous rescue scheme that called for an unprecedented trio of spacewalkers to work together in the unforgiving vacuum of space. The gamble paid off. After an eight-hour struggle, the trio snagged the spinning satellite, wrestled it into the shuttle's cargo bay, attached the booster and sent the satellite on its way.

Elsewhere:

- **Cancer** In a report that stirred controversy and confusion, a University of Toronto researcher claimed that mammography has no demonstrable benefit for women in the age range 40 to 49, though it does for older women. Some early leaks even claimed (falsely) that the study found mammograms were dangerous for those under 50. Vowing to study the matter in more detail, researchers advised women to continue being tested.
- **Smoking** Federal health officials reported that the number of Americans who smoke tobacco had reached a record low and was falling faster than at any other time since government tracking studies began 37 years ago. In 1955, 42% of Americans smoked; now nonsmokers outnumber smokers 3 to 1.

SOCIETY

Schmidt Leaves Yale

After six years as president, he joins a new education project

BENNO SCHMIDT DESCRIBED HIS SURPRISE DECISION to resign his post as president of Yale as "leaping into the abyss." But after six rocky years in New Haven, leap he did—to head up media mogul Christopher Whittle's experimental Edison Project, a bold $2.5 billion proposal to build 1,000 new private schools operated to make a profit and designed to test new curriculums, methods and technology.

PEOPLE

- **Leaning** The Tower of Pisa in Italy could fall down at any minute, alert scientists claimed; they girdled the structure with 18 steel bands and installed 800 tons of lead at the base to halt its precarious inclination.
- **Retiring** Farewell! Johnny Carson took his leave of NBC's *Tonight* show after 30 memorable seasons. The insomniac's friend modestly accepted a nightly shower of accolades and listened misty-eyed as Bette Midler sang a last farewell.

You load 4.5 tons and what do you get? A satellite in the cargo bay.

Goodnight, Johnny

13

JUNE

American/Russian Gothic: look who dropped by!

More than 1 million ballots were cast in a contest to decide whether the new Elvis Presley stamp should feature the King as a young or mature performer. The people's choice: the hip-swiveling rocker of *Return to Sender*.

A Russian Conquers Washington

Yeltsin, denouncing communism, wins new agreements and new respect

CONFOUNDING PREDICTIONS OF A HO-HUM summit, virtuoso politician Boris Yeltsin swept into Washington, surprising and exciting the blasé capital. On his agenda: arms cuts, aid and trade. First Yeltsin and George Bush surprised everyone with a substantial arms-reduction pact. Yeltsin next charmed Congress at a joint session that awarded him 13 standing ovations. Russia's first democratically elected President denounced communism, pledged market reform and more democracy for Russia and asked the Hill to approve a package including $12 billion in assistance.

Clinton Clinches

But Perot surges, keeping major candidates off balance

BILL CLINTON SWEPT THE LAST SIX DEMOCRATic primaries—including Jerry Brown's home state of California—to seize the Democratic nomination. But, to his dismay, Ross Perot was stealing headlines, voters and Clinton's mantle as a Washington outsider demanding change. Perot signaled he was serious—but lost a few of his outsider stripes—by hiring two veteran campaigners, Republican Ed Rollins and Democrat Hamilton Jordan, as advisers.

Late in the month Perot tangled with George Bush when the President accused him of having investigated his children, seeking scandal. "Leave my kids alone," Bush warned. An outraged Perot denied the charge and accused Bush's "dirty tricks crowd" of conducting "a carefully thought out and carefully executed effort to try to damage my candidacy."

The Supreme Court Finds a New Center

In four surprising decisions, the Justices shun extremes

IN ITS FINAL DAYS IN SESSION, THE SUPREME Court surprised observers by issuing a quartet of decisions that showed a distinct and unexpected pro-First Amendment, pro-civil liberties streak. In rulings on free speech, school prayer, tobacco-company liability and college desegregation, the Court rejected the right-wing views of Justices Antonin Scalia and Clarence Thomas. Controlling the agenda was a new centrist trio: Justices Sandra Day O'Connor, David Souter and Anthony Kennedy, all of whom had been appointed by conservative Republican Presidents Ronald Reagan and George Bush.

BLACKBOARD BUNGLE

His attack on Murphy Brown helped position Vice-President Dan Quayle as a newly substantive voice on the issues and a possible 1996 candidate. But when Quayle, visiting a school in New Jersey and relying on a faulty cue card, tripped up by instructing a spelling-bee student to add an *e* to the word potato, he was once again branded a lightweight.

South Africa: 42 blacks were massacred in Boipatong

WORLD

The Danes Say No To Maastricht

A surprising veto clouds the future of the European Community

DANISH VOTERS SURPRISED ALL OF EUROPE when they narrowly voted not to ratify the Treaty of Maastricht, the landmark agreement that pledged the European Community to monetary as well as political union by the end of the century. The stunning vote was a clear warning that the transition to full European unity would be a lengthy, contentious process. E.C. supporters took heart later in the month when Irish voters overwhelmingly approved the treaty with a resounding 69% majority.

Elsewhere:

●**Israel** Voters handed Prime Minister Yitzhak Shamir's Likud Party a resounding defeat; Yitzhak Rabin's Labor Party formed a coalition government pledged to pursue peace.

●**Czechoslovakia** After winning elections in their respective republics, Czech leader Vaclav Klaus and Slovak leader Vladimir Meciar agreed to split the union into two separate nations Jan. 1, 1993.

BUSINESS

SEC Charges Seven With Insider Trading

The social register gets busted

THE SECURITIES AND EXCHANGE COMMISSION accused seven corporate leaders of raking in at least $13 million in illegal profits from stock trading based on inside information. Among those charged were social luminaries Martin Revson and Edward Downe Jr., husband of auto heiress Charlotte Ford.

SCIENCE

Rio Hosts a Summit To Save the Earth

Bush flies down to Brazil, but casts a pall on the green scene

AFTER TWO YEARS OF PLANNING, THE EARTH Summit got under way in Rio de Janeiro with a global guest list of more than 100 world leaders and 30,000 others concerned about the planet. Most delegates felt that the treaties to be signed were not strong enough, and they blamed the U.S. George Bush, after long hesitation, attended the meeting but refused to sign accords he said favored developing countries over American interests.

SOCIETY

Summer Bummer

Apotheosis of the squirt-gun

THE SUPER SOAKER CAUGHT THE FANCY OF kids with its high-pressure air pumps, splashing so hard and squirting so far as to render obsolete all other forms of water weaponry. But when a soaking led to a shooting in Boston, the mayor asked toy stores not to sell the Soakers.

PEOPLE

●**Charged** Amy Fisher, 17, a Long Island high school girl, was accused in the May shooting of the wife of her alleged lover, a 38-year-old auto-body-shop owner, Joey Buttafuoco.

> **❝As one of the few politicians who admits to both having inhaled and having enjoyed it, of course I support it.❞**
> –Rep. Joe Kennedy, *on whether marijuana should be legalized for medicinal use*

Diana, the Princess of Wales, attempted suicide five times, according to a new biography by Andrew Morton that seemed to have been written with her cooperation

JULY

Clinton accepting: Perot's pullout fueled his surge

NATION

Clinton Is Crowned As Perot Bows Out

All aboard! Baby-boomer bus leaves New York City for nation's heartland

DEMOCRATS DOMINATED THE NEWS IN JULY. First, Bill Clinton surprised many by naming Tennessee Senator Al Gore, a fellow Southern Democrat—and fellow baby boomer—as his running mate. A second surprise: the Democratic Convention in Madison Square Garden proved to be well oiled and humming.

It was Clinton's week—until Ross Perot stole the show on the convention's final day with the stunning announcement that he was quitting the race, leaving his supporters feeling betrayed. The unpredictable Perot gave little reason for his July surprise, but said he had been increasingly impressed by a "revitalized" Democratic Party. Seizing the moment, a delighted Clinton adroitly pitched the Democratic tent in the middle-class backyard in his acceptance speech.

The challengers bounced out of the political lovefest way above the incumbents. Clin-

Just that simple: the grand impractical crusade of Perot's legions fell victim to grimly practical considerations

ton had been running a poor third in the polls in mid-June. When he, wife Hillary and the Gores boarded buses for a "double-date" campaign swing through the Midwest the day after the convention, their ticket was suddenly leading Bush-Quayle by 20%.

Supreme Court Upholds Roe v. Wade

Justices approve tough restrictions, but hew to the 1973 ruling

THE SUPREME COURT SURPRISED OBSERVERS by upholding *Roe v. Wade*, the 1973 case that declared a constitutional right to abortion. The decision hewed carefully to the middle ground; yet, coming from a court dominated by conservative apointees of Presidents Reagan and Bush, it was a remarkable declaration of judicial independence.

The co-authors of the majority decision were the newly emerging centrist bloc of Justices, Anthony Kennedy, Sandra Day O'Connor and David Souter. Still, the ruling—on a Pennsylvania state law—permitted the states to impose strong restrictions on abortion.

WORLD

Showdown in Iraq
You blinked! No, *you* did!

AFTER DAYS OF HARD NEGOTIATION AT THE United Nations, a three-week showdown over whether a U.N. inspection team would gain access to the Iraqi Agriculture Ministry ended. Baghdad agreed to admit a team of inspectors—with one important catch: the building would be barred to inspectors from the U.S. and other nations that had fought in

PALATIAL PRISON

Colombia drug kingpin Pablo Escobar escaped from his luxurious "prison" in his hometown of Envigado, after being told he would be transferred to a harsher military facility

the Gulf War. George Bush quickly called the agreement a "cave-in" by Saddam; the Iraqi leader claimed a triumph over the U.S. By the time the team entered the building, the Iraqis had had five days to remove any incriminating material.

- **Algeria** A few seconds after Algerian head of state Mohammed Boudiaf spoke the words "We are all going to die," an assassin in uniform raised his submachine gun and fired, killing the 73-year-old leader.

BUSINESS

New Competition for Cable Companies

After a long fight, the FCC allows phone operators to carry TV signals

IN A CONTROVERSIAL DECISION—AND A MAJOR victory for phone operators—the FCC granted phone companies the right to carry TV programming into millions of homes. The ruling will allow phone companies to transmit TV shows, movies, sports and news formerly carried only by cable and broadcast networks. It is also expected to pave the way for consumer services, including interactive television and home shopping, and to lower cable rates. The cable industry immediately attacked the order.

Elsewhere:

- **British Air** In one of the biggest cross-border deals in history, British Airways agreed to acquire a 44% equity stake in USAir for $750 million. The pact would have created the largest airline alliance ever and accelerated worldwide consolidation of the airline industry. But the deal fell through later, after U.S. Transportation Secretary Andrew Card vowed to reject the partnership.

SCIENCE

The King of Lizards Meets His Match

A new find in Utah makes Tyrannosaurus rex look cuddly

DINOSAUR LORE HAS IT THAT *TYRANNOSAURUS rex*, the king of the giant lizards, was the meanest creature ever to roam the earth. But fossilized claw, skull and jawbones found in a quarry in eastern Utah point to a dinosaur that, while smaller than *Tyrannosaurus*, was probably a lot nastier. Labeled the "Utahraptor" for now, the 7-m (20-ft.), one-ton beast is the largest specimen ever found of Velociraptor, an upright, fast-moving carnivore that sported an enormous claw on the back of each foot for slashing at prey.

Ice-T: not attending the policeman's ball

ARTS

Fire and Ice-T

Protesters demand that Time Warner pull its Body Count album

THE 1,100 SHAREHOLDERS AT COMMUNICAtions conglomerate Time Warner's annual meeting had more than financial statements on their mind. Critics blasted the company for releasing rapper Ice-T's *Body Count* album and *Cop Killer* cut, which contained such lines as "Die Pig, Die!" A few weeks later Ice-T defused the situation by asking Time Warner to recall the CDs and remove the controversial cut from future pressings.

PEOPLE

- **Married** Edward M. Kennedy, 60, bon vivant Senator from Massachusetts, and Victoria Anne Reggie, 38, Washington lawyer, were wed in a ceremony at Kennedy's McLean, Va., home, in the second marriage for each.
- **Annulled** The marriage of Princess Caroline of Monaco, 35, and her first husband, French playboy Philippe Junot, 52, was voided by the Vatican.

> **❝ Actually, I'm a little envious of Murphy Brown. At least she's guaranteed of coming back this fall. ❞**
>
> **–Dan Quayle**

Curtain up! 172 nations—and almost 11,000 athletes— competed as the games of the 25th Olympiad began in Barcelona.

AUGUST

NATION

Mother Nature's Angriest Child

Hurricane Andrew is the costliest natural disaster in U.S. history

> **"The heart wants what it wants. There's no logic to these things."**
>
> **–Woody Allen,**
> *defending his love affair with Mia Farrow's adopted daughter*

LIKE A POWERFUL, PETULANT CHILD, HURRI-cane Andrew rampaged across the Bahamas and the populous tip of southern Florida and into Louisiana's Cajun country. With winds up to 164 m.p.h., Andrew carved out a 20-to-35-mile swath south of Miami that leveled entire city blocks and left residents without electricity, phones, drinkable water, sewage treatment, food or shelter. The hurricane proved the costliest natural disaster in American history. A slow response by state and federal governments was offset by the charity of sympathetic Americans, who rushed money and supplies to the damaged areas.

The G.O.P. Family Goes Schizophrenic

Bush rallies his fractious party for now—but watch out in '96!

After Andrew, homeowners filed suit against contractors for shoddy construction

WHEN REPUBLICANS CONVENED IN HOUSTON for their convention, the show had a schizo-phrenic quality not often seen at G.O.P. gather-

ings. Night after night, the party's fault lines were laid bare for the nation to see. Patrick Bu-chanan's darkly apocalyptic speech Monday night troubled many with its exclusionary tone; it was followed by Ronald Reagan's sun-ny vision of America's future. After days of an-tigay rhetoric, HIV-positive speaker Mary Fish-er hushed the convention by insisting that AIDS victims "have not earned cruelty and do not deserve meanness." Some Republican women protested the party platform's extreme-ly harsh stand on abortion.

Garnering a short-lived bounce, by week's end Bush was narrowing Clinton's lead in the polls. But the strongly factional character of the get-together guaranteed that the G.O.P. was

Children, grandchildren and Barbara Bush join the President at the convention podium

in for some major change before it gathers again in 1996.

Elsewhere:
- **Middle East** George Bush promised new Is-raeli Prime Minister Yitzhak Rabin he would guarantee the repayment of up to $10 billion in bank loans—a guarantee the Ad-ministration had withheld from Israel to force it into a more conciliatory policy with its Arab neighbors.

WORLD

Germany for Germans?

A week of rioting signals a vicious outbreak of xenophobia

IN A HAIL OF ROCKS AND MOLOTOV COCK-tails, skinheads and neo-Nazis in the eastern port of Rostock tried to storm an apartment block housing 200 asylum-seeking Roma-nian gypsies. Local crowds, shouting "Germany for Germans!" let the rock throw-ers disappear into their midst when police chased them. Chancellor Helmut Kohl de-plored the mayhem, and Bonn officials used the occasion to urge once more the adoption of a constitutional amendment that would curtail Germany's liberal provisions for asylum.

Elsewhere:

- **Bosnia** Television images and news reports of torture and starvation in detention camps shocked the world, stirring calls for action to stop the bloodshed.
- **Brazil** Demonstrators marched across the country to show their disgust with the regime of embattled President Fernando Collor de Mello, after investigators uncovered kickback rackets engineered by his aides.
- **Middle East** Peace talks resumed in Washington, with Israel's new Labor-led government adopting a more conciliatory tone on the Golan Heights and the West Bank.
- **Georgia** Eduard Shevardnadze, out of patience with supporters of ousted President Zviad Gamsakhurdia, sent troops into western Georgia, a Gamsakhurdia stronghold.

'CALL THE AMERICANS AND ASK WHAT THEY INTEND DOING ABOUT ALL THIS!'

BUSINESS

The Barriers Come Tumbling Down

Negotiators sign off on the North American Free Trade Agreement

GEORGE BUSH CALLED IT "THE BEGINNING OF A new era." Mexican President Carlos Salinas de Gortari went on early-morning television to praise the deal, while Canadian Prime Minister Brian Mulroney called it "an important step forward." After 14 months of haggling, negotiators for the U.S., Canada and Mexico had put the finishing touches on the North American Free Trade Agreement. But the hard part was still to come: selling the agreement to lawmakers in each country.

Elsewhere:

- **Post Office** After one month on the job, Postmaster General Marvin T. ("Carvin' Marvin") Runyon announced cuts of about 30,000 managerial jobs, including more than half of the top 42 posts.
- **Bankrupt** In back-to-back reversals of fortune, computer maker Wang Laboratories and pharmacy chain Phar-Mor took refuge from their creditors. Wang had struggled after missing out on the personal computer revolution; Phar-Mor claimed its former officers had embezzled from the company.

SCIENCE

Space Shuttle Yo-Yo Is a No-Go

Astronauts reach the end of their rope, abandon difficult experiment

NASA SCIENTISTS HAD PLANNED IT AS ANOTHER of their space spectaculars: astronauts aboard the shuttle *Atlantis* planned to dangle a half-ton satellite on a 20.1 km (12½-mile) tether, forming the biggest single orbiting object in history. Reacting to earth's magnetic field, the Italian-made satellite was to generate up to 5,000 volts of electricity. But after the satellite rose properly from the shuttle on a 10-m (39-ft.) boom, the astronauts first couldn't pull out its auxiliary power cord; then the line jammed like a badly wound fishing reel. Defeated, the astronauts pulled the satellite back inside the shuttle. To the relief of the Italian space agency, the $379 million satellite may one day fly again.

Like these Tokyo sidewalk surfers, kids around the world adopted America's street style. The look: start with sneakers, add big, baggy pants and T shirt. Top off with baseball cap. Optional: flannel shirt for the grunge look. Awesome!

SEPTEMBER

NATION

Bush Feels Generous; Clinton Feels a Draft

Florida rebuilds, with a little help from the White House

FOR THE SECOND TIME SINCE HURRICANE AN-drew tore into the Gulf of Mexico, George Bush journeyed to South Florida to show his concern. He promised to rebuild the gutted Homestead Air Force Base, and said Washington would pick up the full relief tab rather than the usual 75%-25% federal-local split. Cultivating votes, Bush sowed federal largesse around the country, backing the sale of as many as 150 F-16 fighters to Taiwan and announcing the release of more than a billion dollars of federal monies for farmers. In a major speech in Detroit, Bush laid out his economic program for the country, arguing for lower taxes, less federal spending and less regulation.

Bill Clinton, who also traveled to Florida and backed the rebuilding of the air base, found his conduct during the '60s under new attack when the Los Angeles *Times* said that in 1968 his uncle Raymond Clinton had managed to delay the new college graduate's army induction. Momentarily rattled, Clinton alternately denied the import of the piece and maintained that he had already explained his behavior fully. Meanwhile, a revived Ross Perot was sending signals that he might rejoin the campaign.

❝I strongly believe that a baseball commissioner should serve a full term. ❞

–Fay Vincent, *commissioner of baseball, after his firing*

No exit: Shining Path leader Guzmán, put on display by Peru's government after his capture

WORLD

Europe's Common Crisis: Money

The E.C. flag flies at half-Maastricht

IN A KEY REFERENDUM, FRENCH VOTERS GAVE A faint *oui* to the European Community's Maastricht treaty on economic and political union. But their voice was not hearty enough to still the turmoil in Europe; the margin was a sliver-thin 51%, which highlighted ordinary citizens' doubts about union. A week earlier, currency traders had displayed their own doubts about the future, selling off British pounds and Italian lire and buying sturdy deutsche marks. Eventually both the pound and the lira dropped out of the E.C.'s exchange system; both governments were deeply embarrassed. The future of the Maastricht treaty seemed more in doubt than ever.

"My Turn to Lose"

Peru captures terrorist Guzmán, notorious leader of Shining Path

WHEN PERUVIAN POLICE STORMED THE HOUSE in a Lima suburb searching for a legendary guerrilla, they expected bodyguards or caches of weapons—the stock-in-trade of the Maoist guerrillas of Shining Path, South America's most feared terrorist group. Instead they found its overweight and sickly leader, Abi-

mael Guzmán, who surrendered without a fight. "My turn to lose," said the legendary rebel. All Peru rejoiced, as the nation hoped for an end to 12 years of gruesome terror that had killed 25,000 citizens.

Elsewhere:

- **South Africa** In another grisly massacre, 28 people were killed and another 400 wounded when African National Congress supporters demonstrated at the border of the so-called independent homeland of Ciskei.
- **Germany** Attacks against asylum-seeking foreigners continued to spread throughout the country; more than 150 incidents were registered in the last week of August and the first week of September alone. Official calls for special police powers did not seem to deter anyone. Right-wingers threw fire bombs at a house of asylum-seekers a mile from Chancellor Helmut Kohl's Bonn office.

BUSINESS

Muscle Card

GM rolls out a fancy new credit device to help rebuild its auto sales

FOLLOWING THE LEAD OF AT&T AND GENERAL Electric, General Motors began offering its own high-powered credit card to boost sales of its products and grab a share of the $485 billion market for plastic money. Holders of the card will earn 5% rebates on purchases made with the card, up to $500 a year. Cardholders could apply the rebates toward the lease or purchase of GM cars and trucks.

Elsewhere:

- **Insurance** Primerica, the New York City concern known for its Smith Barney brokerage subsidiary, agreed to invest $550 million for a 27% stake in the Travelers insurance company. Travelers had been struggling under the weight of troubled real estate loans, and had paid more than $200 million to victims of Hurricane Andrew. The 129-year-old company had announced 3,500 layoffs, 10% of its work force; Primerica's stake was valued at about half Travelers' book value.

SCIENCE

Children of Chernobyl

Sooner than expected, cancer hits youngsters who were downwind

AFTER THE NEAR MELTDOWN OF THE CHERNO-byl nuclear power plant in 1986, the number of cancer cases was expected to rise in areas affected by fallout. But no one suspected it would happen so soon or that so many of its victims would be children. Two new reports indicated that childhood thyroid cancer in the area had skyrocketed from an average of four cases a year to about 60. Gomel, the first region hit by the radiation, now has a thyroid cancer rate about 80 times the world average.

Elsewhere:

- **Iron** A study from Finland provided strong evidence that too much iron in the body can promote heart attacks.

SOCIETY

A Kid Asserts His Legal Rights

Gregory Kingsley wins a new family and a new name—and makes history

IT WAS AN EXTRAORDINARY VICTORY FOR AN OR-dinary boy: after two days of emotionally charged testimony, a Florida judge granted Gregory Kingsley, 12, his dearest wish. He allowed him to "divorce" his natural parents and be adopted by George and Lizabeth Russ, the foster family Gregory had come to love.

The case attracted national attention, but in the end it was Gregory's small, clear voice declaring "I'm doing it for me, so I can be happy" that resonated in the courtroom. In the past eight years, the child had spent just seven months with his natural mother.

PEOPLE

- **Evolving** Three of pop's grandes dames were singing distinctly different tunes on new releases. Linda Ronstadt opted for the classics of the Caribbean on *Frenesí*, Sinéad O'Connor delivered a sultry series of torch songs on *Am I Not Your Girl?*, and raspy rocker Cher was threatening to go country on her upcoming record in 1993.

Net gain: Manon Rheaume played goalie for the Tampa Bay Lightning hockey team, becoming the first woman to compete in the N.H.L.

OCTOBER

Perot claimed only the pleas of his believers had coaxed him back into the race

Sinéad O'Connor tearing a picture of the Pope on *Saturday Night Live*

NATION

He's Back! Ross Perot Changes His Mind

The candidates debate, the charges fly—and the race heats up

ON THE FIRST DAY OF OCTOBER, MERCURIAL billionaire Ross Perot announced that he was rejoining the presidential race, swayed by his followers' ardent demands. Perot twanged that he was "honored to accept their request." The Texan's performance in the first of three debates was sharp and engaging. But Bill Clinton held on to his strong lead in the race.

Clinton was the clear winner of the second debate, staged in a question-and-answer format with uncommitted voters, as he had suggested. President Bush seemed tired at first, but thrilled his supporters with a much more upbeat performance in the third debate.

The campaign's final days held two sur-

prises. First, Perot charged the Republicans with intending to smear his daughter, though he offered no proof. Then new evidence in the indictment of Casper Weinberger offered further proof that George Bush had been a party to the Iran-*contra* scheme.

Progress on MIAs

Vietnam promises new access and evidence on missing Americans

TO THE RELIEF OF THE FAMILIES OF AMERICAN soldiers and pilots missing in Southeast Asia, President Bush announced that "Hanoi has agreed to provide us with all, and I repeat all, information it has collected on American POWs and MIAs." The President made it clear that Hanoi's cooperation would open the way toward re-establishing diplomatic relations between the nations.

WORLD

Canadians Vote No— In Any Language

They reject a new constitution; Quebec's fate is unresolved

CANADIANS TURNED DOWN A PROPOSED NEW constitution that was designed to have something for everybody. As it turned out, it had something for almost everybody to hate; 54% of voters said no. The pact would have recog-

MEET PROFESSOR JETSON

Excellent! Some TV stations around the country claimed that many Saturday-morning cartoon and kiddy shows were "educational" in nature. Included in the honor roll: *The Jetsons*, *G.I. Joe*, and *Leave It To Beaver*.

nized Quebec as a "distinct society" and guaranteed it 25% of the House of Commons. But the province's Francophones insisted on greater control over tax money, and most English-speaking Canadians bridled at special treatment for Quebec, even though they would have received more power in a new, popularly elected Senate. The biggest loser: Brian Mulroney, already the most unpopular Prime Minister in the history of Canadian polling, who had campaigned heavily for the accord.

Elsewhere:
- **Brazil** The nation celebrated as President Fernando Collor de Mello was impeached by the lower house of Congress.
- **South Africa** President F.W. de Klerk released 150 political prisoners in a deal to entice the African National Congress back to talks on the nation's future government.
- **Hong Kong** A week after he was snubbed by China's rulers in a trip to Beijing, the crown colony's British governor Chris Patten was again attacked by the Chinese over his proposal to give Hong Kong's citizens a greater voice in choosing their legislators.
- **El Salvador** Scientists excavated nearly 60 of several hundred battered skeletons from around a demolished church in the town of El Mozote, confirming that as many as 800 civilians, most of them women and children, had been mutilated, burned and murdered during the civil war in 1981 by soldiers from the Salvadoran army's U.S.-trained Atlacatl Battalion.

BUSINESS

The Corporate Giants Scramble to Survive

GM, IBM and Sears trim their sails

BATTERED BY CHANGING TIMES AND MARKETS, three major U.S. companies announced significant overhauls:
- **General Motors** After months of bitter skirmishing with GM's board of directors, chairman and CEO Robert Stempel finally quit, after a power struggle with his leading critic on the board, retired Procter & Gamble chairman John Smale. The board named a new management team; Jack Smith, the former head of GM's profitable overseas operation, succeeded Stempel.
- **Sears** The retail giant announced it would begin dismantling its $57 billion empire, selling off its real estate and brokerage businesses to concentrate on retailing and insurance.
- **IBM** Big Blue announced that it was doubling—to 40,000—its estimate of the number of workers who would either retire or re-

sign from the company by the end of the year, and that it would reduce its manufacturing capacity 40% by shrinking many of its 30 factories worldwide.

The Toronto Blue Jays celebrate after beating the Atlanta Braves for Canada's first-ever World Series title

SCIENCE

Polar Meltdown

New evidence suggests the ice caps are more fragile than assumed

A REPORT IN THE SCIENCE JOURNAL *NATURE* suggested that large portions of the polar ice caps may have melted as recently as 3 million years ago, when world temperatures rose only a few degrees. The report added fuel to concerns that possible climatic change could melt the caps again. A meltdown of the Antarctic ice sheet could raise world sea levels by about 60 m (200 ft.).

Elsewhere:
- **Milk** The Physicians Committee for Responsible Medicine took on a sacred cow, questioning the value of cow's milk for children and warning it could actually prove harmful to some youngsters. Other scientists labeled the charge irresponsible.
- **RU 486** The French-made drug RU 486 cannot be imported into the U.S. even though it is a safe way of inducing nonsurgical abortions, according to many scientists in the U.S. and Europe. A new study showed that the drug actually prevents pregnancy if taken within 72 hours after intercourse.

SEX: **Madonna's book proved it sells**

23

NOVEMBER

Chums: Barbara Bush escorts Hillary Clinton on a tour of her new home

NATION

Clinton Whispers, but Voters Roar

"Failed governor of a small state" wins the biggest election of all

HE LOST HIS VOICE, BUT IT HARDLY MATTERED. He won just about everything else. The voters had spoken, and the election that briefly looked close was firmly his. Bill Clinton's plurality in the popular vote, 43%—vs. 38% for George Bush and 19% for Ross Perot—was solid rather than spectacular. But his victory nonethless was sweeping. He showed strength in every part of the country, winning 31 states and 357 electoral votes, against only 18 states and 168 electoral votes for Bush. But the Governor's coattails were short; while women did well, Democrats failed to win a "filibuster-proof" majority of 60 in the Senate; in the House they lost 10 seats.

File Under Fired

A search for dirt on Perot and Clinton costs an official her job

SWAMPED BY ALLEGATIONS THAT HER SUBORDI-nates searched the passport records of Ross Perot, Bill Clinton and Clinton's mother Vir-ginia Kelley during the presidential campaign, Assistant Secretary of State Elizabeth Tamposi was forced to resign her post. Tamposi claimed she was only taking orders from higher-ups. A three-judge panel of the federal appeals bench named former U.S. Attorney Joseph diGenova as a special prosecutor to investigate the case.

Elsewhere:

- **U.S. Navy** After a bitter court battle, Petty Officer Keith Meinhold, 30, managed to re-tain his job in the Navy. He had been dis-charged in August after admitting he was gay on national TV.
- **Subic Bay** After nearly a century of Ameri-can military presence in the Philippines, the U.S. Navy steamed out of Subic Bay, leaving the post to the Filipinos.

WORLD

The White Wine War

America and France trade threats over trade policy

TRADE WAR! FRANCE AND THE U.S. SEEMED ready to mount the barricades as they quar-reled over the price of oilseed and white wine. The scrap began when the U.S. threatened to add a 200% tariff (thus tripling prices) on white wine imported from Europe—unless the E.C. agreed to cuts in subsidies that encourage pro-duction of oilseeds. From the sidelines, German Chancellor Helmut Kohl denounced the potential trade war as "the politics of idiocy."

When the European Community and the U.S. reached an agreement aimed at averting the trade crisis, irate French farmers aped Yankee revolutionaries by dumping chickenfeed into the Seine. But Paris was prevented under the rules of the Community from exercising a veto of the agreement.

Elsewhere:

● **Yugoslavia** Angered by the ongoing warfare in the Balkans, the U.N. stiffened sanctions against Yugoslavia, and the West vowed to intercept sanction-busting vessels in the Adriatic.

BUSINESS

A Fiery Flaw

General Motors admits it failed to correct its unsafe trucks

CONTINUING GENERAL MOTORS' STREAK OF BAD news, the company released internal documents indicating that from 1983 to 1987 GM recognized but failed to correct a design flaw in its Chevrolet and GMC pickup trucks. The flaw exposed side fuel tanks during crash impacts, allegedly causing about 300 deaths. The company could face untold costs in settling lawsuits relating to the the hazard. About 5 million of the vehicles are still on the road.

Elsewhere:

● **Economy** Just in time for Bill Clinton to reap the benefit, George Bush's long-promised upturn seemed at hand. Third-quarter figures showed gross domestic product rising at an annual rate of 3.9%. Strong increases were also shown by consumer spending, business investment, house sales and consumer confidence.

FOURTH ESTATE ABUSES FIRST KITTY, FIRST AMENDMENT
Political paparazzi sank to a new low, using catnip to lure Socks, the First Cat-elect, out of the Arkansas Governor's Mansion for a photo opportunity. Socks didn't say no.

SOCIETY

Churches in Change

Modern concerns transform centuries of tradition

IN A MAJOR MONTH FOR RELIGIOUS NEWS, three separate events crystallized the issues transforming the churches.

At a synod in London, Anglicans narrowly decided to allow women to become priests, breaking 19 centuries of tradition and perhaps presaging a split in the church. Soon after, meeting in Washington, U.S. Catholic Bishops failed to approve a letter on the role of women in the church. Designed to please all sides of a contentious debate, the diluted document satisfied no one.

Finally, the Roman Catholic Church issued a new catechism, a 676-page summary of essential beliefs on doctrine and morals. The document confronts such modern sins as test-tube conception, artificial insemination, check bouncing and speeding and drunk driving; it also counsels respect for homosexuals, while calling on gays to abstain from sexual relations.

PEOPLE

● **Arrested** Sol Wachtler, chief judge of the New York State Court of Appeals, was seized by the FBI after a seven-week investigation. He was accused of blackmail and attempted extortion of his ex-mistress, a wealthy Republican fund raiser.

A GM pickup truck in flames after being hit on the side by an automobile

November was a good month for radio shock jock Howard Stern; he wasn't fined for indecency. In October the FCC levied a $105,000 fine against a Los Angeles radio station that carried Stern's show; in December his bosses at Infinity Broadcasting were fined $600,000 and warned against future violations.

DECEMBER

NATION

Errand of Mercy

U.S.-led troops head for Somalia to combat anarchy and starvation

IN A STRIKING DEPARTURE FROM POLICY, THE U.S. embarked on a humanitarian mission in famine-ridden Somalia, where armed gangs

Ready, aim, film! The only shooting on the beaches of Mogadishu was by an army of the press.

had been stealing relief supplies, threatening mass starvation. President Bush offered to organize and command a U.N. force and supply most of the troops; the U.N. gladly agreed. The Marines waded ashore on Dec. 9 (and were greeted by the lights of the world press). After an initial delay, supplies were flowing, and key Somali clan leaders agreed to a truce. But two questions remained: whether long-term peace was possible, and whether troops would be back in the U.S. by the Administration's promised Jan. 20 date.

Bush's Victory Lap

Eyeing history, the President visits Somalia and signs a pact in Moscow

FOR A LAME DUCK, GEORGE BUSH WAS FLYING high and fast—both literally and symbolically. Tidying up his presidency for the history books on Christmas Eve, he pardoned six Iran-*contra* defendants, including former Defense Secre-

tary Caspar Weinberger, who was awaiting trial in January, former National Security Adviser Robert McFarlane, former Assistant Secretary of State Elliot Abrams and three ex-CIA officials.

After Christmas, Bush jetted around the globe, rounding off his term in office with three policy initiatives. First, he visited Somalia, mingling with the troops on New Year's Eve in the capital, Mogadishu, and journeying the next day to Baidoa, in the heart of the famine zone. Next it was off to Moscow, where Bush and Boris Yeltsin signed a treaty that should accomplish the radical cut in long-range nuclear weapons that had long eluded U.S. and Soviet leaders, retiring about two-thirds of their remaining long-range warheads.

During his journey the President disclosed that he had warned the Serbs not to try anything in Kosovo, a mostly Albanian province that the Serbs threatened to subject to Bosnian-style "ethnic cleansing." If Serbia does cause a conflict there, said Bush, the U.S. is "prepared to employ military force" to stop it.

Professor Bill's Class: Political Economy 101

Clinton's summit played well, but his promises are looking harder to keep

IN LITTLE ROCK, BILL CLINTON STAGED A TELE-vised 19-hour talkathon on the economy that served as a remarkable national teach-in: 329 economists, corporate executives and labor leaders got a chance to pitch their favorite nostrums to the President-elect. But offstage, Clinton and his top advisers fretted that his campaign pledge to cut the deficit in half within four years—while cutting middle-class taxes and spending more to fuel growth—looked tougher to meet than they expected. New figures showed the budget deficit would be $100 billion higher than earlier estimates.

Ayodhya: Hindus rejoice as the Babri mosque is razed

WORLD

A Mosque Is Razed And India Divided

Riots between Hindu and Muslim rage across the country

TO THE SOUNDS OF CONCH SHELLS AND CLASH-ing cymbals, a mob of Hindu fanatics swinging pickaxes, crowbars and bare hands descended upon the Babri mosque in the northern Indian town of Ayodhya and razed it. Never mind that the Supreme Court had ordered that the mosque be left alone. Hindus believed the mosque had been built on the spot where the Hindu god Rama was born. The destruction enraged Muslims, roughly 12% of India's population. Riots followed in Bombay, Calcutta and other cities. Prime Minister P.V. Narasimha Rao cracked down on extremists from both factions, arresting nearly 6,000 Hindus and Muslims, but the crisis seemed far from over.

Elsewhere:

- **Russia** In a tough battle for power, the Congress of People's Deputies forced Boris Yeltsin to dump his architect of economic reform, Yegor Gaidar, in favor of Victor Chernomyrdin, a former Communist Party apparatchik.
- **Serbia** Defying world opinion, voters reelected President Slobodan Milosevic over opponent Milan Panic, giving the militant nationalist 55% of the vote.

BUSINESS

Big Blue Company, Big Red Ink

IBM downsizes again, and its stock continues to fall

COMPUTER GIANT IBM ANNOUNCED ITS MOST traumatic cutbacks to date. In its fifth major restructuring in the past seven years, it planned to shed more unprofitable and ill-fitting assets and slash its work force in 1993 more than 8%, or 25,000 employees. The latest round of cuts will include the first layoffs in the company's 78-year history and will lead to a $6 billion pretax charge for the fourth quarter. IBM was expected to post a net loss of about $4.8 billion for the year; it also announced it intends to pare its spending on research and development by $1 billion, or 17%. The bad news reverberated on Wall Street, where it hastened the company's decline—by Dec. 18 the value of IBM stock had dropped 63% since February 1991.

SOCIETY

A Cross to Bear

Cincinnati's Christmas is haunted by the Ghost of Hatred Present

FOR NINE DAYS A CROSS RAISED BY THE KU KLUX Klan inspired a festival of civil disobedience in Cincinnati's Fountain Square. Four times the Klan put it up; three times protesters knocked it down before the Klan's permit to display the cross expired. Ironically, the Klan was backed by a federal court decision that required the city to permit the placement of a Hanukkah menorah in another part of the square.

PEOPLE

- **Convicted** Former CIA chief Clair George was found guilty of lying to Congress in the Iran-*contra* affair. Simultaneously, the Supreme Court refused to review a lower-court ruling that overturned the 1990 conviction of former National Security Adviser John Poindexter.

Taking Aim On Jupiter

Fly-by distance: 304 km (189 mi.)

SUN

EARTH

Galileo's trajectory

Astroid belt

JUPITER approach: December 1995

For the second time since its launch in 1989, the Galileo spacecraft has streaked past the earth on its round-about voyage to Jupiter. Employing a crack-the-whip-like maneuver, the probe gathered momentum for the remaining 874 million miles of its journey.

PANDA'S PASSING

Ling-Ling, the crowd-pleasing panda for two decades at the National Zoo in Washington, died of unknown causes at age 23. Ling-Ling, a gift from the Beijing government, was the oldest giant panda outside China. She was survived by her mate Hsing-Hsing, the initially reluctant father of her five cubs—all of which died within days of their birth.

27

FOR THE RECORD

BESTSELLING BOOKS

Fiction
1. *Gerald's Game* Stephen King
2. *The Pelican Brief* John Grisham
3. *Delores Claiborne* Stephen King
4. *Mixed Blessings* Danielle Steel
5. *Waiting to Exhale* Terry McMillan
6. *The Tale of the Body* Thief Anne Rice
7. *Jewels* Danielle Steel
8. *Star Wars, Vol. 2: Dark Force Rising* Timothy Zahn
9. *The Stars Shine Down* Sidney Sheldon
10. *Mexico* James A. Michener

ACADEMY AWARDS

Movies premiering in 1991

Best Picture
The Silence of the Lambs

Best Actor
Anthony Hopkins,
The Silence of the Lambs

Best Actress
Jodie Foster,
The Silence of the Lambs

Best Director
Jonathan Demme,
The Silence of the Lambs

Best Supporting Actor
Jack Palance, *City Slickers*

Best Supporting Actress
Mercedes Ruehl,
The Fisher King

Lifetime Achievement
Satyajit Ray

MOST POPULAR FILMS

Based on box-office receipts
1. Batman Returns
2. Beauty and the Beast
3. Lethal Weapon 3
4. Sister Act
5. Wayne's World
6. Hook
7. Basic Instinct
8. Home Alone 2
9. Home Alone 2
10. A League of Their Own

TONY AWARDS

Best Play
Dancing at Lughnasa

Best Muscial
Crazy for You

Best Revival
Guys and Dolls

Best Actress, Play
Glenn Close,
Death and the Maiden

Best Actor, Play
Judd Hirsch,
Conversations with My Father

Best Actress, Musical
Faith Prince, *Guys and Dolls*

Best Actor, Muscial
Gregory Hines, *Jelly's Last Jam*

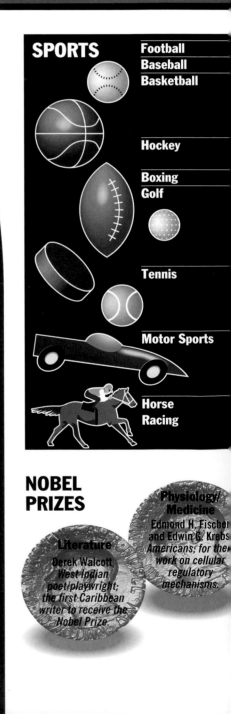

SPORTS

Football
Baseball
Basketball

Hockey

Boxing
Golf

Tennis

Motor Sports

Horse Racing

NOBEL PRIZES

Literature
Derek Walcott,
West Indian
poet/playwright;
the first Caribbean
writer to receive the
Nobel Prize.

Physiology/Medicine
Edmond H. Fischer
and Edwin G. Krebs,
Americans; for their
work on cellular
regulatory
mechanisms.

Non-Fiction

The Way Things Ought to Be Rush Limbaugh

It Doesn't Take a Hero H. Norman Schwarzkopf with Peter Petre

Sex Madonna

A Return to Love Marianne Williamson

Diana: Her True Story Andrew Morton

Silent Passage Gail Sheehy

Every Living Thing James Herriot

How to Satisfy a Woman Every Time Naura Hayden

More Wealth Without Risk Charles J. Givens

I Can't Believe I Said That! Kathie Lee Gifford

Source: Waldenbooks (February–December 1992)

TOP 10 TV PROGRAMS
Fall Season, 1992

1. Roseanne
2. Jackie Thomas
3. 60 Minutes
4. Murphy Brown
5. Coach
6. Murder, She Wrote
7. Cheers & NFL Monday Night Football (tie)
9. Home Improvement
10. Full House

Superbowl XXVI	Washington Redskins over Buffalo Bills, 37-24
World Series	Toronto Bluejays over Atlanta Braves, 4 games to 2
NBA Championship	Chicago Bulls defeated the Portland Trailblazers, 4 games to 2
NCAA Championship	Duke defeated Michigan, 71-51
NCAA Women's Championship	Stanford defeated Western Kentucky, 78-62
Stanley Cup	Pittsburgh Penguins over Chicago Blackhawks, 4 games to 0
Heavyweight Title	Riddick Bowe defeated Evander Holyfield in Las Vegas
The Masters	Fred Couples
U.S. Open	Tom Kite
LPGA Championship	Betsy King
PGA Championship	Nick Price
British Open	Nick Faldo
Australian Open	Monica Seles, Jim Courier
French Open	Monical Seles, Jim Courier
Wimbledon	Steffi Graf, Andre Agassi
U.S. Open	Monica Seles, Stefan Edberg
Daytona 500	Davey Allison
Indianapolis 500	Al Unser, Jr.
Le Mans	Derek Warwick, Yannick Dalmas, Mark Blundell
Formula One	Nigel Mansell
Kentucky Derby	Lil E. Tee
Preakness Stakes	Pine Bluff
Belmont Stakes	A.P. Indy

TOP 10 VIDEOS
RENTALS

1. Father of the Bride
2. Fried Green Tomatoes
3. The Hand That Rocks the Cradle
4. Wayne's World
5. White Men Can't Jump
6. Cape Fear
7. Deceived
8. The Fisher King
9. The Prince of Tides
10. Thelma and Louise

SALES

1. Beauty and the Beast
2. 101 Dalmatians
3. Sister Act
4. Beethoven
5. Hook
6. Wayne's World
7. The Rescuers
8. Ferngully
9. The Great Mouse Detective
10. Batman Returns

Physics
George Charpak, Polish-born French; for devising an atomic detector to trace the trajectories of subatomic particles.

Economics
Gary S. Becker, American; for work linking aspects of economics to human behavior.

Chemistry
Rudolph A. Marcus, American; for his mathematical analysis of the causes and effects of electron movement.

Peace
Rigoberta Menchu, Guatemalen Quiche Indian; for protesting government abuse of indigenous peoples.

Sources:
Sports: The 1993 Information Please Sports Almanic; Nobel Prizes: Facts on File; Videos: *Video Business*; Oscar Awards: *Variety*; Tony Awards: Facts on File; Books: *Publishers Weekly*; Television: Nielsen Media Research

WINDS OF CHANGE

What's wrong with the weather? Mother Nature's deadly show

ALASKA
Giving scientists only 30 minutes warning, Mount Spurr erupted violently in August. On the same day, earthquakes rocked Alaska's Andreanof Islands and Kyrgyzstan in the former U.S.S.R.

WASHINGTON
Seattle had its driest May in history.

COLORADO
A dry, hot April set record high temperatures, but snow fell on June 1.

EAST COAST
One of the fiercest storms of the century struck the East Coast in mid -December, causing record coastal floods and snowfalls.

CALIFORNIA
In February torrential rains and heavy mountain snows caused the worst flooding in Southern California since 1938.

GULF OF MEXICO
In late August Hurricane Andrew's 164 m.p.h. winds battered Florida and Louisiana in America's costliest storm ever.

HAWAII
Hurricane Iniki blew through in mid-September, destroying one third of the homes on Kauai and causing an estimated $1.2 billion in damage.

TEXAS
In January the Southern U.S. from Texas to Georgia got twice as much rain as usual.

MEXICO
In January Guadalajara received 10 in. (254 mm) of rainfall, a record. The previous high for that month was 4 in. (94 mm).

EL NINO
This warm ocean current can disrupt jet streams and affect weather patterns on five continents.

NICARAGUA
An earthquake in the Pacific Ocean 30 miles west of Nicaragua sent tsunamis as high as 45 ft. along 200 miles of coast and caused more than a hundred deaths.

BRAZIL
For each of five days in May, it rained more in southern Brazil than it usually does in a month.

THE PERIOD FROM DECEMBER 1991 TO MARCH 1992 went into the National Weather Service's record books as America's warmest winter in at least 97 years. It hardly rained at all in rainy Seattle in May. Africa is having its worst drought in 50 years, and Melbourne had its coldest January in 137 years.

What's wrong with the weather? Cautious scientists point to three main suspects: El Niño, the recurring buildup of warm water in the Pacific; the eruption of Mount Pinatubo in the Philipines, which heaved ash into the atmosphere and created a global haze; and the accumulation of greenhouse gases, which may have raised the world's average temperature. However, these phenomena interact in complex ways and may even cancel one another. In short, no one knows why Mother Nature put on such an unpredictable—and deadly—show in 1992.

PARIS
The worst rainstorm in a decade battered Paris in May, flooding the sewers and clogging the Seine with 300 tons of dead fish.

FRANCE
Flash floods in late September killed 38 people. Hardest hit: the Southeastern region of Vaucluse.

ITALY
Unusually low pressure together with winds from Africa caused the canals of Venice to overflow in late March. Water filled the Piazza San Marco to ankle depth every day for a week.

PAKISTAN
Flood waters building up over a month created a vast brown inland sea; by mid September more than 2,000 had drowned.

HONG KONG
The first five months of 1992 were the wettest in a century in Hong Kong. A killer rainstorm on May 8 triggered flooding and mud slides.

MIDDLE EAST
The region experienced its coldest winter in 40 years. In January it snowed in Amman, Damascus and Jerusalem.

PHILIPPINES
Mount Pinatubo's blowup, perhaps the largest volcanic eruption of the century, may lower temperatures around the world for the next three or four years.

AFRICA
A swath of Africa stretching from Cairo to Cape Town is suffering its worst drought in 50 years.

AUSTRALIA
Sydney endured its wettest December in two decades, and Melbourne its coldest January in at least 137 years.

TIME Graphic by Joe Lertola

SAY WHAT?

Gossip, gaffes and gab: the year's best sound bites

"Who am I? Why am I here?"
—Admiral James B. Stockdale, Ross Perot's running mate, at the vice-presidential debate

"If you've got a better idea... I'm all ears."

—Ross Perot, second presidential debate

"FIGHT THE REAL ENEMY."
—Sinead O'Connor, tearing up a photo of the Pope on *Saturday Night Live*

"I think it's about time we voted for Senators with breasts. After all, we've been voting for boobs long enough."
—Claire Sargent, candidate for Senate in Arizona, in September

"The Governor's jogging motto is, start slow and taper off."
—James Carville, on the candidate's exercise regimen

"I'm in trouble because I'm normal and slightly arrogant. A lot of people don't like themselves, and I happen to be totally in love with myself."
—Mike Tyson, following his conviction for rape

"It is about a socialist, anti-family political movement that encourages women to leave their husbands, kill their children, practice witchcraft, destroy capitalism and become lesbians."
—Evangelist Pat Robertson, speaking about the proposed Equal Rights Amendment, at the Republican Convention

"OH, SQUIDGY!"

—Ex-car salesman James Gilbey to Princess Diana, in an intercepted telephone conversation

"I suppose I could have stayed home and baked cookies and had teas."
—Hillary Clinton, describing her decision to pursue a career while raising a child

"You should draw a mushroom cloud and put underneath it, 'Made in America by lazy and illiterate Americans and tested in Japan.'"
—Senator Ernest Hollings of South Carolina in reaction to the President's trip to Japan

"I will cut off the head of my baby and swallow it if it would make Bush lose."

—An Iranian housewife, on the election

"I didn't expect to meet her. But then, she didn't expect to meet me."

—Walter Cronkite, on being seated next to Madonna at an Oscar-night party in Hollywood

"That's fine phonetically, but you're missing just a little bit."

—Vice President Dan Quayle, to Trenton, N.J., student William Figueroa after the sixth-grader successfully spelled "potato" in a spelling-bee

"It showed the rumors about the Vice President are true—that he's an idiot."

—William Figueroa, upon reflection

"Old Mc-Donald had a farm, e-i-e-i-o....e."

—Iowa Senator Tom Harkin, on how Quayle might handle an old song

"I want my name in the press. Why? Because I can make a lot of money. I figure if I'm going through all this pain and suffering, I'm getting a Ferrari."

—Amy Fisher, the "Long Island Lolita," hours before being sentenced in a plea bargain for shooting the wife of her alleged lover

"In the next life, I should like to come back as your trousers."

—Prince Charles, reportedly to confidant Camilla Parker-Bowles in a phone conversation

" 'DIDN'T INHALE?' "

—A dubious Billy Crystal, on Bill Clinton's marijuana experience, during the Oscar Awards telecast

"He's ... very evolved; more than his linear years. He plays like a Zen master. It's very in the moment."

—Barbra Streisand on tennis pro Andre Agassi

"I mean, if black people kill black people every day, why not have a week and kill white people?"

—Rap singer Sister Souljah, quoted in the Washington *Post*

"As you know, I planned a trip out here for some time, so it fits in very nicely."

—George Bush, on his visit to South Central L.A. following the riot

"NOT!"

—Wayne, *Wayne's World*

Fed up with politics as usual, American voters change the terms of the election and take a chance on a political unknown

BY MICHAEL KRAMER

HE ENTERED THE RACE UNKNOWN OUTSIDE THE South, a second-tier candidate facing an invincible President. Most assumed his candidacy was a dress rehearsal for 1996, a first-time-around-the-track adventure designed to acquaint the electorate with Bill Clinton and to teach Clinton something of the world beyond Arkansas. The risks seemed slight—but they became great. Charges of the kind that had hobbled others quickly attended Clinton's fledgling candidacy. He was written off more than once, politically dead in a country that barely knew him. How many times did he die? "Several at least," Clinton recalled. "Maybe more. But I always came back, didn't I?"

From Gennifer Flowers to the draft to charges that he waffled on the issues and massaged his rhetoric to conform to the expectations of his varied audiences, Clinton persevered. He survived because of his toughness. Not tough in the sense of ruthlessness or crudity, rather tough in the sense of purpose and mission. That focus, combined with an innate self-confidence, led Clinton to move quickly. He thought as he talked and rarely wavered: What's the question? Here's the response. He went immediately to the core of a problem, a fluent mind at the height of its power.

Besides his iron will, the key to Clinton's success was his uncompromising centrism. Ronald Reagan was gone and in many quarters derided, but Clinton knew that his ideological legacy endured. The nation's political balance had shifted rightward, and Clinton went with the flow. To a nation strapped economically and an electorate depressed psychologically because of it, Clinton routinely preached an activist politics—but one nonetheless rooted firmly in the center. In tone and content he often appeared as an endangered species—a moderate Republican. He called himself a "new kind of Democrat," and welfare reform, especially, was the talisman of his stance. He had read the American voter well and disciplined himself to stray only episodically for calculated (and temporary) advantage as he dealt with the shifting state of play.

To a degree the best political scientists came to envy, Clinton had gone to school on the failings of the losers who preceded him, and to anyone interested he proudly recounted the lessons he drew from his study. Thus, when it was his turn, he was ready. He calmly tacked to the left to meet the primary challenges of Paul Tsongas and Jerry Brown, and he sounded populist chords against George Bush when his innate strategic sense told him it was wise. But in every major pronouncement Clinton stayed squarely in the middle—where the votes were. Enough were charmed by this deftness that eventually they came to believe Clinton's tireless intonation that the 1992 contest really was a "watershed" election. They voted in record numbers, thus rendering foolish yet another bit of conventional wisdom.

What was act, what was real? Four years will tell the tale, a term during which welfare reform, national service

and a host of other initiatives will probably play peripheral roles in the country's evaluation of its new leader. Clinton has been elected to fix the economy. By 1996, if the electorate continues to view the nation as on the wrong track, Clinton will become a very young ex-President.

Whatever Clinton's personal fate, the country's politics seems changed forever in two significant ways. The first involves the candidates' increasingly creative use of television. Never again will presidential contenders content themselves with standard press conferences, tarmac photo-ops or Sunday-morning talk-show appearances. MTV, Arsenio, Donahue and Larry King have reshaped the way one strikes for the White House. Voters crave contact with the candidates, who have heretofore appeared to them mostly through slickly produced television commercials.

Now the sultans of gab offer the illusion of intimacy. With civilians asking questions—over the phone or from a live audience—the electorate has come to perceive these encounters as more "real" than when reporters do the grilling. No matter that follow-up interrogations are a rarity or that ordinary people often lack the policy sophistication necessary to pry a revealing response from a practiced politician. The perception is what counts, and the ease with which a candidate navigates these electronic town meetings will, from now on, materially affect his prospects.

THE OTHER CHANGE IN AMERICAN POLITICS INvolves Ross Perot. With 19 million people voting for the Texas billionaire despite his demonstrated nuttiness, something fundamental has happened. As party loyalty disintegrates, as the electorate's distrust of Washington-centered solutions increases, as the nation's disgust with packaged candidates and the media filter through which they are apprehended grows, the temptation to roll the dice with an outsider will increase. It could happen again, and perhaps as soon as 1996 if the new, self-described "policy-wonk" President proves less than a match for the country's problems.

Perot (as well as Clinton) was conceivable as President because two core pivots have changed. First, the end of the cold war has dampened the country's fear of selecting a candidate unsuited to the role of nuclear custodian; a life-ending conflict seems a distant nightmare. Second, many Americans are worried, for the first time, that the lives of their children may be worse than their own. Taken together, these two central factors, one an upper, the other a downer, open the presidential sweepstakes to a wider array of players. Whether any untraditional pretender gets a chance to contest credibly for the White House will turn in large measure on whether Clinton, as the champion of governmental action, can prove that an institution many voters viewed as irrelevant (and even harmful) before the campaign can be seen to work. In a real sense, then, the future of America's political system is Clinton's to define. ∎

Off and Running

Against all odds, Bill Clinton won the right to challenge George Bush for the presidency

ONLY 20 MONTHS BEFORE, GEORGE BUSH HAD been basking in the glow of the Gulf War victory and enjoying the highest approval ratings ever recorded for an American President. That he might even stand a chance of losing the presidency seemed improbable; that he might lose to the young (just 44 at the time), virtually unknown Governor of one of the smallest and poorest states in the nation—well, nobody would have believed it.

Yet when Americans went to the polls on Nov. 3, 1992, they voted overwhelmingly for change, electing the Democrat, Arkansas Governor Bill Clinton, to the presidency with 43% of the popular vote and 370 electoral votes. The voters gave the incumbent President only 38% of the popular vote and a meager 168 electoral votes. Independent candidate Ross Perot finished a strong third in the race, with 19% of the popular vote but no electoral votes. Although Clinton's percentage of the popular vote was not high, the combined total who voted for Clinton and Perot—and thus against the President—was a strong 62%. The mandate for change was clear.

Reflecting the nation's deep dissatisfaction with "politics as usual," the election broke many of the rules of recent presidential contests. Candidates blazed new media paths to speak directly to the public; Perot's strong candidacy shook the Washington political establishment; and,

in a heartening development, the campaign engaged cynical voters, a higher percentage of whom made their way to the polls than had in many other years.

NEW HAMPSHIRE'S ANGRY VOTERS

As 1992 began, many of the Democrats' strongest potential candidates were holding back from entering the race, perhaps owing to President Bush's high approval scores in the polls. Three key contenders—New York Governor Mario Cuomo and Senators Lloyd Bentsen and Sam Nunn—never did enter the race; Virginia Governor Doug Wilder exited early. The early pack of Democrats included former Senator Paul Tsongas of Massachusetts, a cancer survivor and preacher of pro-growth programs; Clinton, a young centrist often accused of seeming facile; Senator Tom Harkin of Iowa, an unreconstructed liberal; former California Governor Jerry Brown, who refused to accept campaign contributions of more than $100; and Nebraska Senator Bob Kerrey, who won the Congressional Medal of Honor in Vietnam. None of the candidates were national figures; of them, Clinton had the strongest organization and the most funding.

Clinton's campaign almost ended in New Hampshire, however, when an Arkansas state employee, Gennifer Flowers, told a tabloid newspaper (which reportedly paid her more than $100,000 for the recollection) that she had maintained a 12-year sexual relationship with the Governor. When the charges became public, stirring enormous national coverage, Clinton and his wife Hillary went on television's 60 *Minutes* to counter the charges. Clinton branded the allegations false, and the couple successfully conveyed a sense of togetherness and purpose.

Just as that flap died down, another began: the first sto-

ries about how Clinton had avoided the draft as a young Rhodes scholar at Oxford began to surface. On Feb. 12 Clinton suddenly called a press conference in a hanger at the Manchester, New Hampshire, airport and handed out a faded photocopy of a letter written by the young Clinton to an ROTC officer in Arkansas expressing his agony over the Vietnam War. The candidate never did put the draft issue to rest; his statements in New Hampshire were the first of a long series of incomplete and sometimes conflicting remarks on the subject that would fuel a widespread distrust of Clinton well into the fall.

When primary day came in New Hampshire, it was the voters' turn to make headlines: they chose their tough-talking neighbor, Tsongas, giving him 33% of the vote. It was the beginning of a strong stretch for Tsongas, who went on to victories in primary contests in Massachusetts and Maryland before running out of money and energy in March. Clinton survived in New Hampshire, running second with 25% of the vote and claiming to be "the Comeback Kid."

REPUBLICAN RUCKUS

The results of the Republican primary in New Hampshire were even more noteworthy. With a cry of anger, disgust and pain that was, above all, a warning to George Bush, Republican voters gave only 53% of their vote to the incumbent President, while lavishing 37% on right-wing commentator and gadfly Patrick Buchanan, a former speechwriter for both Richard Nixon and Ronald Reagan. The votes were less an expression of faith in Buchanan than an angry gesture directed at Bush's broken promises ("Read my lips: no new taxes") and at what many saw as his almost bizarre disconnection from the realities of American life, particularly the country's economic straits.

Paul Tsongas: the Speedo candidate meets the press

They Also Ran

CALL IT THE "EX-FACTOR." THE 1992 CAMPAIGN WAS enlivened by the contributions of an ex-Senator, an ex–White House insider and an ex-Governor.

PAUL TSONGAS Paul Tsongas was the Democratic Party's underdog of choice. The former Senator from Massachusetts possessed a power of glamourlessness, a nerdy, basset-hound anti-image that gave hope to those voters who despaired of American politics as all sound bites and video bursts. Tsongas' astringent message was that Santa Claus in whatever extravagant form (Ronald Reagan or the Great Society) was not coming back.

Part of Tsongas' appeal sprang from his personal history. He had apparently beaten the lymphoma that drove him from the Senate in 1984, and his TV ads showed him vigorously doing the butterfly stroke in a swimming pool. Though he did well in the early primaries, he suspended his campaign after stinging defeats in Illinois and Michigan. In November Tsongas admitted that he had experienced a recurrence of his cancer, saying "Whatever strength I brought to the campaign was in my head, not my lymph nodes."

PAT BUCHANAN Politicians are candid at their peril; a gaffe occurs when one of them inadvertently says what he actually thinks. By that standard, conservative Republican candidate Patrick J. Buchanan was a veritable gaffemeister, insisting that Watergate was "a bunch of Mickey Mouse misdemeanors," Congress was "Israeli-occupied territory" and Oliver North "a hero." His regular stump speech extolled isolationism, protectionism and fiscal stinginess. The former White House speechwriter demonstrated Bush's weakness with a strong showing in New Hampshire, then refused to withdraw from the race, though he lost in every primary. In a final blow to Bush, Buchanan's hard-

"For twelve years I was his girlfriend, and now he tells me to deny it."
—Gennifer Flowers

"The story is just not true."
—Bill Clinton

By mid-March, the President's campaign seemed in turmoil and the Republican race had settled into a two-man contest—between Bush and his lesser self. Bush repudiated his budget compromise of 1990, saying he regretted breaking his "no new taxes" pledge. His campaign operation was divided over tactics; backbiting and finger pointing were rife. Meanwhile, the pace of the economic recovery was glacial.

It was not until May that Bush finally shook off Buchanan, who—no doubt with an eye to 1996—refused to withdraw from the campaign, though he never won a primary. His persistence badly damaged Bush, whom he painted as an unprincipled pragmatist who would rather win re-election than lead the nation. Buchanan's supporters, overwhelmingly white, male and angry, reveled in his harangues against gays, environmentalists and foreigners. His cry of "America First" appealed to those who thought the country was headed in the wrong direction.

Ironically, it was not Bush but his Vice President, Dan

Quayle, who capitalized on those concerns for the Administration, striking a nerve with his attack in May on TV's *Murphy Brown* show for its "glorification" of single motherhood and with his denunciation of America's "cultural élite." Alert to voters' concerns about Clinton's character, the Republicans decided to make the issue of "family values" central to their campaign.

THE DEMOCRATS THIN OUT

After New Hampshire, the Democratic race accelerated, as the candidates endured a long string of primaries scattered about the country. Here Governor Clinton's strong organization and funding tilted the scales. He had always been favored to win the cluster of Southern and Border state primaries in early March, since that was his home region. But, learning a lesson from the failed campaign of Senator Al

Jerry Brown: 1-800-pound guerrilla

nosed speech at the Republican Convention all but declared a social war in the country and horrified mainstream viewers.

JERRY BROWN In 1992 Brown, the former two-term Governor of California, made his third bid for the White House. With a forthrightness bordering on naiveté and an all-too-California tendency to let it all hang out, Brown did not even try to protect himself from the perceptions raised by his esoteric passions. "I don't know which image you have of me," he told new audiences, "Governor Moonbeam?

Pat Buchanan: always lead with your right

The Governor who drove a Plymouth? Slept on the floor?" Brown's unshakable counterculture image undercut his fervent message, a call for a full-scale American political reformation.

Brown's tactics were certainly revolutionary: he pioneered the use of a telephone 800 number to solicit funds and support, vowing to accept no donation over $100. As other Democrats dropped out, Brown became the focus of the Anybody-but-Clinton crowd. His high point came when he won the Connecticut primary, but Clinton finally beat Brown in his home state of California, ending his run.

Gore of Tennessee in 1988, Clinton from the very first had poured money and organizational effort—and his personal time—into Illinois and Michigan. If he could follow up a Southern sweep with big March victories in these important states, he figured, he could sew up the nomination.

Almost. But first, Nebraska's Kerrey had a moment of glory. A week after the New Hampshire vote, he won the South Dakota primary ("We've struck gold in the Black Hills!" he declared) and attracted a scattering of contributions, but not enough to keep him in the race. When Bill Clinton took his first victory, winning Georgia by a wide margin in early March, Kerrey withdrew. Tom Harkin, whose war chest had emptied early, soon followed.

Paul Tsongas seemed to lose some momentum after his New Hampshire victory, but rallied with victories on March 10 in Utah, Maryland and Washington, demonstrating he could win outside New England. Now he and

Clinton were the front runners, with Jerry Brown waging a pesky guerrilla operation well to the left of their centrist campaigns. Clinton still suffered from voter doubts about his character, while Tsongas continued to surprise many with his appeal, which was based on his honest message that the nation had overdue economic bills to pay.

By the end of March, the Clinton-Tsongas duel was over; Clinton's advance work paid off when he took the Illinois and Michigan primaries. Exhausted and in debt, Tsongas suspended his candidacy. Suddenly the nomination was Clinton's to lose: he had nearly half the delegates he needed, and only Jerry Brown stood in his way. Unlike Tsongas, Brown couldn't be starved out of the race. He lived off the land, foraging for petty cash with his 800 number and vowing to wage war "for the soul of the Democratic Party" in the remaining primaries.

Brown didn't beat Clinton, but he made him work for the nomination. The two engaged in a bruising street fight in April's New York primary. There Clinton shot himself in the foot, admitting to a reporter that he had tried marijuana while a graduate student in England, but "didn't inhale," touching

See How They Run
The pulse of the polls: Clinton's rise, Bush's fall, and the ins and outs of Ross Perot

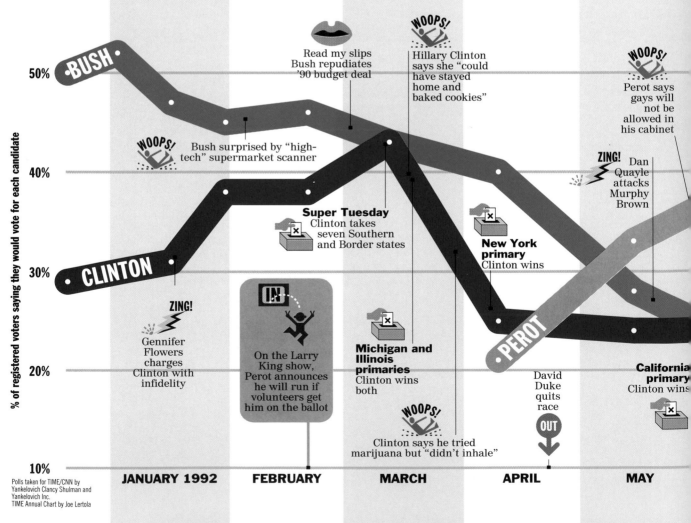

Read my slips
Bush repudiates
'90 budget deal

Hillary Clinton
says she "could
have stayed
home and
baked cookies"

Perot says
gays will
not be
allowed in
his cabinet

WOOPS!
Bush surprised by "high-tech" supermarket scanner

ZING! Dan
Quayle
attacks
Murphy
Brown

% of registered voters saying they would vote for each candidate

50%

40%

30%

20%

10%

Super Tuesday
Clinton takes
seven Southern
and Border states

New York
primary
Clinton wins

WOOPS!
Gennifer
Flowers
charges
Clinton with
infidelity

IN
On the Larry
King show,
Perot announces
he will run if
volunteers get
him on the ballot

Michigan and
Illinois
primaries
Clinton wins
both

David
Duke
quits
race

OUT

California
primary
Clinton wins

WOOPS!
Clinton says he tried
marijuana but "didn't inhale"

JANUARY 1992   FEBRUARY   MARCH   APRIL   MAY

Polls taken for TIME/CNN by
Yankelovich Clancy Shulman and
Yankelovich Inc.
TIME Annual Chart by Joe Lertola

Spring in New York: Clinton adviser James Carville and Brown adviser Jacques Barzahi do the Primary Shuffle

Clinton won in New York with 41%; but in a surprise, Paul Tsongas placed second with 29%, despite the suspension of his candidacy. Though Clinton had won, two-thirds of New York Democrats said they wanted another candidate in the race; many in his party believed the doubts about his character would lead to disaster against George Bush in November. Still, Clinton went on to victory in the Pennsylvania primary and finally beat Brown in the Californian's home state on June 2 to clinch the Democratic nomination with 285 delegates to spare.

But Clinton, ordinarily a cockeyed optimist, was forcing his smile the day he clinched the Democratic nomination. He was running last in the polls, not merely in second place, but in third. Ahead of him was the incumbent President. And ahead of George Bush—topping the June polls—was a surprise independent candidate whose race transformed the campaign, Texas electronics billionaire Ross Perot. ■

off skeptical guffaws from his fellow baby boomers. However, Clinton assiduously worked two key blocs of voters, blacks and Jews, and successfully attacked Brown's eccentric economic plan, based on a proposed "flat tax" of 13% on income.

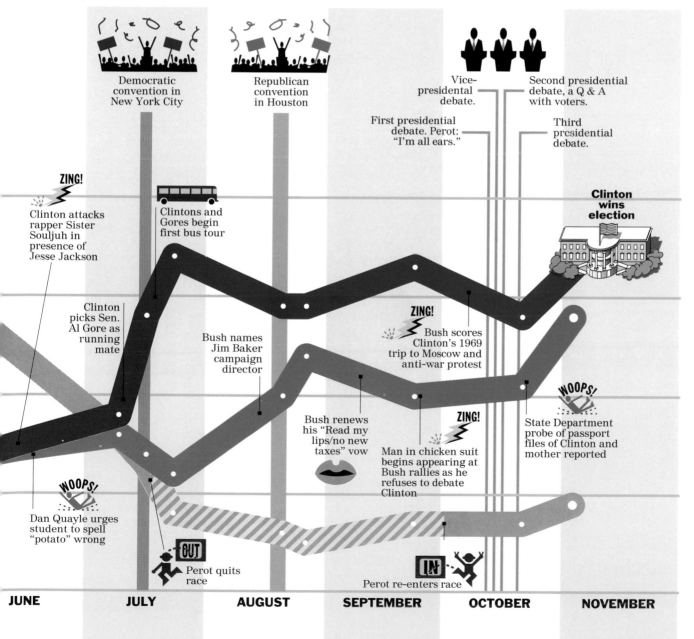

Democratic convention in New York City

Republican convention in Houston

Vice-presidential debate.

Second presidential debate, a Q & A with voters.

First presidential debate. Perot: "I'm all ears."

Third presidential debate.

ZING!
Clinton attacks rapper Sister Souljuh in presence of Jesse Jackson

Clintons and Gores begin first bus tour

Clinton wins election

Clinton picks Sen. Al Gore as running mate

Bush names Jim Baker campaign director

ZING!
Bush scores Clinton's 1969 trip to Moscow and anti-war protest

Bush renews his "Read my lips/no new taxes" vow

ZING!
Man in chicken suit begins appearing at Bush rallies as he refuses to debate Clinton

WOOPS!
State Department probe of passport files of Clinton and mother reported

WOOPS!
Dan Quayle urges student to spell "potato" wrong

OUT Perot quits race

IN Perot re-enters race

JUNE   **JULY**   **AUGUST**   **SEPTEMBER**   **OCTOBER**   **NOVEMBER**

Perot Crashes the Party

A can-do billionaire shook up the
parties, woke up the voters,
and climbed to the top of the polls

T HREE MONTHS BEFORE, IN FEBRUARY, H. ROSS
Perot had been just another TV talk-show guest, a
blustery businessman holding forth on the economy on Larry King's talk show on CNN. Asked at the
outset whether he planned to run for President,
Perot gave a typically forthright answer: "No." But 45 minutes later, Perot—by all evidence impulsively—dropped a
bombshell. Yes, he'd run, and run hard, if his supporters
would put him on the ballot in all 50 states as an independent. That "if" was answered by an enormous outpouring of
volunteer enthusiasm. Perot established an 800-number operation to enlist support; in the month between March 13 and
April 13, he claimed to have received 1.5 million calls.

In those early days, Perot did the seemingly impossible: he crafted a credible national presidential campaign out of two dozen TV interviews and half a dozen speeches. His folksy, no-nonsense manner and outsider status attracted many who were disenchanted with both major parties. Volunteers registered him in state after state: by May, Perot was actually leading the polls at 33%, with Bush at 28% and Clinton at 24%.

THE BILLIONAIRE BOY SCOUT

Ross Perot held court in the 17th floor of a North Dallas office tower, a memorabilia-filled aerie that radiated almost preternatural calm. Yet the man was notoriously complex. Was he simply what he purported to be: the ultimate straight arrow, the billionaire who never lusted after money, a self-effacing idealist, a brilliant problem solver and political outsider? Or, as his many critics charged, was he thin-skinned, self-righteous, unwilling to compromise, a sucker for conspiracy theories?

The son of a small-town cotton broker in Texarkana, Texas, Perot attended the U.S. Naval Academy, spent four years in the Navy and in 1957 joined the white-shirted brigades of IBM as a computer salesman. The Perot myth was born when he broke with the rigid corporate culture and inflexible commission system of IBM in 1962 to found Electronic Data Systems—and became a just-folks billionaire seven years later, shortly after he took his company public. During the 1970s and '80s, the intense Perot tangled with a host of foes: the North Vietnamese, Iranian revolutionaries, the Reagan and Carter Administrations and the General Motors board.

This real-life Crusader Rabbit boasted several formidable political assets. He had a political bull detector that cut through Washington-style obfuscation, and his one-liners could be devastating. He also took stands that ran counter to the timorous can't-tell-the-truth-to-the-people philosophy of both parties. He favored means testing for Social Security and Medicare and kept the focus of the campaign on his pet peeve, the deficit, throughout the contest.

Yet some of Perot's ideas bordered on the demagogic. He advocated a constitutional amendment to bar Congress from raising taxes without a vote of the people. He was entranced by a grandiose notion of electronic town meetings, a high-tech gimmick that seemed to step outside America's traditional system of representation. Worst of all, Perot seemed unable to stand the glare of media scrutiny and public criticism that came with the territory of running for President. Like a salesman whose primary product is his own reputation, Perot hated adverse comment.

Perot confirmed the worst assessments of his character when he suddenly withdrew from the campaign only two months after formally entering it, crushing the expectations of his loyal volunteers. Oblivious to the stunned cries of betrayal, Perot insisted that he was interested only in the good of the country, and said he was impressed with the "revitalized" Democratic Party. But many Americans concluded Perot had taken Harry Truman's advice: unable to take the heat, he had made tracks from the kitchen. ■

Barnstorming on The Boob Tube

CALL IT THE TOUCH-TONE REBELLION, THE MTV Uprising, the Arsenio Insurrection. Prompted, perhaps, by 1991 polls showing voter alienation at a 25-year peak, candidates found new ways to reach out and touch voters, and voters found new ways to dial their populist rage right into the political system.

800 NUMBERS Jerry Brown was the first to discover the power of the 800 number. His nagging campaign against Bill Clinton was fueled by his small-contributions-only phone number, which kept his ascetic crusade alive. By the end of March, Brown's call-in had generated $3.5 million in pledges and $2 million in actual contributions. But he was soon supplanted by a new king of phone-call frenzy, Ross Perot. At one point, Perot claimed that his own 800 number was generating 500,000 calls in a 24-hour period.

Saxman Clinton warbles for Arsenio

TALK SHOWS Hail, King Larry King! Ross Perot was not only a favorite guest of King's on his nightly CNN talk show; he announced his availability as a candidate on the program. Before too long, George Bush and Bill Clinton were putting on pancake for the show. King was only one of many TV and radio hosts who benefited from the candidates' desire to appear in an unbuttoned format, as opposed to the standard Sunday morning "issues" programs. Clinton advisers traced his comeback to his casual appearance on the Arsenio Hall show, where he donned shades and played rock saxophone. Even MTV got into the picture, offering a regular political segment with reporter Tabitha Soren. Baby boomers

Perot's poetry: folksy-charm, low-tech charts

"Elvis" Clinton and Al Gore were happy to appear on the music network. By the end of the campaign, even the President wanted his MTV time—and got it.

INFOMERCIALS It took the unpredictable Perot to demonstrate that more than 11 million American homes would tune in to a 30-minute dry-as-dust lecture on the sorry state of the U.S. economy. His first infomercial had a bigger audience than the National League baseball playoff game that followed. Characteristically, Perot scripted and extemporized the entire no-frills production himself.

Down to The Wire

While Bush rallied and Perot dallied, Bill Clinton forged on to the Big Prize

AS THE DEMOCRATS HEADED for their convention in New York City, the polls were moving as well. In the month after Ross Perot had topped the polls in June, Bill Clinton's stock had risen; now he was actually leading at 28%, with 26% each for Perot and George Bush. Steadily repeating his centrist message, Clinton had positioned himself above the fray as Perot and Bush traded charges in late June that each had investigated the other's children, seeking scandal.

Four days before the opening of the convention, Clinton made another sound move. Defying the unwritten law that the primary purpose of the vice-presidential candidate is to balance the ticket, he chose, of all potential running mates, the one closest to being a carbon copy of himself: Tennessee Senator Al Gore. Besides hailing from neighboring mid-South states and swimming in the centrist mainstream of their party, they were close enough in age to form the first all-baby-boom ticket.

LOVEFEST IN MADISON SQUARE GARDEN

To seasoned observers, the Democratic Convention seemed like a Republican Convention. Everything worked. The television was good. The words were good. The propaganda, especially, was good. The also-rans performed well, and the delegates in Madison Square Garden cheered like paid extras. On display was a reformed party that had healed its incessant factional splits. Then, to the astonishment of all, Ross Perot stole the show.

On the day of Clinton's acceptance speech, Perot threw his thunderbolt, suddenly and inexplicably shutting down his campaign with all the brutality of a plant manager pink-slipping loyal workers at Christmas. But Perot cheered Clinton's camp when he spoke of having been impressed in recent weeks by a "revitalized" Democratic Party.

Bush and Clinton reacted to the Texan's surprise like political ambulance chasers, each inviting Perot's folks to

Sleazy Business

ARLY IN THE PRESIDENTIAL CAMPAIGN, GEORGE Bush publicly ordered his political operatives to "stay out of the sleaze business." Voters endorsed the impulse. Even so the race was marred by a series of allegations that placed the focus on innuendos rather than issues:

FLOWERS OF EVIL In January the supermarket tabloid *Star* paid Arkansas state employee Gennifer Flowers more than $100,000 for a story in which she claimed that she and Bill Clinton had had a 12-year affair.

FEELING THE DRAFT In February a letter Clinton had written to the director of the ROTC program at the University of Arkansas in 1969 surfaced. In it, Clinton thanked the officer for "saving me from the draft."

PRIVATE EYES In June, Ross Perot and Bush traded charges that each was employing private investigators to find damaging revelations about the other's family. "Leave my kids alone!" the President stormed.

REDS UNDER THE BEDS In October, Bush told Larry King on his talk show that Clinton should "level with the American people on the draft, on whether he went to

Moscow, how many demonstrations he led against his country from a foreign soil." The comments marked the climax of a well-orchestrated campaign of rumors, leaks and innuendos aimed at Clinton's patriotism.

DOCTORED PHOTOS In the campaign's final week, Perot came up with a new explanation for why he had withdrawn from the race in July: he wanted to save his daughter Carolyn from a smear. Offering no proof, he claimed the Republicans had plotted to portray his daughter as a lesbian by circulating a doctored photograph, then to "disrupt" her August wedding.

UNSTATELY SEARCH After the election, State Department officials admitted they had searched the passport files of both Clinton and Clinton's mother Virginia Kelley during the campaign, at the request of officials in the Bush campaign. In December former U.S. Attorney Joseph diGenova was named to conduct a probe of the incident.

"sign on." But the timing was in Clinton's favor; in his ringing acceptance speech that night, in which he challenged the President, "If you won't use your power to help America, step aside. I will," he included an invitation to Perot's supporters to join the Democrats. The next morning Clinton, his wife Hillary and Senator Gore and his wife Tipper embarked on yet another unconventional campaign foray: a six-day bus jaunt from New York City to St. Louis, Missouri.

The bus tours—six more were to follow—were an enormous success. They drew an unsubtle contrast between the patrician Bush's alleged loss of contact with heartland America and the Clinton-Gore close-to-the-people pitch. The journeys cemented the relationship between the couples, drew huge and enthusiastic crowds and allowed the candidates to relax and campaign in an easy, friendly manner. Meanwhile, polls showed a huge postconvention "bounce" for Clinton that put him ahead of Bush by 24 points. He would never trail again.

REPUBLICANS MEET IN HOUSTON

While the Democrats barnstormed Middle America, the President wasted August. He was late getting organized, late appointing Secretary of State James Baker to be the new campaign manager and pull his floundering organization together, late settling on a theme—a good three months behind on almost everything.

In contrast to the lift Clinton got out of the Democratic Convention, Bush got almost none from the Republican meeting. Though the President played the stature card in his acceptance speech, pointing out his foreign policy achievements, he skipped gingerly around any discussion of the economy. Worse, the convention laid bare the deep divisions within the party. Patrick Buchanan's opening-night speech all but raised the specter of race war, only to be followed minutes later by Ronald Reagan's soaring tribute to Bush and America's future.

Bush did manage to narrow Clinton's lead in the polls a bit after the convention. But a slow federal response to Hurricane Andrew's devastation of Florida and Louisiana gave voters renewed concern about the President's reflexes, even though Bush visited the damaged regions twice. Clinton was also losing ground as new details about his avoidance of the draft again raised concerns about his credibility. But Clinton's team scored big points when Bush refused to agree to a plan for televised debates between the two; Clintonites in chicken suits were sent to Bush's rallies to showcase his supposed fear of facing their man. Through September the candidates barnstormed around the nation, with Bush finally delivering a detailed, forceful speech on his economic plans for the nation in Detroit in mid-month.

THE RETURN OF PEROT

In September the Third Man emerged from the woodwork: Perot began signaling that he might get back in the

Top: George Bush, in his just-plain-folks mode, samples the blue-plate special at a diner in Spartanburg, S.C. Below: country boys Bill Clinton and Al Gore hit the hay.

race. The Texan seemed driven by two forces: the desire to rehabilitate the reputation he had tarnished by his sudden withdrawal in July, and a profound dislike of Bush. Managing to manipulate events like a master puppeteer, he invited top Clinton and Bush advisers to Dallas, where they pitched their respective candidate's policies to his centurions. Three days later, on Oct. 1, the mercurial billionaire announced that his followers around the country, having found Bush and Clinton wanting, were demanding his active candidacy. He allowed that he was "honored to accept their request," and introduced his running mate, retired Vice Admiral James Stockdale.

Once again the man who had been written off as "the

"The people have spoken, and we respect the majesty of the democratic system."
—George Bush

yellow Ross of Texas" had completely altered the shape of the contest, essentially turning it into a one-month campaign. Perot further surprised the country when his no-nonsense 30-minute TV infomercials drew large audiences.

Perot's re-entry also upset the complicated debate calculus that the Bush and Clinton teams had finally compromised on. Four debates were to be crammed into a nine-day period; now they would be three-way affairs. In the first, Perot was the consensus winner, charming the nation with his folksy mannerisms and down-to-earth words, while Clinton deftly handled Bush's attack on his alleged lack of patriotism during the Vietnam days.

It was Dan Quayle's turn to attack in the single vice-presidential debate. The Vice President and Gore tore into each other with a zest that frequently left Perot's running mate Stockdale a tongue-tied bystander. Two nights later, the three presidential candidates debated again, this time in the question-and-answer-with-voters format suggested by Clinton. In this congenial atmosphere, Clinton was a clear winner. To some viewers, Bush seemed to adopt an almost elegiac tone, as if he knew he had lost. The President rebounded, however, with a much sharper performance in the third and final presidential debate, finding new energy and focus in his appeals for support.

INTO THE HOMESTRETCH
Visibly elated and upbeat after his strong performance in the final debate, Bush hit the campaign trail in the last week of October, while polls showed Clinton's long-held lead beginning to slip. Again and again the President hammered home his message: that voters should not entrust their government to a small-state Democratic Governor whose public policies and statements, Bush charged, amounted to "a pattern of deception." Bush tied his fate to the Slick Willie issue.

In Dallas, Perot was profiting from his three engaging debate performances and his well-received infomercials. He had restored most of the favorable image he had trashed by his July withdrawal, and was climbing in the polls. Then, in the campaign's final week, his fatal flaw surfaced again, with his unproven charge that the Republicans had planned to smear his daughter with a doctored photograph. The Texan's vagaries stopped but did not reverse his meteoric rise in the polls; he was putting on a last-gasp TV advertising blitz like none ever seen before.

The final days of the campaign held another surprise. Former Defense Secretary Caspar Weinberger was indicted by a Washington grand jury on a count of making false statements to Congress. Evidence in the case suggested that contrary to his frequent assertions of ignorance, President Bush had been "in the loop" on the notorious arms-for-hostages deal in the Iran-*contra* affair. The revelation raised a spate of new questions at a most delicate time for the President. He turned uncharacteristically shrill, repeatedly castigating Clinton and Gore as "bozos."

MANDATE FOR CHANGE
Finally, after all the shouting of the campaign, it was the voters' turn to speak. On Tuesday, Nov. 3, they cast their ballots in record numbers, reversing a 20-year declining trend. Their choice: Bill Clinton.

"The people have spoken," said Bush from the White House, "and we respect the majesty of the democratic system." Clinton accepted the President's declaration with thanks, as he, Hillary and the Gores stood before a cheering throng of Arkansans in front of the state capitol in Little Rock. In his moment of triumph, the man who had come so far from his trials in New Hampshire appealed for unity. "If we have no sense of community," said the President-elect, "the American Dream will continue to wither." ■

Election Results at a Glance

PRESIDENT

How the States Voted 🐴 Democratic 🐘 Republican

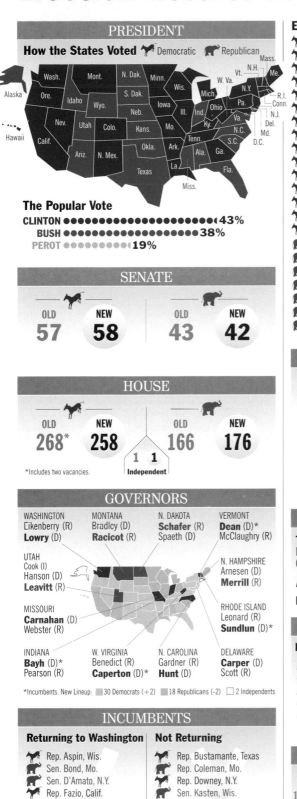

The Popular Vote

CLINTON ●●●●●●●●●●●●●●●●●●●●●● **43%**
BUSH ●●●●●●●●●●●●●●●●●●● **38%**
PEROT ●●●●●●●●●● **19%**

SENATE

	OLD	NEW		OLD	NEW
🐴	57	58	🐘	43	42

HOUSE

	OLD	NEW		OLD	NEW
🐴	268*	258	🐘	166	176

1 1
Independent

*Includes two vacancies.

GOVERNORS

WASHINGTON	MONTANA	N. DAKOTA	VERMONT
Eikenberry (R)	Bradley (D)	**Schafer** (R)	**Dean** (D)*
Lowry (D)	**Racicot** (R)	Spaeth (D)	McClaughry (R)

UTAH		N. HAMPSHIRE
Cook (I)		Arnesen (D)
Hanson (D)		**Merrill** (R)
Leavitt (R)		

MISSOURI		RHODE ISLAND
Carnahan (D)		Leonard (R)
Webster (R)		**Sundlun** (D)*

INDIANA	W. VIRGINIA	N. CAROLINA	DELAWARE
Bayh (D)*	Benedict (R)	Gardner (R)	**Carper** (D)
Pearson (R)	**Caperton** (D)*	**Hunt** (D)	Scott (R)

*Incumbents. New Lineup: ▮ 30 Democrats (+2) ▮ 18 Republicans (-2) ☐ 2 Independents

INCUMBENTS

Returning to Washington	**Not Returning**
Rep. Aspin, Wis.	Rep. Bustamante, Texas
Sen. Bond, Mo.	Rep. Coleman, Mo.
Sen. D'Amato, N.Y.	Rep. Downey, N.Y.
Rep. Fazio, Calif.	Sen. Kasten, Wis.
Rep. Gingrich, Ga.	Rep. Kostmayer, Pa.
Sen. Glenn, Ohio	Rep. Mavroules, Mass.
Sen. Hollings, S.C.	Rep. Oakar, Ohio
Sen. Packwood, Ore.	Rep. Patterson, S.C.
Sen. Specter, Pa.	Sen. Sanford, N.C.
Rep. Wilson, Texas	Sen. Seymour, Calif.

Electoral Votes

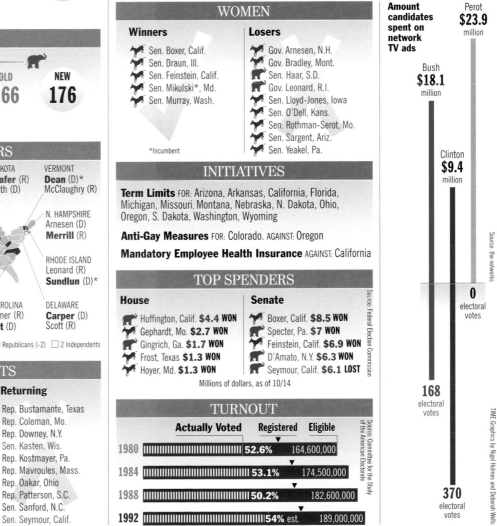

CLINTON: 370

BUSH: 168

WOMEN

Winners	**Losers**
Sen. Boxer, Calif.	Gov. Arnesen, N.H.
Sen. Braun, Ill.	Gov. Bradley, Mont.
Sen. Feinstein, Calif.	Sen. Haar, S.D.
Sen. Mikulski*, Md.	Gov. Leonard, R.I.
Sen. Murray, Wash.	Sen. Lloyd-Jones, Iowa
	Sen. O'Dell, Kans.
	Sen. Rothman-Serot, Mo.
	Sen. Sargent, Ariz.
*Incumbent	Sen. Yeakel, Pa.

INITIATIVES

Term Limits FOR: Arizona, Arkansas, California, Florida, Michigan, Missouri, Montana, Nebraska, N. Dakota, Ohio, Oregon, S. Dakota, Washington, Wyoming

Anti-Gay Measures FOR: Colorado. AGAINST: Oregon

Mandatory Employee Health Insurance AGAINST: California

TOP SPENDERS

House	**Senate**
Huffington, Calif. **$4.4 WON**	Boxer, Calif. **$8.5 WON**
Gephardt, Mo. **$2.7 WON**	Specter, Pa. **$7 WON**
Gingrich, Ga. **$1.7 WON**	Feinstein, Calif. **$6.9 WON**
Frost, Texas **$1.3 WON**	D'Amato, N.Y. **$6.3 WON**
Hoyer, Md. **$1.3 WON**	Seymour, Calif. **$6.1 LOST**

Millions of dollars, as of 10/14

Source: Federal Election Commission

TURNOUT

	Actually Voted	Registered	Eligible
1980		52.6%	164,600,000
1984		53.1%	174,500,000
1988		50.2%	182,600,000
1992		54% est.	189,000,000

Source: Committee for the Study of the American Electorate

Amount candidates spent on network TV ads

Perot **$23.9** million

Bush **$18.1** million

Clinton **$9.4** million

0 electoral votes

168 electoral votes

370 electoral votes

Source: the networks

TIME Graphics by Nigel Holmes and Deborah Wells

The fury of nature and man combined to create
two great convulsions in a doubt-ridden America. But the
country remembered its Samaritan soul
in time to come to the aid of starving Somalis.

By HUGH SIDEY

THOMAS JEFFERSON, AGELESS VOICE OF REASSESS-
ment on every subject from cosmic theories to the
production of the humble garden pea, would have
relished 1992. Little seemed settled or certain.
New thoughts and formulations of old ideas abounded,
and a new order was aborning. But painfully.

It was a time of political transition from one generation
to another, accompanied by arguments on the purpose of
public life and the use of national wealth—the U.S. still
claiming rank as the world's largest treasury but not growing fast enough to keep up with its wants. The presidential
election, a constitutionally mandated forum designed to
doubt and nag the status quo, limned the demands to cut
the $300 billion defense expenditures. The world might no
longer have a communist military ogre on the loose, but it
did offer menacing economic competitors across each
ocean. In or out of the defense industry, a fellow could lose
his job overnight—in fact, his whole career orientation. It
was a year of frayed nerves.

Nothing in the broad U.S.A. could claim full status as a
national crisis, like a war or a depression; instead, a collection of aches, pains and imagined miseries spread from
coast to coast. Call it a national angst, at least until a few
good economic indicators intruded at the end of the year.
About the same time, the American voters decided to cast
out George Bush, an old-style élitist of inherited means
and social standing, and try Bill Clinton, a New Age élitist
raised to power on his brains, with considerable assists from
public trusts and positions.

Against that background, two great convulsions rocked
the country. One was man-made. The other was an act of
God.

On an April afternoon, a superior court jury in California's Simi Valley, a bedroom community northwest of Los
Angeles and home of Ronald Reagan's new presidential library, acquitted four white policemen on trial for brutalizing a black motorist. The violence done to Rodney King

had been caught on amateur videotape and was soon
broadcast to a shocked world. It showed King being beaten
senseless in a bizarre and mindless frenzy as an unseen
minicam looked on. After such documentation, few people
expected the jury's sweeping exoneration.

Within hours of the verdict, fury raced down the sunny
streets of Lotusland. Gangs ran wild, looting and burning
and expending their anger on anyone of any race or color
in their sights. The harsh truth so starkly etched in those
sad hours was that the greater Los Angeles melting pot, a
once promising experiment in modern America, lay a reek-
ing, smoldering wreck. The final tallies showed 52 dead
and a billion dollars in property destroyed. It was the most
damaging riot in U.S. history.

Echoes were heard in a dozen other cities, though nothing compared with the uprising in the City of the Angels.
For a few weeks ranking officials of state and federal governments (including Bush and Clinton) tramped through
the ruins, conferred, appointed study commissions and voted money to help rehabilitate the ravaged streets. A new
federal prosecution on civil rights violations was launched
against the police officers.

But then, almost as if the riot had been just another Hollywood series on inner-city violence, the nation seemed to
turn away and seek the next thrill in a three-ring presidential race, featuring the in-out-in-again performance of Ross
Perot, the billionaire populist. The larger question in the
Los Angeles tragedy was barely addressed in the campaign.
Economic hopelessness, which robbed millions of minority Americans of even a glimpse of the great dream, was
now deepened by what appeared to be a system of justice
too often manipulated against race and too often controlled by affluence. Rodney King's haunting plea, "Can
we all get along?" remained unanswered in the streets
where men and women and children crowded together in
fear and poverty.

Nature vented its own fury above the southern Atlantic

Ocean, where a hurricane formed, crossed the Bahamas, gained muscle as it went and then slammed into southern Florida with shrieking wind gusts up to 169 m.p.h. After cutting a 20- to 35-mile swatch south of Miami, Hurricane Andrew—such a stately name—blew on into Louisiana's Cajun country and into the history books as the costliest disaster in American history. Andrew had been dutifully tracked since birth and identified as a truculent child, but no one was prepared for the monster that hit the mainland. Yachts and trucks were tossed about like toys. Flimsy mobile homes were obliterated. The tantrum's final toll: 59 dead and 250,000 homeless, and more than $20 billion in damages.

Andrew also left its share of long-range questions about life and life-style along the vulnerable coastal fringes. Should population density be controlled in these delicate regions where nature punches ferociously at man's creations with alarming regularity? And what of the codes designed to give buildings and homes enough strength and resiliency to protect inhabitants in that kind of storm? In many instances, safety requirements for both regular dwellings and mobile homes had been callously ignored. The result was that thousands of homes virtually flew apart at Andrew's first touch. Somewhere in this ravaged landscape there seemed to be a voice warning the republic to slow down and plan ahead.

America's West Coast also felt nature's fury. In mid-August, California's drought-stricken Calaveras County, once the heart of the gold rush, broke into flame, causing 15,000 residents to flee. As that blaze was being brought under control, another kindled in Northern California, which had also been devoid of significant rainfall for the first time in years. Soon after, tornadoes ripped through the South and Midwest, sometimes accompanied by deluges that sent rivers wild, scrambling planting and harvesting plans. The wild weather ignited anew the speculation that abuse of the earth was changing its climate.

One enduring controversy that promised to become a consuming fire in the combustible political atmosphere fizzled out surprisingly at year's end. With the Supreme Court deliberating a challenge to a Pennsylvania abortion law, more than half a million pro-choice activists, liberally populated with Hollywood stars, had gathered on the Washington Mall in the spring to voice their affirmation of *Roe v. Wade*, the court's 1973 decision upholding the right to abortion. It was the largest rally in the history of the movement.

Maybe the august court, judged after the five Reagan-Bush appointments to be solidly conservative and splendidly entrenched in its marble hall, did hear the cries from below after all. The court ruling in the summer did virtually no damage to *Roe* and showed again how difficult it is to harness the minds of court members to political ideology.

And as if to make the point perfectly clear, the court in November refused to review an appellate court ruling that struck down a Guam law making abortion a felony. With Clinton headed for the White House, the basic right to abortion under the Constitution seemed for the time being firmly guaranteed.

B UT AS ALWAYS IN THE TUMULTUOUS RITES OF FREE-dom, no sooner is one controversy eased than another rises to take its place. As bright decorations and carols heralded the coming of Christmas, 3,000 U.S. troops were shouldering their weapons, bidding goodbye to teary families and soberly anticipating the holidays in Somalia in the far-off Horn of Africa. Operation Restore Hope was in theory a peacekeeping mission designed to bring order out of anarchy and allow help to reach a people dying at the rate of a thousand a day from starvation, disease and the bullets of heartless thugs. But it carried with it a hard lesson: though no villainous superpower stalked the globe, it starkly reminded this nation, in its rituals of thanks, that Peace on Earth is still a distant dream. ∎

RAGE IN L.A.

A surprising verdict ignites a riot—and exposes America's racial divisions

CALIFORNIANS WERE RELAXING A little on Wednesday, April 29. The week before, they had been rattled by two substantial earthquakes and their rumbling aftershocks. But now the ground had stopped shaking. And then, at midafternoon, came the seismic news: a Superior Court jury in Simi Valley, a bedroom community northwest of Los Angeles, had acquitted on all but one count—and deadlocked on that—the four white Los Angeles policemen on trial for beating and otherwise mistreating black motorist Rodney King.

The verdict prompted amazement and disbelief. The King case was not another garden-variety allegation of police brutality. Everyone in the world within eyeshot of a television set had seen the amateur video-tape made by a witness on the night of March 3, 1991, when, after a

Chief Daryl Gates claimed his officers could cope with the rage, but at first the police abandoned the city to a mob.

high-speed chase, King was forced out of his car and encircled by police. The 81-second video recorded what happened next: a danse macabre of casual, almost studied, violence. King, writhing on the pavement, was kicked by his uniformed assailants, jolted with a stun gun and hit with nightsticks 56 times.

Yet seeing, for the jurors in the King trial, was not believing. Legal experts scrambled to explain the unexpected outcome. Some cited a lackluster prosecution, which did not call King to testify, did not raise the issue of racism until late in the 29 days of testimony and may have assumed that the stark video alone guaranteed convictions. Others pointed to a crucial decision last Nov. 26, when the judge granted a defense motion for a change of venue, from Los Angeles County to neighboring and overwhelmingly white Ventura County. Before a jury of 10 whites, one Asian and one Hispanic, defense lawyers portrayed the accused policemen as the "thin blue line" between law-abiding citi-

zens and the rebellious, intransigent forces embodied, so the argument implied, in Rodney King.

In the beginning, the verdict was greeted with righteous indignation. Just three hours after it was announced, thousands of shocked black residents of South Central Los Angeles gathered at the First African Methodist Episcopal Church. Speaker after speaker denounced the injustice and alienation that are part of their everyday life. Each community leader acknowledged that institutions designed to protect law-abiding citizens had failed them this time, but still some appealed for calm. It was already too late. By the time the two-hour meeting broke up, the first fires had been set. As weary parishioners left the prayer meeting, some were shot at by thugs. "Nothing you're talking about is going to do any good," one young man told the departing crowd. "Come with us—let's burn."

For more than 48 hours, an urban nightmare came true as hatred ruled the streets. During that time, parts of the city virtually ceased to function. Hundreds of thousands of citizens were sent home from schools, offices and public facilities. Much of the destruction hit the depressed South

Central area, a 46-sq.-mi. part of town plagued by gangs, poverty and the drug-dealing criminals who dominate life there. Not surprisingly, it was the besieged black community that suffered the most.

Almost immediately after the rioters took to the streets—many chanting "No Justice, No Peace"—Angelenos experienced the brutality of mob rule. At 6:30 Wednesday evening, an airborne television camera captured the beating of Reginald Denny, a white truck driver who made the mistake of stopping at a red light in the neighborhood where the first riot erupted. At least five black men pulled Denny from his sand truck, bashed him with the vehicle's fire extin-

"People, can we all get along? We're all stuck here for a while. Let's try to work it out."

—RODNEY KING

guisher, punched him and stole his wallet. Another fired a shotgun into him at close range. As a blood-soaked Denny called for help, he was hit with beer bottles and karate-kicked in the head. The whole macabre scene, like a mirror-image replay of the King beating, was broadcast live on a local TV station. Denny was eventually rescued by four black bystanders and taken to a hospital, where he underwent four hours of brain surgery.

Many residents assumed that the mayhem would be restricted to the South Central neighborhood. But by midday Thursday, fires were breaking out in scattered areas all across Los Angeles. In a racially mixed neighborhood just west of downtown, looters and arsonists hit stores, including the upscale I. Magnin on Wilshire Boulevard. Nearby apartment buildings caught fire. "We pick up from one fire and go on to another," explained fire captain Mike Castillo shortly after evacuating 15 residents from a burning building. Castillo's four-man crew stayed on the job for 48 consecutive hours, tracking arson activity as it moved north and west through the city.

The firepower wielded by gun-toting gang members and frightened citizens also hindered law-enforcement efforts. Traffic was snarled on one South Central street after a car careened out of control when a motorist was killed by a sniper. Several roadways were cordoned off by police to prevent destruction from spreading north to Hollywood and Beverly Hills from the poorer regions of the city.

Though the King verdict clearly sparked the explosion, the black community's rage had long been building. Citing numerous incidents, black leaders charged that local police forces had systematically brutalized and mistreated blacks. During the 1970s, 16 blacks died as a result of choke holds administered by Los Angeles police. Police chief Daryl Gates defended the use of the procedure at the time, suggesting that blacks had some anatomical weakness that made them especially vulnerable to that method of restraint.

End of the dream: sheriff's deputies monitor suspects after a store was looted on Martin Luther King Jr. Boulevard

THIS LAND IS YOUR LAND . . .

What the middle class is fleeing from: charred remains in Los Angeles

THE L.A. RIOTS UNDERSCORED A PAINFUL TRUTH: A relentless exodus from the cities has split the country. Suburbanization, the most irresistible demographic trend of the past 40 years, has reduced America's inner cities to hollow shells peopled largely by poor nonwhites. The process began after World War II, accelerated during the 1960s and '70s, when malls diverted shoppers from downtowns, and peaked during the 1980s, when employers transferred millions of jobs to suburban office parks. Now about half of America's 250 million people live in the suburbs, and only one-quarter in central cities.

The result is an America that is rapidly dividing into two worlds separated by class, race and drive time. Sheltered in tree-lined streets where the fantasy of a homogeneous middle-class society can still be entertained, many suburbanites know the city mainly as a skyline glimpsed from an overpass or as the place of the shooting reported on the evening news. As workers and employers have retreated to their homes and industrial parks beyond the city line, the poor left behind have become more destitute than ever. In 1990 and 1991 welfare rolls in Los Angeles climbed to historic levels. Nearly 1.4 million Angelenos, a seventh of the county's population, depend on one or more of the county-administered relief services. Meanwhile, federal aid to cities declined from $47.2 billion in 1980 to $21.7 billion 10 years later.

As many African Americans have flowed into the middle class, they too have sought refuge in the suburbs. Their departure has deprived black youths in the ghetto of living examples of the steady work and stable family life of middle class blacks.

Just as Gates was the target of protests following King's beating, he found himself accused of slow response—and worse—in his handling of the violence. In large measure, the riots got out of hand because the 7,800-strong police department was slow to respond to many of the initial disturbances. Although Gates had earlier indicated that $1 million had been set aside for police overtime, the force was virtually invisible in the early hours of the rioting, allowing many looters to smash storefronts and torch buildings with impunity. A follow-up panel, headed by former CIA chief and FBI director William Webster, rapped Gates for failing to take personal command of the response.

Lee's Market was one of the many stores to be cleaned out by looters. Dozens of black and Hispanic men, women and children emerged from the jagged front windows laden with groceries as an L.A.P.D. cruiser moved past the area, its occupants, vastly outnumbered, making no attempt to intervene. "They should go and destroy Beverly Hills," said one rioter. "Hey, the police don't even bother to stop." A minute later, someone lit a match, and what was left of the store went up in flames. Watching the destruction, neighborhood resident Verdis Barnes expressed rage over the King verdict: "The video tells it all. They didn't have to do him like that. But these people should have gone somewhere else to do this."

After nightfall, police responded only to life-threatening situations, escorting fire fighters but standing a safe distance from rampaging gangs as they cleaned out stores in dozens of malls. Gates initially claimed that his force was simply overwhelmed, but his department had not identified potential trouble spots and did not have enough officers on standby for riot duty—standard procedure for some big-city forces, particularly those that have experienced racial unrest. Other law-enforcement units were also slow to react. Though California Governor Pete Wilson deployed about 2,000 National Guard troops on Wednesday evening, it took almost 24 hours for the extra men to reach the streets. They were followed by hundreds of California highway patrolmen on loan from other parts of the state. By the time President Bush dispatched 4,500 federal troops to the area at week's end, the violence had largely abated.

Not all the black rage was directed at the police force. Many rioters targeted Asian-owned businesses. Relations between the black and Asian communities have been tense for years, mainly because of a perception that Korean merchants have been exploiting poor neighborhoods by establishing shops in ghetto areas while refusing to hire blacks to work in them.

Store owners in the prosperous Koreatown district, five miles north of the initial flash point, were ready for action. In the absence of effective police protection, the merchants resorted to vigilante tactics. At a large mall featuring a food outlet, a pharmacy and a liquor store with Korean-language signs, men with pump shotguns and high-powered pistols defended their businesses. A barricade of shopping carts was arranged in the parking lot, which was patrolled by armed Koreans. As a pair of looters approached the mall, the guards fired 12-gauge rounds into the air to chase them away. Elsewhere a security guard was killed defending a Korean-owned store from attack.

The area's most prominent blacks had virtually no ability to restore calm. Los Angeles Mayor Tom Bradley deplored the King verdict at the Wednesday-night church rally when he declared, "We have come tonight to say we have had enough!" But the following night, a subdued Bradley appealed for order on a broadcast of the *Arsenio Hall Show* and issued a warning: "Don't break the law, or we will put you in jail." But most Los Angeles viewers knew that was a promise the mayor could not keep.

In the California primary in June, voters approved a referendum calling for comprehensive police reform. Known as Charter Amendment F, the measure called for civilians on the police-review board and a five-year limit to the police chief's term, subject to a one-time reappointment by the mayor. When the riot broke out, police chief Gates was attending a reception in the affluent suburb of Brentwood, trying to raise money to fight the proposal. As criticism of his performance mounted in the weeks following the riot, Gates finally retired from his post on June 26. The new chief was one of the nation's most prominent black police officials: former Philadelphia police commissioner Willie L. Williams.

In the days following the riots, campaigners George Bush and Bill Clinton toured the devastated areas. The President's guardians were so concerned for his security that they would not tell TV crews what route he would take, lest live coverage draw hostile demonstrators. But some showed up anyway, chanting "Go Home" or "No Justice." In response, Bush delivered a many-sided message. "Just wanton lawlessness," he said, viewing the twisted skeletons of washers and dryers in a torched laundromat. But he also told police officers that he wanted to "get at the root cause" of the unrest, and he promised federal help in rebuilding Los Angeles—while yet remarking that "dumping largesse" from Washington on the community was not the answer. Sturdier values are needed, said the President, and the Federal Government cannot teach youths how to tell right from wrong.

The last word on the riots came from the figure whose beating had prompted them. For more than a year he had been a writhing body twisting on the ground under kicks and nightstick blows. Then on Friday afternoon television finally gave Rodney King a face and a voice: a hesitant, almost sobbing voice that yet was more eloquent than any other that spoke during the terrible week. "Stop making it horrible," King pleaded with the rioters. "Can we all get along?" The nation's leaders, of both races, could not seem to find such plain but heartfelt words. ∎

. . . THIS LAND IS MY LAND

What the middle class is fleeing to: Silver Firs, a placid Seattle suburb

NOW THE SUBURBS CONTROL THE NATION'S DESTINY. Voters there will punish any candidate who would have them transfer tax revenue back to the cities. In the mostly homogeneous suburbs, people have less stake in solving the problems of people unlike themselves in the dimly remembered cities. It is also more tempting for them to dump their own problems there. Until the summer of 1991, Westchester County, a prosperous suburb of New York City, was exporting some of its homeless to a hotel in Manhattan. In 1990 New Jersey Governor Jim Florio, a Democrat, raised taxes to redirect funds from suburban to inner-city schools through tax hikes. In 1991 voters elected a veto-proof Republican majority in both houses of the legislature to roll back the program.

When hard-pressed cities try to tax their citizens more to pay for needed services, it often backfires, provoking another wave of middle-class flight to the suburbs. Moreover, urban governments' attempts to expand their revenues—through extending the city limits or applying payroll taxes on commuters—are often thwarted.

There are two approaches that might begin to alleviate the poverty of the city. One way is to move money to the cities through court-ordered revenue sharing. Another way to dissolve knots of urban poverty is to disperse the poor to the suburbs in manageable numbers, a prospect that makes homeowners shudder. Yet the same self-interest that has made them turn away from the cities may eventually force them to recognize that the larger health of America requires the cities to be rescued. Even in a nation as spacious as the U.S., people are running out of places to escape.

TIME Map by Paul J.Pugliese

ONCE AGAIN THOUSANDS OF American soldiers were donning flak jackets and moving into harm's way on a far-off continent. The soldiers of Operation Restore Hope would be spending Christmas in Somalia; some might even die there. Under the United Nations' aegis but their own flag, they would be conducting an experiment in world order: armed peacemaking, rather than peacekeeping. Anarchy ruled in Somalia, and the U.N. had resolved specifically to intervene in a nation's domestic affairs to rescue a civilian population that was dying at a rate of a thousand a day, not just from starvation but from bullets as well.

Announced abruptly by George Bush, America's mission to the Horn of Africa was intended to be a quick fix, a jolt of military muscle to make the country safe for humanitarian aid. According to the plan, once the so-called secure environment for relief operations was achieved, U.S. troops were supposed to hand over their responsibilities to a smaller, traditional force of U.N. peacekeepers, not yet formed or financed. President Bush announced the campaign, dubbed Operation Restore Hope, on Dec. 4; White House spokesman Marlin Fitzwater even suggested that the U.S. military operation could be over by Inauguration Day, Jan. 20.

That all sounded too easy to be true. George Bush, a lame-duck President, had sprung a very big operation on Americans without clearly defining his short- and long-term goals. Washington talked about a swift and simple job of pacification that would leave the difficult—and in the end essential—rebuilding of the country to others, and President-elect Bill Clinton said he stood behind the President's decision. But from specific details about the military operation to large issues of global responsibility, the decision to intervene raised important questions about what it would really take to restore hope to Somalia.

THE ROAD TO STARVATION

On one issue, however, there was no argument: Somalia's need was desperate beyond measure. The country is a sickle-shaped expanse on the Horn of Africa, stretching across an unforgiving desert. Limited natural resources and internal disputes have historically kept stability at a distance, and the clans of Somalia have regularly battled with one another. Under the one-man rule of Mohammed Siad Barre, Somalia waged war with neighboring Ethiopia in the 1970s, backed by Moscow. But Somalia lost both Moscow's backing and the war, suffering enormous losses.

DAWN OF HOPE

U.S. troops land in embattled Somalia to feed the hungry and restore hope. But how deeply would they become involved in local politics? And when would they return?

Burdened by nearly a million refugees, years of drought and an enfeebled economy, Siad Barre turned to the U.S., which was eager for a strategic outpost near the Arabian oil fields. For the next 10 years the U.S. poured millions of dollars into arming the country, but Siad Barre's regime began to crumble. Three clan factions united to oppose his rule, and after three years of civil war he fled the capital, Mogadishu, in January 1991. Somalia was left a shambles: thousands had been killed, the countryside was destroyed and hundreds of thousands of refugees had fled the country.

With the clans now fighting each other and the land fallow, a man-made famine took hold, and a horrified world saw image after image of stick-thin, starving children. The U.N. and others mounted relief operations, but workers could not get the aid through; armed gangs loyal to the clan warlords stole the donated food supplies. U.N. Secretary-General Boutros Boutros-Ghali had repeatedly urged the world to step forward. Now Bush made the U.N. an offer it could not refuse: the U.S. would organize and command a U.N. force and supply most of the troops. In his address to Americans announcing his decision, Bush stressed that the American interest was "humanitarian," and said "only the U.S. has the global reach" to cope with the crisis.

Bush announced that "about a dozen countries" would contribute troops; France made a quick offer of 1,700. The U.S. was prepared to send 28,000 Marine and Army fighters, who would secure airports, ports and

roads and chase away the looters. But when an advance guard of 1,800 U.S. Marines began landing in Somalia in early December, there was no agreement on whether they and other U.N. troops to follow would try to disarm the war bands.

THE MARINES HAVE LANDED: "SAY CHEESE!"

The first images cast an antic light on Operation Restore Hope. As Navy SEALs waded ashore in the moonlight on the night of Dec. 9, their faces blackened with camouflage paint, their bodies braced for confrontation, they were met and blinded by the glare of television lights. But the farcical aspect of this first military landing broadcast live around the world soon faded as the troops fanned out from their beachhead into the anarchy-ridden city of Mogadishu. The airport was secured, the city port occupied, and for the first time in two years most of the firepower belonged to friendlies. The sense of a dangerous mission rapidly gave way to a more human drama. Everywhere the U.S. troops turned, they found themselves hemmed in by Somalis eager to touch American flesh, gesture their relief, smile their thanks. Declared Fatima Mohammed, 32, a mother of seven: "I'd like the U.S. troops to stay here for life."

That was precisely the problem. The Bush Administra-

tion had repeatedly stated that its sole objective was to open a food pipeline to feed the starving, not to wage war on the country's armed gangs or impose political solutions. The Somalis, however, expected nothing short of a Marshall Plan. They wanted the Americans to stay long enough to fix not only their diet, but also their broken government and lawless society. Between the objective and the dream lay much room for disappointment.

As the operation slowly got under way, the first 3,000 U.S. troops found themselves spread thin. Most of the capital's armed thugs crept away, but soldiers had yet to impose more than a veneer of security. Urgent calls for help came from good samaritans trapped in their compounds in outlying towns, where marauding gunmen were still stealing, fighting and killing. By Dec. 11, Robert Oakley, the U.S. special envoy, had brokered a temporary reconciliation between the country's two most powerful clan leaders, General Mohammed Farrah Aidid and Ali Mahdi Mohammed, who had not spoken in more than a year. Emerging from their meeting at the U.S. liaison office, the two warlords agreed to an immediate cease-fire, though no one believed their hostilities had ended for good. Neither warlord called on his followers to surrender their weapons.

The rules for disarmament seemed porous and confusing. Marines understood that they were authorized to seize any weapons in their zone of security, yet were sometimes ordered not to. Within 36 hours of the troops' arrival, sniper fire and gun battles resumed. On Saturday, Dec. 12, American troops first exchanged fire with local gunmen. A Somali armed personnel carrier fired on two U.S. Cobra gunships, which returned the fire, destroying three armed vehicles and causing several Somali casualties.

More serious was the delay in moving troops into the countryside. Original plans called for units to relieve Bai-

A lame-duck President had sprung a very big operation on Americans without defining its goals

Left, U.S. troops disarm a gang member. Right, the face of starvation. Below, Bush prays with GI's.

INTO BAIDOA

Finally, on Wednesday, Dec. 16, 70 trucks, jeeps and armored vehicles carried U.S. Marines and French Foreign Legionnaires into Baidoa as helicopter gunships buzzed overhead. After the frustrating initial delay following their landing, the U.S.-led forces were now under way. Running two weeks ahead of schedule by their own reckoning, they began moving into the final four of the eight towns where distribution of food and supplies would be centered, including Kismayu. On the road to one of the centers, Bardera, a land mine caused the first American casualty: a ci-

vilian Army employee was killed, and three State Department personnel were wounded. U.S. commanders said their troops were moving fast because there had been no opposition from armed gangs. Under an agreement with clan leaders, their heavy weapons—trucks and jeeps mounted with machine guns, called "technicals"—were withdrawing from towns the multinational force controlled.

U.S. Marines had a visitor for New Year's Eve: George Bush, who was in the middle of an extended last overseas tour. The President spent New Year's Eve in Mogadishu behind razor-wire barriers, and journeyed the next day to Baidoa. Essentially a photo opportunity, the visit still underlined a major policy challenge that Bush will leave for his successor: the use of American military force for purely humanitarian missions in countries where the U.S. has no economic or strategic interests at stake. Bill Clinton's more pressing challenge will be to bring the troops home in timely fashion. As the year ended, the White House boast that the U.S. forces would be back by Inauguration Day seemed naive at best. In a splashy joint appearance just four days before Bush arrived, Somalia's two top warlords announced a new thrust for peace. But only a few hours later, warring clans were exchanging unusually heavy mortar and artillery fire. ■

doa, one of the chief feeding centers, 150 miles northwest of Mogadishu, within a few days. Fighting there had intensified as gunmen, flushed from the capital, turned on one another and terrorized the town with killing and looting. Relief workers barricaded themselves in compounds, but local citizens, starving and in the line of fire, had nowhere to hide. The situation to the south, in Kismayu, was also grim; 60 people were killed there in early December, and all but a handful of relief workers had to be evacuated.

Abortion:

The Obstacle Course

It may be legal—but abortion is not available to many U.S. women

JUST BECAUSE ABORTION IS LEGAL IN ILLINOIS doesn't mean that Sheela Paine can easily get one. At the age of 30 she already has five children. In the spring of 1992 she was in the 19th week of a pregnancy she couldn't afford; her husband is unemployed, and the family lives on welfare. She also couldn't afford the reduced $425 price of a second-trimester abortion at the clinic near her home in East St. Louis. During her last pregnancy Paine tried to induce miscarriage by taking quinine pills. She ruled out a cheap illegal abortion because a girlfriend had bled to death after getting one. But the prospect of trying to support yet another child made her sick with worry. "My hair started coming out," she says. After many anxious days, she finally got an abortion when she was able to borrow the money.

Abortions are still legal in Texas too. But that doesn't mean doctors can easily perform them. Four years ago, Dr. Curtis Boyd's Dallas clinic came under siege for weeks by antiabortion demonstrators. One day one of the protesters began asking after Boyd's children by name. "How's Kyle?" the man would inquire. "Has he had any accidents?" Then came the handwritten death threat in his mailbox. Boyd moved his family out of town for a while, and on Christmas Eve his clinic was torched. Boyd is back in business today, but with a sharper sense of the odds against him. "What professionals would continue to do a service that subjected them to this kind of abuse?" he asks.

Boyd's comments were made just two months before the Supreme Court's long-awaited ruling on a crucial case in the ongoing pro-life/pro-choice debate: a Pennsylvania law that established restrictions on abortion. In its decision the court narrowly upheld *Roe v. Wade*, the landmark 1973 case that found a constitutional right to abortion; at the same time, the Justices permitted greater restrictions on abortion by the states. Among the Pennsylvania restraints: a requirement that teenagers show the consent of one parent or a judge, and another that stipulates a 24-hour waiting period for a woman after hearing a presentation from her doctor of alternatives to abortion. The court struck down a provision that would have required women to inform their husband.

But for all the attention paid to Supreme Court rulings on abortion, that is not where the issue is really being decided. Even as the court ruled on the Pennsylvania case, abortion was not available in 83% of America's counties, home to nearly a third of American women of childbearing age. For reasons of professional pride, or fear, or economic pressure, doctors have backed away from the procedure even where it remains available.

In Gulfport, Miss., local officials have prevented Dr. Joseph Booker, above, from completing work on a new abortion clinic

63

The reality in most American communities is that two decades of moral and religious reflection, legal maneuvering and political assaults have combined to do precisely what conservatives promised when *Roe* was handed down: roll back the Supreme Court ruling until it is no longer the law of the land. Now, in the noisy streets and legislatures and the bare chambers of the individual conscience, that most fundamental question—Who decides whether a woman can have an abortion?—must itself be redecided. With that, America is entering new moral and political territory, rough and uncharted, but lighted by the phosphor of righteous certainties. And as the combatants square off with their irreconcilable notions of life and liberty, the middle ground, what there is of it, promises to become scorched earth.

Each year there are 1.6 million abortions carried out in the U.S., representing almost a fourth of all pregnancies. It is estimated that more than 46% of American women will have had an abortion by the time they are 45. But while there are about 2,500 places around the country that provide abortions—down from a high of 2,908 ten years ago—they are mostly clustered around cities, leaving broad areas of the country unserved. A single clinic serves 24 counties in northern Minnesota. Just one doctor provides abortions in South Dakota.

For a glimpse of the future, look at Mississippi. Three of the state's four clinics are clustered around the capital and largest city, Jackson. But their survival is threatened by a new law that would require clinics to have advance transfer agreements with hospitals to care for patients who may suffer complications—a provision designed to capitalize on the resistance among many hospitals to associate themselves with anything as controversial as abortion.

A law requiring a 24-hour waiting period is scheduled to go into effect now that the Supreme Court has upheld the Pennsylvania law. Though it sounds benign enough, it can confound poor women who already have to travel long distances to find a clinic, only to discover they must also scrape together the price of overnight accommodations. Often by the time they get the money together, they have advanced into

The Shouting of the Lambs

Although not as widely known as Operation Rescue, The Lambs of Christ are perhaps the most zealous of pro-life groups. Above, the Rev. Normal Weslin leads a prayer vigil for jailed lambs in Fargo, N.D.

the second trimester, when the cost is higher. (Only 12 states—Mississippi is not one of them—routinely provide Medicaid financing for abortion.) Nancy Rogers owns one of the clinics near Jackson. Two years ago, when she went to the capital to argue against the bill before a state legislator, she got a sense of what she was up against. "His exact words were, 'I have no sympathy for anyone who cannot afford a motel room.'"

There's one other clinic in Mississippi, but lately it has not been open for business. When Dr. Joseph Booker first moved to the coastal town of Gulfport to set up a gynecology practice in 1988, local officials granted him every permit he needed to start a business. But when he moved to new offices in 1992, local officials, citing the abortions he performed, denied the permits he needed and encoded an antiabortion zoning ordinance.

TARGETING DOCTORS

Discouraging the doctors who provide abortion has become one of the characteristic tactics of the most militant antiabortion groups. In a widely publicized protest staged by Operation Rescue in Buffalo, New York, in April, the Rev. Robert Schenck pushed a fetus in front of abortion-rights demonstrators and threatened to stand outside restaurants frequented by doctors from abortion clinics, holding banners announcing ABORTIONISTS EAT HERE. Other leaders threatened to picket the schools attended by the doctors' children.

Death threats, obstruction and broken windows have taken their toll, but the medical profession has also tiptoed away from abortion because many doctors see it as routine work that's poorly paid by their standards. Hospitals have also been withdrawing from the abortion business. In the years after *Roe* was handed down, more than half of all abortions were performed in hospitals. By 1988, 86% were done in neighborhood clinics and an additional 4% in the offices of individual doctors. Some hospitals shy away from the procedure because of opposition from potential donors or members of their governing boards. At the same time, groups like Planned Parenthood encouraged the move to clinics as a way to keep abortion cheap and accessible. But clinics tend to be small outposts that offer easy targets for the sit-ins, arson and bombings that a large, well-guarded hospital is better suited to resist. And as the work has fallen largely to clinic doctors who specialize in abortion, it has dropped off the list of skills that a woman's regular physician can be expected to have.

As older physicians retire, the medical profession is also losing its institutional memory of the days before *Roe*. A generation raised in the era of safe and legal

ABORTION LAWS STATE-BY-STATE

Laws affecting the availability of abortion, as of May 1992. Some, like the outright bans and husband notification, were not being enforced at the time, pending consideration by the Supreme Court.

 Bans
Laws that prohibit virtually all abortions. Most date from before *Roe*.

Counseling Bans
Laws that prevent certain health-care providers from giving advice or referrals regarding abortion.

Notification of Husband
A requirement that a woman must gain consent from or notify her husband.

Notification of Parent
Laws that require minors seeking abortions to notify one or both parents or obtain consent.

Informed Consent/Delay
Laws that require women be counseled and/or given state-prepared materials. Often they must wait up to 24 hours or more before proceeding.

Public Facilities/Employees
States that prohibit the use of public facilities for abortion, or that prohibit public employees from participating in an abortion.

Public Funds
States that will not provide Medicaid funding for abortions unless the woman's life is in danger.

States where both houses support keeping abortion legal
States where both houses favor criminalizing abortion
Houses split or very close
○ Governors who favor criminalizing abortion

TIME Graphics
by Nigel Holmes

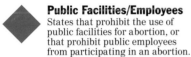

Alabama ✕ ● 📄 $
Alaska 📄
Arizona ✕ ◆ $
Arkansas ✕ ● $
California ✕
Colorado ✕ ♂ $
Connecticut
Delaware ✕ 📄 $
D.C. ✕ $
Florida ♂ 📄 $
Georgia ● $
Hawaii
Idaho 📄
Illinois ♂ $
Indiana ● 📄 $
Iowa
Kansas ✕ ● 📄 $

Kentucky ♂ 📄 ◆ $
Louisiana ✕ ⊖ ● 📄 ◆ $
Maine 📄 $
Maryland ✕ 📄
Massachusetts ✕ ● $
Michigan ✕ ● $
Minnesota ●
Mississippi ✕ 📄 $
Missouri ⊖ ● 📄 ◆ $
Montana ♂ 📄
Nebraska ● 📄 $
Nevada 📄 $
New Hampshire ✕ $
New Jersey
New Mexico ✕ $
New York
N. Carolina

N. Dakota ⊖ ♂ ● 📄 ◆ $
Ohio ● 📄 $
Oklahoma ✕ $
Oregon
Pennsylvania ♂ 📄 ◆
Rhode Island ♂ ● 📄 $
S. Carolina ♂ ● $
S. Dakota 📄
Tennessee 📄 $
Texas ✕ $
Utah ✕ ♂ ● 📄 $
Vermont ✕
Virginia 📄
Washington
W. Virginia ✕ ●
Wisconsin ✕ 📄
Wyoming ●

Source: NARAL

abortion is less likely to produce doctors ready to go to the barricades at the first sign of women being forced to undergo illegal—and dangerous—abortions. "I have personally taken care of women with red rubber catheters hanging out of their uterus and a temperature of 107°," says Dr. David Grimes, 45, of the University of Southern California School of Medicine. "Once a physician has watched that happening, he or she will never be willing to watch the laws go back."

The new state restrictions allowed by the court are likely to make it take longer for women to afford and arrange an abortion, which makes the procedure more dangerous. They also have the effect of sending a message. To abortion opponents, the message is that abortion on demand is immoral, and so should be illegal. But abortion-rights advocates see a different subtext. Instituting a waiting period suggests that women seeking abortions do so blithely and without reflection—a notion belied by the experience of women who have endured the private, wrenching process of deciding to terminate a pregnancy. Experts calculate that 93% of married women who have abortions talk to their husbands about it.

The idea of parental notification has a logic to it in communities where high school girls cannot receive aspirin from a school nurse without a parent's approval. But again, abortion rights advocates argue that a girl who does not want to tell her parents she is pregnant may have profound reasons for her silence, and no new law is likely to overcome that immediate fear.

Fearing a possible rollback of *Roe v. Wade* in the Pennsylvania case, pro-choice women staged the largest protest in the capital's history in April. But before the year was out, the battleground was to change substantially. First came the court's surprising endorsement of the 1973 ruling—a sign of a newly dominant centrist bloc consisting of Justices Sandra Day O'Connor, David Souter and Anthony Kennedy. Then came the victory of the pro-choice Democratic ticket in the presidential election. With Bill Clinton poised to name new Justices to the court, the possibility of an overturn of *Roe v. Wade* has faded. For the next few years, it seems, the battle that has so sundered the nation will be played out not within the confines of Washington's Beltway, but in the legislatures and courthouses of the states. ∎

ANDREW'S

The costliest hurricane in U.S. history devastates Florida and Louisiana

I T'S AN ODD PRACTICE, THE NAMING OF HURRICANES. Yet anthropomorphizing nature's brutal forces somehow seems to help people cope with the otherwise incomprehensible devastation wreaked by these storms. So it was with Andrew, a simple name for people to curse, fear, blame and remember. From Sunday morning, Aug. 23, into Monday, Aug. 24, Andrew rampaged across the Bahamas and the populous tip of southern Florida and into Louisiana's Cajun country with strength enough to hoist trucks atop buildings, destroy houses and vaporize mobile homes, impale yachts on pier pilings and even strip paint off walls. Propelled by winds up to 164 m.p.h., the storm damaged about 80% of the area's farms and dealt some $400 million in losses to its foliage industry, vegetable crops and tropical orchards. Andrew proved far more expensive than Hurricane Hugo, which ripped through the Carolinas in 1989, and more destructive than any of the recent California earthquakes—in sum, the costliest natural disaster in American history.

Almost like a tornado, Andrew cut a 20-to-35-mile-wide swath south of Miami that leveled entire city blocks and left residents without electricity, phones, drinkable water, sewage treatment, food and shelter. Armed troops patrolled the streets to stop looters, some of whom brought in rental trucks to haul away booty.

The response by state and federal governments was slow and disjointed. President Bush cut short a political trip to New Jersey and hurried to Florida to view the damage just hours after the hurricane blew through. He stayed an hour and a half and spent only a few minutes chatting with Florida Governor Lawton Chiles during a photo opportunity. Two days later, Bush hustled off to Louisiana in Andrew's wake; he returned to both sites the following week to ex-

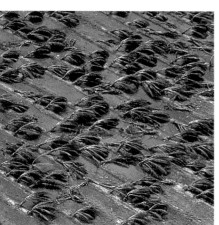

DISASTER VICTIMS: Above, young palms at a tree nursery are racked by savage winds. Right, in Homestead, Gary Davis and his dog stand among the ruins of his mobile home.

WRATH

press his concern. But in Florida, which took the hardest hit, local officials blamed Washington for the slow response, while federal bureaucrats retorted that the state had failed to ask formally for military help. Not until Transportation Secretary Andrew Card met with Chiles and an angry Florida congressional delegation on Thursday did Bush move beyond motion and into action. That night he ordered the Pentagon to rush everything from food to field hospitals to South Florida. But by then, four days had passed. Bush, like nearly everyone else, had badly underestimated the damage.

By Friday, Aug. 28, troops poured into the disaster area with mobile kitchens, tents, electrical generators, water and blankets to help more than 200,000 of the newly homeless—some sleeping in their cars or in campers— try to pick up the pieces of their shattered lives. A second army of carpenters and contractors was soon heading to Florida to mine a $20 billion bonanza in reconstruction and clean-up work. Citing a staggering total of 117,000 homes, nine public schools, 59 hospitals and health-care facilities, countless malls and a couple of city halls destroyed or damaged, Dade County's economic development agency called for a "mini Marshall Plan."

In the long run, pluck and perseverance may prove to have been the strongest ally for Andrew's survivors. Mitch and Penny Burke, newly wed, emerged from a closet after the storm ripped through their home in southern Dade County to find they had lost almost everything—dining-room furniture, bed, clothes, wedding gifts. The damage was so bad that their entire neighborhood faced the likelihood of being razed. "We've got new wallpaper, but no walls," said Penny with resolute humor. "I told the neighbors not to bother knocking when they come visit." ■

FLORIDA WRECKAGE:
Flood waters roar through the town of Homestead, which took the hardest hit from the hurricane. Above center, a wary gun toter backs up his claim to any potential looter. In Cutler Ridge, pleasure boats stacked up in a canal on Paradise Point give testament to the savagery of the storm. At Saga Bay, the winds, which reached a maximum speed of 164 m.p.h., turned an apartment building into a grotesque parody of a child's playhouse.

69

WORLD

Queen Elizabeth called 1992 an *annus horribilis* for the
royal family; the term also fit the human family.
And matters are not likely to improve until the world
finds a better formula for dispelling chaos.

By G E O R G E J. C H U R C H

N O ONE WILL CONFESS TO MISSING THE COLD WAR:
Who could feel nostalgic about the threat of nuclear annihilation? But there are grounds for missing, or at least casting around desperately for
something to replace, the pattern of order that the rivalry of
the superpowers long imposed on world affairs. Alas, no
substitute came into sight during 1992, the first full year of
the post–cold war era.

Instead trends toward cooperation and chaos battled for
supremacy—with chaos for the moment winning. Some
nations continued to forge new cooperative links: the U.S.,
Canada and Mexico initialed a treaty setting up a North
American Free Trade Association, and the European
Community at year's end removed the last remaining barriers to free movement of capital and goods among its 12
members. But these victories for order were outnumbered
by triumphs for disintegration. Ethnic and religious hatreds flared into noxious bloom, producing growing death
lists in nations as widely separated as India, Somalia and
Bosnia. Separatist movements broke up even 74-year-old
Czechoslovakia, which split into independent Czech and
Slovak nations at the end of the year. Peacekeeping operations by the United Nations and other multicountry
groups, though unprecedentedly large and numerous,
were often ineffective. Khmer Rouge guerrillas in Cambo-
dia repeatedly kidnapped blue-helmeted U.N. personnel;
in Liberia, a multinational African peacekeeping force
came under fire in a continuing civil war.

The most portentous explosion (or implosion) was the
one that shattered the Other Superpower. What as recently
as 1991 had been one nation, the Soviet Union, splintered
into 15 countries that went their separate ways. The Com-
monwealth of Independent States supposedly formed at
the end of 1991 to foster unity among 11 of them never really came into existence. Ethnic feuds fueled savage fighting
in Moldova, on the Romanian border; in Tajikistan in
Central Asia; in the Caucasus republic of Georgia; and be-

tween Armenia and Azerbaijan over the enclave of Nagorno-Karabakh. In most cases, truces were quickly made and
just as quickly broken, and by year's end none of the under-
lying conflicts seemed near solution.

Russia made some progress toward both a free-market
economy and political democracy—but unhappily the two
came into conflict. The freeing of prices and the setting up
of incentives toward private ownership of land and industry
were accompanied by rapid inflation, declines in production and shortages of goods. The backlash was so strong that
President Boris Yeltsin at year's end had to drop Yegor Gaidar as his Prime Minister, caving in to forces that want a
much slower move toward dismantling the command
economy. True enough, this was the outcome of debates in
the Congress of People's Deputies that were democratic in
the sense of being loud and uninhibited—one degenerated
briefly into a pushing and shoving match—but hardly
pointed toward stability. Old-line communists and right-
wing nationalists formed an unholy alliance bent on restor-
ing authoritarian rule; at year's end they were being kept at
bay but had not quite been defeated.

At least in Russia and the former Soviet Union, worse
never quite came to worst. But it came to just that in what
was once Yugoslavia. There a horrified world witnessed a
replay of some of the ghastliest scenes from World War II:
concentration camps, mass executions, men, women and
children sealed into boxcars like cattle for deportation and
exile. Having conquered parts of Croatia, Serbia turned its
attention to Bosnia and Herzegovina, which declared independence in March. Serbian forces conquered about two-
thirds of Bosnia, and Croats took much of the rest. By year's
end Bosnia had shrunk to a few small, disconnected slivers
of land around a few major towns and the besieged capital,
Sarajevo. Worse than the fighting was the Serb policy of
"ethnic cleansing," meaning the killing or deporting of
non-Serbs in the conquered areas. By year's end hundreds
of thousands of refugees (mostly Muslims, who constituted

45% of the population of prewar Bosnia) were wandering the country without shelter, facing death from starvation and exposure during the harsh Balkan winter.

Though the U.N. repeatedly denounced Serbia, it could never agree on any way to stop or even slow the aggression. But in the African nation of Somalia, U.S. initiative raised hopes for a far more effective type of future U.N. intervention. The U.S. got U.N. blessing for organizing and dispatching a mixed force—28,000 U.S. troops, 2,000 French, smaller contingents from more than 30 other countries—to that anarchic land, where famine had been killing 1,000 people a day. The aim was to ensure distribution of food to the starving by suppressing the armed gangs that had been looting supplies. It was an entirely new kind of U.N. operation, undertaken for humanitarian reasons (neither the U.S. nor any other major power has any economic or strategic interest in Somalia), an exercise in so-called peace enforcing rather than peacekeeping (there is no peace to keep), all initiated without any invitation from a host government (there is no Somali government). As such, it may well set a precedent for U.N. intervention in situations of a kind that the world body earlier had merely wrung its hands over. First, though, the U.N., having in effect abandoned the old doctrine that anything happening inside one country's borders is no one else's business, must define a new doctrine to govern where, when and under what circumstances such intervention is justified. That definition has not even been started.

Meanwhile, even those areas of the world that had been experiencing growing togetherness hit some ups and downs in 1992. In South Africa, President F.W. de Klerk won a 2-to-1 majority in a March referendum—possibly the last whites-only vote to be held there—for continuing efforts to form a multiracial government. But the African National Congress broke off the talks in June, charging that government security forces had participated in a massacre of blacks in the township of Boipatong. The talks were re-

sumed in December, and later that month De Klerk announced a purge of top-level right-wingers in the military, including two generals and four brigadiers. "We are closing the year on a high note," said Nelson Mandela. In India, Hindu fanatics tore down a 464-year-old mosque in the northern town of Ayodhya, setting off Hindu-Muslim riots that left more than 1,000 dead and the Indian traditions of secularism and toleration of all religions in grave danger.

WHILE THE EUROPEAN COMMUNITY VIRTUALLY completed economic unification, the Maastricht treaty, intended to promote political and social unity, was rejected by Danish voters and won only a "*petit oui*" in a French referendum. Even if it passes a second Danish referendum and a British parliamentary vote next spring, many of the treaty's most ambitious clauses may never go into effect. A common currency also seems far off: its supposed precursor, the exchange-rate mechanism that once kept all 12 currencies in a fixed relationship, blew apart in September. Britain and Italy had to pull out because the pound and lira could not keep pace with the deutsche mark. Britons were further unpleasantly diverted by a series of royal scandals that caused the Queen to call 1992 an "*annus horribilis.*"

By contrast, after Israeli elections replaced hard-line Prime Minister Yitzhak Shamir with the more moderate Yitzhak Rabin, Mideast peace talks actually made some ever-so-tenuous progress. It was another instance of the previously unthinkable becoming reality, which has been happening regularly since the end of the cold war, for both good and bad. Mostly for good: hundreds of millions of people have been freed from communist oppression, and there is no longer a threat that some local conflict will start a showdown between nuclear powers. But the proliferation of local conflicts underlines again the need of a world no longer organized around ideological alliances to find some other integrating principle that might diminish chaos. ■

While the world refused to intervene, Serbia drenched Yugoslavia's former republics in blood

BOSNIA, 1992. FOR THOSE WHO lived there, it was a child's worst nightmare, a land where horror was the custom. Fathers disappeared. Friends died. Neighbors fled. Food was short, bombs fell, and suffering was a way of life. The familiar names of cities and towns turned into symbols of destruction, siege, massacre and "ethnic cleansing."

Like an addiction, hatred consumed the people who used to call themselves Yugoslavs. Every throat slit made someone else thirst for blood. "They killed my husband and son," said a tearful Bosnian refugee. "They burned our home. But they can never rest easy, because one day we will do the same to them, or worse. My children will get their revenge, or their children."

The world's revulsion at the barbarity was genuine and appropriate, but its response was confused and tentative. Political considerations were at odds with military realities. What could outsiders do? While the world watched, the blood continued to flow.

HERITAGE OF HATE

Throughout its 74-year existence, Yugoslavia was a powder keg of ethnic, national and religious hatreds that go back for centuries. The country that vanished in the fighting was an artificial creation of two cultures, patched together in the wake of two world wars. Orthodox Serbs, Catholic Croats and Muslim Slavs were held in check only by strongman Josip Broz Tito's centralized communist system. By the time of his death in 1980, the country was already unraveling. Political power had decentralized, the relatively prosperous economy was faltering, and old tensions began to rise. The richer republics of the northwest, Slovenia and Croatia, felt their development was hampered by the poorer republics of Montenegro, Macedonia,

Slaughter In the BALKANS

Bosnia and Herzegovina, and Serbia. Serbia was hated by the rest for dominating the government and the army; in turn it saw preserving unity at all costs as a mission, given weight by fears that Serbs in other republics were threatened by emerging nationalist regimes.

Slovenia departed first, and the federal government's attempt to hold it by force was cut short by a feisty military defense and the fact that Slovenia had no Serb minority to justify Belgrade's interference. That successful bid for freedom emboldened Croatia, where Serbs are a widely dispersed minority. Croatian President Franjo Tudjman's inflammatory and nationalistic rhetoric also stirred Serb fears of a reprise of the genocidal campaign against them by Croat fascists during World War II. Bosnia, largely Muslim and Croat but with a 1.4 million Serb ethnic component, seceded on March 3, 1992, and Serbia saw the pattern repeating. Once again, Serbs felt victimized while an uncaring world looked on.

Centuries of simmering ethnic hatreds were now so fully aroused that each group was convinced that its opponents—many of whom were friendly neighbors up until a few months before—were guilty of unbounded perfidy. In Bosnia, for example, Croats, Serbs and Muslims had lived peaceably side by side for decades. But now the Serbs, under their fiercely nationalistic leader Slobodan Milosevic, forced Muslim President Alija Izetbegovic to agree to a tripartite division of the newly independent country into ethnic regions. The Serbs laid claim to one-third of Croatia and about 70% of Bosnia's territory.

In early April, Serb guerrillas began to wage what they termed an "ethnic cleansing" campaign in Muslim towns along Bosnia's eastern borders with Serbia and Montenegro. In Croatia, Serb irregulars expelled Croats from areas near the Danube where Serbs predominated. Croats and Muslims responded in kind against the Serbs. By June the violence had spread south and east, igniting Bosnia and Herzegovina, and threatening to engulf the other republics. Hope evaporated that sanity would prevail.

The war's toll mounted. A June estimate had 12,000 people dead, tens of thousands missing and wounded, and 1.5 million men, women and children forced to flee their homes. From Bosnia came daily tales of gut-wrenching savagery, particularly from the besieged capital city of Saraje-

"They killed my husband and son. They burned our home. But they can never rest easy ... my children will get their revenge, or their children."

Top right, pictures of inmates in detention camps flashed around the world in August, heightening calls for intervention. Bottom right, women recoil during a mortar attack in Sarajevo in July.

vo. In May civilians there were lured from their homes by a lull in the fighting, and had lined up for bread and ice cream when three 82-mm mortar shells smashed into the crowd. At least 25 people were killed and an additional 100 injured. Just the night before, shells had slammed into a maternity hospital, killing three newborns. All summer, the world watched the siege of Sarajevo in horror. U.S. Secretary of State James Baker characterized the scene as a "humanitarian nightmare."

SCENES OF HORROR

The turning point in world opinion came in August, when journalists provided new, ghastly images of the slaughter: terrified

babies tied to bus seats, the funeral of two toddlers killed by snipers, a sudden, apparently intentional mortar attack on the mourners. Then came persistent reports of torture and starvation in detention camps and more terrible television images, this time of skeletal, bruised men behind barbed wire. The pictures seemed to come from another time—the Dark Ages, the Thirty Years' War, Hitler's heyday.

A political uproar was sparked by emotional new charges that each faction in Bosnia was running a network of internment camps where beatings, torture, starvation and even murder were commonplace. International observers scrambled to investigate the claims. Bosnian officials claimed that the Serbs were running at least 105 camps, through which 260,000 people had passed since April, with 17,000 deaths, and that 130,000 were still incarcerated. Serbs countercharged that Muslims and Croats were running 40 camps of their own, where more than 6,000 Serbs had died. A Bosnian report, possibly exaggerated, told of a primary school in Bratunac where Serbs were accused of bleeding 500 Muslims to death so Serbs could get transfusions.

According to a former prisoner interviewed in the New York City newspaper *Newsday*, more than a thousand Muslim and Croat civilians were held by Serbs in metal cages stacked four high, without food or water. He said groups of 10 to 15 were removed every few days and shot; many others were beaten to death. British television footage of an open-air jail at Trnopolje showed thousands of prisoners who were dirty, dazed and emaciated. The camera team found evidence of beatings, torture, dysentery and scurvy. There were also "impromptu killing grounds," said a Western diplomat, "where massacres take place, then the killers move on. This is not the kind of murder the U.N. or Red Cross can monitor."

THE WORLD WATCHES

While the world was recoiling in shock from the visible inhumanity, Western reaction was more rhetorical than real. For months, leaders in Europe and the U.S. engaged in hand wringing over the human tragedy in the Balkans yet shied away from facing the hard choices that any effort to stop the killing would entail. On May 31 the U.N. took action, imposing economic sanctions intended to force the

A British diplomat told the victims in Bosnia, "There is no cavalry coming over the hill . . . there is no force coming."

Sarajevo stories: top, a cellist played each day amid the ruins of the National Library. Bottom, when a sniper fired into a crowd, a Muslim soldier shot back.

Serbs to end their belligerency. But the embargo leaked; Bulgarian officials claimed in November that 100,000 tons of crude oil and gasoline had passed into Serbia by rail alone since the embargo was declared. Heavy truck traffic and considerable small-time smuggling added to the illegal influx.

Finally, the powerful August pictures of dead children and imprisoned adults that captured the cruelty and suffering of the conflict succeeded in raising moral outrage throughout the world. Under pressure to do something—anything— the U.N. Security Council passed a vague resolution that provided for "all measures necessary" to ensure delivery of relief supplies. Observers could be forgiven if they somehow got the idea that the U.N. had authorized the use of force to end the barbarities. U.S. Deputy Secretary of State Lawrence Eagleburger spelled it out carefully: "What we are talking about is the provision of humanitarian

assistance. We are not talking about going beyond that."

In mid-August a NATO contingency plan calling for 100,000 alliance troops to hold a land corridor from the Adriatic coast was rejected. Britain's Deputy Foreign Minister Douglas Hogg flew to Sarajevo to tell Bosnia's President Izetbegovic "that there is no cavalry coming over the hill, that there is no international force coming." In the U.S., Democratic candidate Bill Clinton demanded that George Bush take a more active role in stopping the slaughter, as did former Secretary of State George Shultz.

Early in October the U.N. imposed a ban on military flights over Bosnia. In November the Security Council tightened the sanctions, approving plans to bar all shipments of strategic goods through Serbia and Montenegro, including fuel, steel and chemicals. NATO and the nine-nation Western European Union authorized a naval blockade to intercept sanction-busting vessels in the Adriatic Sea. Many feared, though, that the sanctions would only deepen the state of economic extremity for most people in Serbia and Montenegro without affecting the power of Serbian President Milosevic.

In December that power was tested at the polls when Milosevic ran for re-election as President of the Serbian republic; his principal opponent was the Prime Minister of Yugoslavia, Milan Panic, a naturalized American citizen. The U.S. and other Western nations strongly supported Panic's effort to oust Milosevic's brutal regime. The week before the election, Eagleburger, newly sworn in as U.S. Secretary of State, attempted to cast further disfavor on Milosevic and his minions by releasing a list of alleged war criminals in the fighting. Included on it were Milosevic, General Ratko Miadic, commander of the Serb military forces in Bosnia, and Radovan Karadzic, Milosevic's chief political operative in Bosnia. The West also threatened tougher boycotts if Milosevic was re-elected.

However, when militant Serbs went to the polls on Dec. 20, they gave Milosevic a wide majority. Panic denounced the election as fraudulent and said he would demand a new vote. In a written statement, he claimed the voting was invalid "because of fraud, theft and cheating in the counting of ballots." Election monitors from the Council on Security and Cooperation in Europe described the campaign and election as "riddled with flaws and irregularities . . . tainted by shameless propaganda in the state-run media," without endorsing Panic's charges. But like the countries that had stood by as Yugoslavia progressed deeper into barbarity, both Panic and the European observers were powerless to overturn the election results.

As the deadly year drew to a close, the talk was only of harder times to come: U.S. and European diplomats threatened tighter sanctions or even military action; the Serbs promised more complete ethnic cleansing. Western officials began to fear that Belgrade might next turn its attention to Kosovo, the predominantly Albanian province that is a disputed part of southern Serbia. Some feared that a conflagration in Kosovo could spread beyond Serbia to involve Albania and perhaps Macedonia, Greece, Bulgaria, even Turkey. It would not be the first time that slaughter in the Balkans had forced a reluctant world to war. ■

The Winter of Discontent

RUSSIA IS FIGHTING THREE REVOLUTIONS AT ONCE:

"It's winter here," said Boris Yeltsin to Bill Clinton in a telephone conversation just after the U.S. election. "And you know, winter is always hard for us."

THE PRESIDENT OF RUSSIA WAS NOT JUST TALKING ABOUT the weather; he was acknowledging a force of history. The Romanovs' throne, Alexander Kerensky's provisional government and Mikhail Gorbachev's Soviet Union all came crashing down when the snows were swirling, the days cold and the nights long. In each case the implications for the world—and the U.S.—were immense.

Now it is Yeltsin's turn to contend with the conspiring adversities of nature, economics and politics. Once again, the whole world has a huge stake in the outcome. When temperatures fall in Russia, food is harder to find in the cities and prices rise. The sting in the air makes shopping even more of a hardship. As citizens trudge from store to store in the dark, their frustration is, as it has always been, aimed at their leader in the Kremlin. But unlike the Czars and the General Secretaries before him, Yeltsin does not rely on terror to enforce the passivity of the populace. Instead, he has to address its grievances and contend with its elected representatives. Real democracy, however primitive and messy, has come to Russia. That achievement, imperfect though it is, is nothing less than a miracle. But it is a miracle wrapped in danger inside a dilemma.

Yeltsin is sometimes said to be presiding over the second Russian Revolution. But that understates and oversimplifies the challenge facing him and his people. Russia is actually in the throes of three transformations at once: from totalitarianism to democracy, from a command economy to a

**From totalitarianism to democracy
From command economy to
a free market
From multi-national empire
to a nation-state**

79

Yeltsin's

free market, and from a multinational empire to a nation-state. Any one of these would be arduous enough all by itself. Undertaking three revolutions simultaneously with so little warning and preparation has overloaded the circuits. Russia is trying to cast off, virtually overnight, the legacy of more than a thousand years of absolutism; and it is trying to create, virtually from scratch, the institutions, traditions and political culture associated with the rule of law and popular government. No wonder the winter of 1992-93, more than any in years, was the winter of Russia's discontent.

TOWARD DEMOCRACY

After seven years of political turbulence, Russia is highly sensitized to trouble. As the Congress of People's Deputies met in Moscow early in December, rumors of a coup, a dictatorship, social upheaval raced through the capital. But something else happened as well. Most of Russia's 150 million citizens were taking the latest crisis in stride, indifferent to all the fuss in Moscow. However imperfect their experiment in democracy had proved so far, they were confident that one day it would succeed.

This winter, their faith was pinned on Boris Nikolayevich Yeltsin. He never aspired to the role of Sun President, around whom everything in the realm turns. But he so dominated the political landscape that it would be no exaggeration to say that as Yeltsin goes, so goes the nation. Under his leadership, Russia has taken major strides toward becoming a free and open society. The disastrous state of the economy Yeltsin inherited has made the transition exceptionally difficult, but his reform team is doing much better than many Western analysts expected.

The trouble is that one year after the collapse of the Soviet Union, Russia still lacks the kind of political institutions that would ensure the continuity of reforms without Yeltsin. Attempts to establish a system of checks and balances are not faring well. The legislature is paralyzed by unending battles with the executive branch. The new constitutional court must work without a proper constitution. The government has to listen to such a deafening chorus of calls for its resignation that ministers cannot concentrate on the business of reform. It falls to the President to keep the operation of state on track. Says Gennadi Burbulis, Yeltsin's chief political strategist: "The majority of Russians have confidence not in institutions like the parliament and government but in the person of the President. During a transformation of such magnitude, this kind of personification of power can be positive, but it is also dangerous."

Yeltsin has proved immune to efforts by sycophantic followers to turn him into an uncrowned Czar. He is a true man of the people—a real muzhik, as the Russians say— who works in his own garden and loves to eat herring with boiled potatoes. To maintain the common touch, he often stops his official motorcade to chat with people on the street. Although he has an unfortunate habit of making promises dictated by the feelings of the moment, he has been courageous in supporting unpopular economic poli-

HARDLINERS A collection of unrepentant communists, disgruntled military men, ultranationalists and Old Guard apparatchiks is gathering strength and slowing reform. Among the toughest: Civic Union boss Arkadi Volsky, an adviser to each of the past three Soviet leaders, and Dmitri Vasiliev, president of Pamyat, a rabidly nationalist, anti-Semitic group espousing a return of the Czar.

OTHER REPUBLICS In 1992 new Presidents were overthrown in Georgia, Azerbaijan and Tajikstan. The 25 million ethnic Russians now living outside Russia but within the borders of the old union are now treated as second-class citizens. 80,000 Russian troops are stuck in the Baltics, where they are regarded as foreign occupiers. Disputes with Ukraine continue over control of nuclear weapons and the navy.

Gremlins

...ajor problems when the Soviets fell

THE ECONOMY Free enterprise is stalled between reform and reaction. In January of 1992 the government freed prices of consumer goods and began selling state property into private hands. But the reforms have ripped Russia's social safety net, worsening inflation, unemployment and living standards, and even creating nostalgia for communist rule. One-third of the population lives below the poverty line.

THE ENVIRONMENT Six years after Chernobyl, 19 similar graphite-moderated nuclear reactors are still in operation. For more than 30 years the Soviets dumped enormous quantities of radioactive rubbish into the atmosphere; four of their nuclear-powered subs sank accidentally. Above, in 60-second shifts, soldiers clad in lead clear debris from Chernobyl. Radiation damaged this black-and-white photo.

cies that have eroded his standing among ordinary citizens.

Yeltsin has tried out a variety of roles in his quest to be the kind of strong executive he thinks Russia needs. After he was chosen chairman of the Supreme Soviet in May 1990, he did a stint as parliamentary leader. A year and one month later, he became the first popularly elected President in the country's history. He even took on the second job of Prime Minister for several months in October 1991. None of these has quite fit the bill. Ironically, Yeltsin is haunted by the same problem that plagued Mikhail Gorbachev when the former Soviet President was trying to create a new structure of power to replace Communist Party rule: he has more authority on paper than in practice. Yet whenever Yeltsin begins to talk tough in response to turmoil in the ethnic enclaves of the Russian federation or the latest challenge from parliament, the opposition immediately warns of a coming dictatorship.

Russia desperately needs a new constitution to codify the nation's guidelines. The project has been caught in a dispute between Yeltsin and the parliament over what kind of state structure to enshrine in the new basic law. Yeltsin wants a strong President, who will have a free hand to organize new government structures and appoint ministers. Legislators want to give parliament the power to control government appointments and to make the head of state a figurehead that Yeltsin supporters claim would be akin to the British Queen.

Far from being a driving force for change, the current two-tier parliament, made up of a permanently working Supreme Soviet and a larger Congress of People's Deputies that meets at least twice a year, has turned into a major bastion of communist and conservative opposition to reform. The legislature is a cross section, frozen in time, of political forces active in the Soviet Union back in 1990, when the last elections were held and Communist Party influence remained strong. Parliamentarians asserted their strength by summoning the People's Deputies into session—over Yeltsin's heated opposition—on Dec. 1, the very day his mandate to rule by decree expired.

The Congress soon became as a battleground between Yeltsin and the forces opposing reform; at one point a fistfight broke out on the floor. At the end of the first week the Congress only narrowly turned aside a constitutional amendment that would have stripped Yeltsin of his power to appoint a government. Then the Deputies refused to confirm Yeltsin's key deputy, Yegor Gaidar, as Prime Minister. After eight days of haggling, Yeltsin finally took the podium and proceeded to heap buckets of scorn on the legislators. Then he played his strongest card, calling for a referendum to end the political stalemate. "I am asking the citizens of Russia to make it clear," he said, addressing the electorate. "Which side are you on?" When confronted with the stark choice of submitting or facing the President at the ballot box, the balky Deputies under leader Ruslan Khasbulatov became more inclined to deal. So, on reflection, did Yeltsin. On the last day of the Congress, he named Viktor S. Chernomyrdin, 54, as the new Prime Minister. The move was deplored by Yeltsin's allies in reform; many claimed it was a serious blow to his stature. He also agreed to modify his referendum. Now

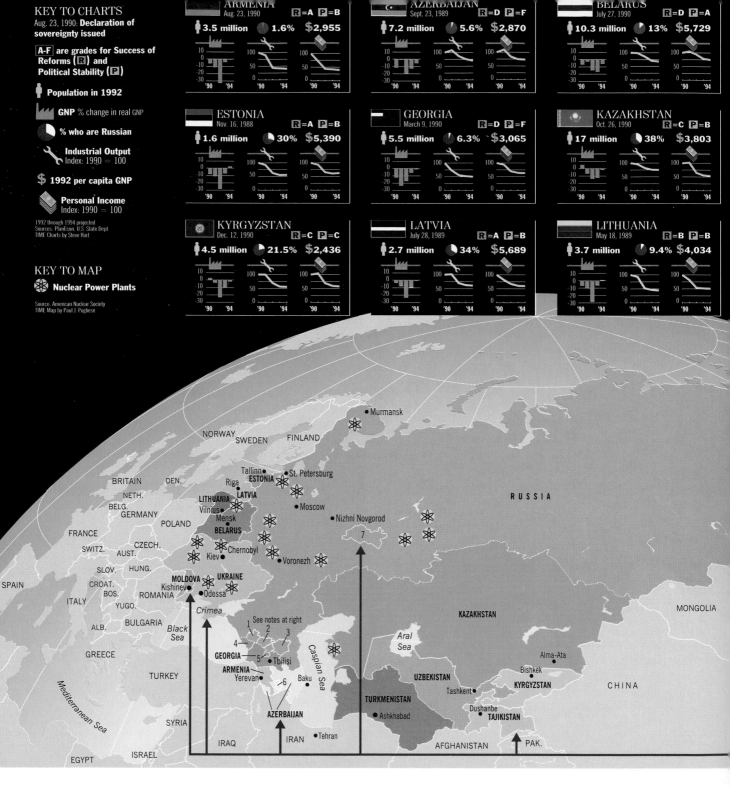

KEY TO CHARTS

Aug. 23, 1990: **Declaration of sovereignty issued**

A-F are grades for Success of Reforms (**R**) and Political Stability (**P**)

👤 Population in 1992

🏭 **GNP** % change in real GNP

◗ % who are Russian

🔧 Industrial Output Index: 1990 = 100

$ 1992 per capita GNP

💵 Personal Income Index: 1990 = 100

1992 through 1994 projected
Sources: PlanEcon, U.S. State Dept
TIME Charts by Steve Hart

KEY TO MAP

✴ **Nuclear Power Plants**

Source: American Nuclear Society
TIME Map by Paul J. Pugliese

ARMENIA Aug. 23, 1990 **R**=A **P**=B
3.5 million 1.6% $2,955

AZERBAIJAN Sept. 23, 1989 **R**=D **P**=F
7.2 million 5.6% $2,870

BELARUS July 27, 1990 **R**=D **P**=A
10.3 million 13% $5,729

ESTONIA Nov. 16, 1988 **R**=A **P**=B
1.6 million 30% $5,390

GEORGIA March 9, 1990 **R**=D **P**=F
5.5 million 6.3% $3,065

KAZAKHSTAN Oct. 26, 1990 **R**=C **P**=B
17 million 38% $3,803

KYRGYZSTAN Dec. 12, 1990 **R**=C **P**=C
4.5 million 21.5% $2,436

LATVIA July 28, 1989 **R**=A **P**=B
2.7 million 34% $5,689

LITHUANIA May 18, 1989 **R**=B **P**=B
3.7 million 9.4% $4,034

Russians will not be asked to choose directly between him and the Congress. Instead, they will determine who should have more power by voting on a new constitution in April 1993.

TROUBLED NEIGHBORS

Russia is not the only part of the former Soviet Union to find the transition from totalitarian rule to democracy rocky. The new states have learned that it is not enough to establish a presidential form of rule if there are no local democratic traditions to sustain it. During 1992, new Presidents were overthrown in the republics of Georgia, Azerbaijan and Tajikistan. In the Central Asian nation of Turkmenistan, President Saparmurad Niyazov is reviving the tradition of the communist personality cult, complete with marching columns of youths dressed in T shirts emblazoned with his portrait.

Russia's behavior toward other parts of the old Soviet Union is a troubling matter. In trying to redefine their own nationhood, many Russians have not yet been able to ac-

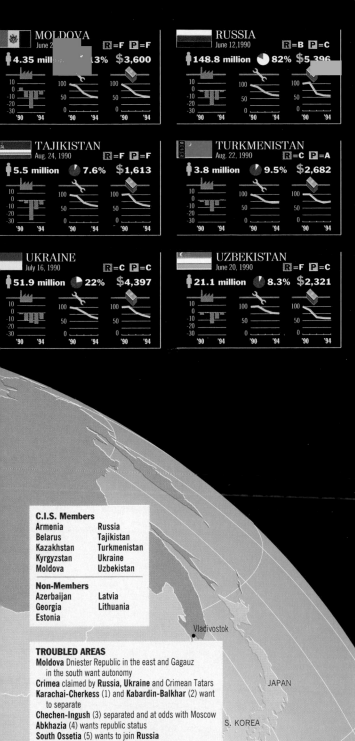

MOLDOVA
June 2
4.35 mill...   ...3% $3,600
R=F P=F

RUSSIA
June 12, 1990
148.8 million   82% $5,396
R=B P=C

TAJIKISTAN
Aug. 24, 1990
5.5 million   7.6% $1,613
R=F P=F

TURKMENISTAN
Aug. 22, 1990
3.8 million   9.5% $2,682
R=C P=A

UKRAINE
July 16, 1990
51.9 million   22% $4,397
R=C P=C

UZBEKISTAN
June 20, 1990
21.1 million   8.3% $2,321
R=F P=C

C.I.S. Members
Armenia	Russia
Belarus	Tajikistan
Kazakhstan	Turkmenistan
Kyrgyzstan	Ukraine
Moldova	Uzbekistan

Non-Members
Azerbaijan	Latvia
Georgia	Lithuania
Estonia	

Vladivostok

JAPAN

S. KOREA

TROUBLED AREAS
Moldova Dniester Republic in the east and Gagauz in the south want autonomy
Crimea claimed by **Russia, Ukraine** and Crimean Tatars
Karachai-Cherkess (1) and **Kabardin-Balkhar** (2) want to separate
Chechen-Ingush (3) separated and at odds with Moscow
Abkhazia (4) wants republic status
South Ossetia (5) wants to join **Russia**
Armenians in **Nagorno-Karabakh** (6) want independence from **Azerbaijan**
Tatarstan (7) wants economic and political antonomy
Tajikistan engaged in civil war

The notion that Russia has a mission to protect those kinsmen is by no means confined to extremists; it is a mainstream sentiment and a powerful force in the deliberations of the Congress. The U.S., the West Europeans and the United Nations must use their considerable influence with the newly independent states to protect the rights of the Russian minorities there. Otherwise, Russia may take matters into its own heavy hands. If so, the world would surely suspend whatever help it is giving to any government in Moscow, which would only deepen the crisis in Russia and accelerate the vicious cycle of economic distress and political extremism.

TO MARKET, TO MARKET

Cumbersome and corrupt, the Soviet economy functioned, such as it did in the past, because it had its own internal logic. Moscow once decreed the production of every tank, shoe and potato; every working-age person was supposed to have a job; prices were stable. No such coherence and vision applies to the new Russian economy. Since Yeltsin decapitated the old command system without putting something in its place, Russia has become a battlefield on which the concepts of free enterprise and state control went to war.

In January 1991, Yeltsin freed prices of consumer goods and began selling state property into private hands. The reforms began well. Despite the hardship inflicted on consumers, the high prices lured goods to market and shortages all but disappeared. The big setback came when the Russian central bank began funneling money to cash-starved state industries. That kept the old behemoths in business but whipped up inflation and sent the ruble plunging to more than 400 to the dollar. Now Russia is undergoing the most severe economic hardship since World War II. The gross domestic product declined 23% in 1992, while inflation may hit a monthly annualized rate of 2,200%. Meanwhile the number of jobless workers surged from 59,000 to 905,000 in 1992 alone.

Initial promises of support from the West remain largely unfulfilled, and Yeltsin is still waiting for $13 billion of the $24 billion in Western assistance that the major industrialized countries pledged in April 1992. The political and economic turmoil hurt Russia's ability to attract desperately needed investments from Western firms. "It's like the Wild West," says John Kiser, a Washington technology-trade expert. "There's no law and no contracts. The only thing you have to build on is your confidence in the people you're dealing with."

Democracy, nationalism, the economy: the three revolutions converge in the figure of Yeltsin, a master politician who is determined to get politics off the national agenda so that Russia can finally buckle down to work. Many of his tactical moves appear to be prompted by a desire to hold the forces of reaction in check long enough for a new society to emerge, where economic self-interest will prevail over the political passions of the past. He also seems to be sincere in his intention to devolve power from a small group of players in Moscow out into the vast reaches of the country. But the paradox Yeltsin must ultimately resolve is whether he is willing to use his own political power to the full in order to one day give power back to the people. ■

cept the idea that the 14 non-Russian republics of the U.S.S.R. are today independent foreign countries. Russian politicians have even coined a new phrase—the near abroad—to distinguish between the former Soviet republics and the rest of the world. The Russian sense of special rights and responsibilities in the near abroad is more than a matter of imperial postpartum depression. Some 25 million ethnic Russians live outside Russia but within the borders of the old union. The dominant local nationalities now treat those Russians as second-class citizens or worse.

England's royal family endures a year of marital hassles, burning castles and restless vassals

The Bi

AS A SORROWING QUEEN ELIZABETH and her family watched the flames consume the halls and treasures of Windsor Castle on Nov. 20, it seemed a cruel metaphor for the events of 1992. Britain's House of Windsor was under fire as it had not been since 1936, the year Edward VIII abdicated the throne. The notion of the family monarchy, a Victorian-era invention that accorded a symbolic and public role to royal offspring and consorts as well as to the crown, seemed on the brink of collapse. None of the four children of Queen Elizabeth II had sustained a stable marriage. The heir to the throne, Prince Charles, and his striking bride Diana announced their separation in early December. Princess Anne, who had divorced earlier in the year, was remarried only a week after the Waleses' shocker. Prince Andrew was separated from his cavorting duchess, and Prince Edward has not approached the altar or shown signs that he ever will. There was scandal as well: the uproar over Diana's secretly taped phone coos to a friend was overshadowed by reports of a steamy conversation between Prince Charles and a longtime companion.

Speculation about adultery, love affairs, "Dianagate" followed by "Camillagate"— the headlines were hurricanes buffeting a fragile, archaic institution that may not be able to withstand the impact. Each new revelation elicited more serious calls from a restless public for the monarchy to be taxed, for a cut in its numbers who are paid a government stipend and—to entertain the unthinkable—for the whole institution to be abolished. The Queen herself, in an unusually personal speech at a banquet given by the Lord Mayor of London, exclaimed, "1992 is not a year on which I shall look back with undiluted pleasure . . . it has turned out to be an *annus horribilis.*"

A HOUSE DIVIDING

The horrible year reached a climax in its last month with the announcement of the royal separation. Princess Diana broke the news to her sons at Highgrove, the hated country house she visited for the last time to remove her possessions. Prince Charles sought out the boys at their boarding school to reassure them. Then, on Wednesday, Dec. 9, Prime Minister John Major announced the split in the House of Commons, hoping to get the worst of the press coverage over with before the little princes' Christmas break.

The fairy-tale marriage of the Prince and Princess of Wales was finally over after 11 years, and people were sorry

GULF WAR
The Prince and Princess of Wales in South Korea in November 1992. Only weeks later they separated.

ing to be a conversation between her and her too-close friend James Gilbey, usually described as a man-about-town.

The tabloids were howling. Whatever rules of taste and fairness once governed even their coverage of the royals had been consumed in the feeding frenzy. Then, in November, the newspapers got hold of a second tape, this time allegedly of an intimate chat between a lonely Prince Charles and Camilla Parker-Bowles, a married woman with whom he had been linked since well before his marriage to Diana. Thus began Camillagate. Newspaperman John Casey wrote that he had learned that part of the tape included a discussion of the transmigration of souls. "In the next life," he quotes Charles as saying, "I should like to come back as your trousers."

For her part, Diana had made it clear that she relished the prospect of going her own way. On the weekend of Nov. 14, while Charles was home celebrating his 44th birthday, Diana launched a high-profile trip to Paris that turned into a triumph. Looking relaxed and radiant, she spent nearly two hours with the Mitterrands, much of it with the President himself. She appeared confident discussing humanitarian and social issues in such powerful surroundings. Invariably she wins the rapt attention of Presidents and ministers with a distinctly honest way of speaking and asking questions—a far cry from her earlier repertoire of girlish smiles and playing dumb.

Diana plays to the hilt her role as an independent woman. She has become an ardent patron of many causes, especially involving AIDS patients, deprived children and the infirm. Those close to her say the princess is very savvy and streetwise and, when not in the grip of frustration or rage, well able to size up her position. She is a warm, demonstrative mother to her boys, but they know who's boss. Never try to put anything past her, says an ex-employee who wishes her well. Diana's contemporaries, especially women, see her as a kind of feminist heroine, a fighter who knows her own worth, what she wants out of life and how to flaunt traditional protocol to get it. The revelations of Morton's book and the Dianagate tape did nothing to diminish her enormous public appeal. Some 1992 polls ranked her as the royal family's most popular member.

But her directness and warmth, so charming to outsiders, may be the qualities that alienated the remote Prince

g Chill

to see the last gleaming gossamer fade into cobweb. But not even the most reverent monarchist could feign surprise. The Waleses' problems had become public knowledge when Diana went public with her marriage troubles, allowing her brother and close friends to talk to Andrew Morton, whose best-selling book, *Diana: Her True Story*, detailed her depression, bulimia, suicide attempts and estrangement from her prince. In August, a tape surfaced purport-

Charles. His downfall, it seems, was marrying a superstar, a charismatic beauty, perhaps the world's most photogenic woman. Thirteen years his junior and barely out of her teens when they married in 1981, Diana quickly discovered her extraordinary hold on the public. Especially in the past few years, while her two sons were in school, she has defined her own life and goals with scant reference to her husband's. More and more, Charles prefers living in the country and working behind the scenes. He has adopted the environment and architecture as his passions, and his railing against the ugliness of London's new buildings struck a chord in the common man. He is often pictured sketching in Scotland or communing with plants at Highgrove.

TERMS OF ESTRANGEMENT

When the separation was announced, human sympathy was quickly outdistanced by more practical doubts. Exactly what did the palace's separation announcement accomplish? While it insisted that the decision was amicable and that there had been no third parties involved, it was clear that the two had scarcely been able to look at each other, never mind speak, in public. And, of course, each had been caught in indiscreet phonefests with a "confidant."

The real boggler was the statement that "there is no reason why Her Royal Highness should not become Queen." That message caused gasps in Parliament; few believed the Waleses' assurance that they have no plans to divorce. The Archbishops of Canterbury and York released a joint statement that the breakup does not affect Charles' future position as head of the Church of England. But that church still frowns on divorce. As to remarriage, the stricture is so firm that Princess Anne went to Scotland to wed Commander Timothy Laurence, a former equerry to the Queen.

Even the timing of the separation was ridiculed. Prime Minister Major had to cancel a meeting with Jacques Delors, president of the European Commission, to make the announcement—just before an Edinburgh summit meeting of the European Community nations. And the palace's plea in the official announcement for diminished press coverage of the royals was considered naive wishful thinking. The separation announcement confirmed that the tabloids were right, a tough fact for the royal family to face. The palace clung to the one thing Charles and Diana undoubtedly have in their favor: both conduct their public lives energetically and responsibly. Now, despite official denials, there will be separate "courts" of competing loyal

cadres. Yet the couple have great vested interests in common: the throne must be secure for their son.

Diana seemed to be the victor in the separation deal. Care of the children will be shared, but Diana will receive a reported $1.5 million a year, the Kensington Palace apartments, a staff that is mostly her own, continuance of her status as a senior member of the royal family and a life free from Charles' glower. She may have insisted on Major's underscoring her right to be Queen, although with the clamor in Parliament, this may be an unrealistic notion. But Diana should not be counted out; more and more she

DYSFUNCTIONAL FAMILY?

In Queen Elizabeth's *annus horribilis*, controversy engulfed the royal family, here shown at the 1986 wedding of Prince Andrew and Sarah Ferguson. The tally: Prince Charles and Princess Diana separated; Prince Andrew and "Fergie" separated; she was later photographed topless. Princess Anne separated and remarried. Windsor Castle burned, and the Queen agreed to begin paying taxes. The Queen Mother still smiled on.

moves on center stage. Quips Anthony Holden, a biographer of Prince Charles: "If she manages to pull down the monarchy by mistake, she will be elected the first President of the People's Republic of Britain."

THE UNEASY HEAD

The Waleses' woes were only one thorn in Queen Elizabeth's crown of misery. The turmoil of '92 began when Sarah Ferguson, or Fergie, the notorious Duchess of York, decided that a cramped, duty-bound life-style was not for her, and bolted, leaving a trail of dubious liaisons, outsize bills and scandalous tabloid shots of her cavorting topless with a boyfriend in front of her two children.

Then, it seemed, even nature turned against the royals. On Nov. 20 a savage fire struck Windsor Castle,

RESTORATION TRAGEDY

The Windsor Castle fire raged for nearly 30 hours; later, Britons burned when they heard they would pay for the restoration.

raging for 30 hours. The flames jeopardized its priceless art collection and, though limited to one section of the vast structure, completely gutted St. George's Hall, one of the most elaborately ceremonial rooms in the castle. The inferno also heated up another long-simmering issue when it was announced that the public would bear the $100 million cost of restoring the structure. The marital problems of the Queen's family had already focused public resentment on what was coming to be considered the royals' free ride. The Queen has long paid no tax on her personal fortune, and the active members of her family receive nearly $15 million annually to support their public duties. But that is not all the Crown costs. The government maintains royal buildings and grounds, the yacht *Britannia* with its crew of 256, as well as the royal train and various planes and helicopters. It all added up to more than $100 million a year. Commentators often point out that Scandinavian monarchies cost a fraction of that, but Britons revel in pageantry, elaborate parades and huge royal weddings—and no one in the world puts on a better show.

As recently as 1990, Parliament had voted against taxing the Queen. But 1992 polls showed that some 80% of Britons thought the Queen should pay something. Finally, no doubt with an eye on the sagging public image of the monarchy, she yielded, announcing in November that she would begin paying taxes on her private income in 1993.

Even so, 1993 can hardly prove a more taxing year for the royals than 1992. Yet the Windsors' prospects may improve if they can weather the next several years. Charles and Diana are due for a rough passage; but as their new lives take shape, the direction of the Crown may also become clear. In the meantime, Queen Elizabeth, 66, must somehow hang on, as she has for 40 years; her family has not allowed her an easeful old age. Prince William of Wales, scion of Charles and Diana, may prove to be the savior of the monarchy. But he is only 10. ∎

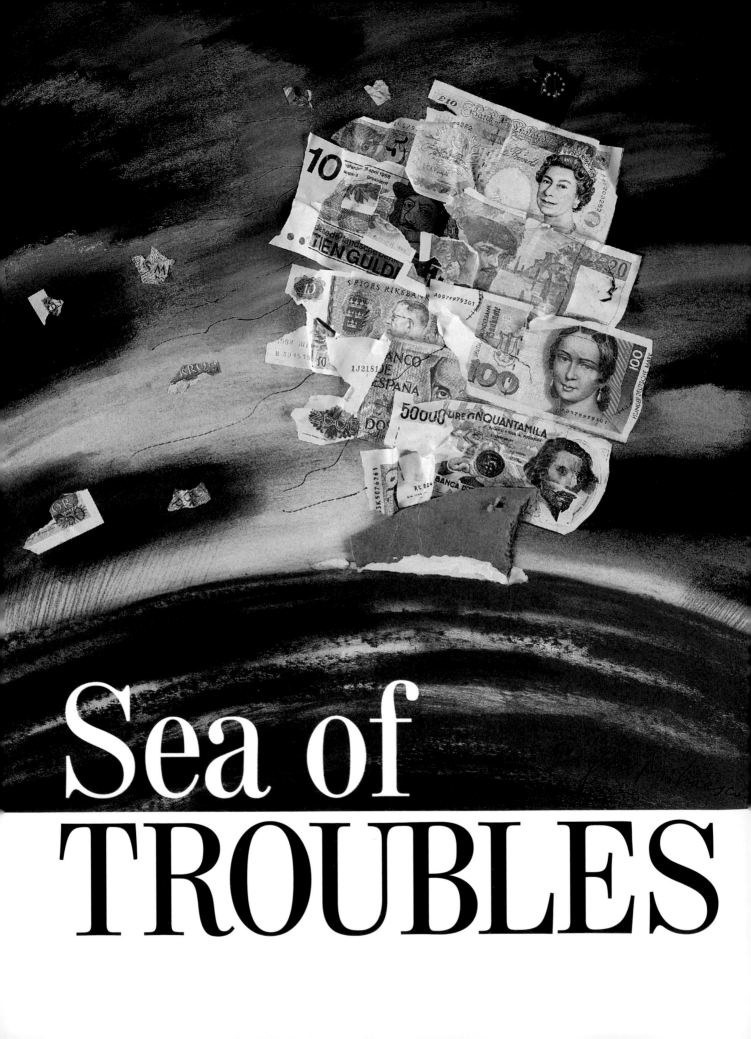

Sea of
TROUBLES

On the eve of 1993, a currency crisis and spreading fear of federalism drove the European Community off course

AS THE EUROPEAN COMMUNITY PREPARED IN THE final months of 1992 to launch its much hyped but still vitally important barrier-free internal market, the whole enterprise was looking very shaky. The EC's political leaders were perched precariously at home, its leading economies were in the doldrums, and social tensions were rising toward red alert. Member governments were divided over strategies, and the once proud European Monetary System was in danger of being battered into oblivion by the markets.

The confidence and self-belief that only a year before had appeared to guarantee economic growth and political direction were suddenly as hard to find as a smiling French farmer. The leaders of the Community met in Edinburgh in December; the summit was valuable group therapy, easing neurosis and doubt by improving prospects for the controversial Maastricht treaty, which provides for eventual political union of the European Community, a common foreign and security policy and a single currency by 1999. But whether the treaty's objective of monetary union by 1999 is attainable will continue to be debated, not least because of fears that the semi-fixed exchange-rate system cannot be salvaged in time to underpin the new Single Market. Nor did Edinburgh do much to bury doubts that governments can produce growth strategies that will put the 16 million unemployed to work, much less offer anything but a closing door to the disturbing inflow of economic and political refugees.

MAASTRICHT IN PERIL

The go-go years of the late '80s generated a bracing political ozone that gave European nations the guts to free up markets and stamp out inflation, to sweep aside hitherto insoluble budgetary problems and set ambitious goals. Although Britain under Margaret Thatcher was plainly operating with a different compass, the majority determinedly fixed their bearings on the destination of deeper political and economic integration.

At first 1992, the target year for completing the construction of a barrier-free internal market, was the banner that appeared to mark the finish of this ambitious journey. Then in Maastricht in 1991, the wording on the banner was changed to read ECONOMIC, MONETARY AND POLITICAL UNION BY 1999. Since torn by some very rough winds, the banner is still flying—but only just. There is doubt that the Twelve can muster the political energy and strength of purpose to carry it further.

They have been weakened by combined punches: the widespread public fear of the political union encoded in Maastricht and the economic weaknesses exposed in the currency crisis of mid-September. The political concern was rammed home when Denmark narrowly voted in June against the Maastricht treaty, unleashing forces that revealed the shallowness of public support for the plan in France, Britain and Germany. Though the treaty squeaked through a September vote in France, the sliver-thin majority of 51% revealed that almost half the electorate challenged the wisdom of forefeiting many of its cherished national prerogatives.

Concern over union was growing again in Britain, where former Prime Minister Margaret Thatcher had always been skeptical. Her successor, John Major, captured the new mood in a speech to a special session of Parliament. "There are fears throughout Europe," he said, "that the Community is too centralized, that it is too undemocratic, that the leaders of the Community are trying to develop it too fast." Sir Charles Powell, formerly the chief foreign affairs aide of both Major and Thatcher, claimed in December that Maastricht "represents yesterday's thinking, yesterday's future," and will be "looked back upon as the high-water mark of federalism in Europe before the tide began to ebb."

CURRENCY CRISIS

The second blow was the revelation in September that an important pillar of the E.C.'s economy, semifixed exchange rates, had become an obstacle rather than a cornerstone of stability and prosperity. By binding Europe's currencies so tightly to the powerful deutsche mark, the EMS forced upon Germany's partners monetary policies that may have been appropriate for curbing German inflation but that were savagely deflationary for everybody else.

When, on Monday, Sept. 14, Germany's central bank allowed a key interest rate to slip for the first time in five years, from 9.75% to 9.5%, it set off foreign-exchange traders already nervous about Maastricht's future. The markets surmised that the German central bank really wanted a fundamental realignment in the exchange-rate mechanism. Within 24 hours, traders drove the British pound below the minimum level agreed on by governments, and Major was forced to take his currency out of the rate-settling mechanism.

The Italian lira found itself under attack too, even though Rome had tried to anticipate traders with a 7% devaluation at the beginning of the week. Italy followed Britain out of the European Monetary System. The Spanish peseta was devalued by 5%, and the French, Danish and Irish currencies all found themselves struggling at the bottom of their permitted exchange rates. It was the worst week ever for the European monetary system, and a deeply embarrassing one for the British and Italian governments.

In Edinburgh, diplomats regrouped, crafting a new form of Maastricht for Danes to approve in May 1993. They also hammered out a compromise spending plan to aid the poorer Mediterranean partners. Germany and France stated their determination to set in motion the machinery for monetary union by June 1, 1993, whether all 12 members go along, or just 10, or even five.

Despite the multiple shocks, despite the ill effects of a spectacularly stubborn slump, in no sense is the European Community on the eve of destruction; it remains a formidable engine of prosperity. Five hundred years after Columbus, the challenges Europe is facing on its own are already making it a historic new frontier. ∎

BUSINESS

The cry of the year was "The economy, stupid!"
America's long slump played havoc with
pocketbooks and politics, but the big question remained:
When will the real recovery begin?

By JOHN GREENWALD

HOW BAD WAS THE U.S. ECONOMY IN 1992? SO BAD that sluggish growth and relentless layoffs cost President George Bush his job. So bad that a desperate General Motors, the world's largest company, forced its chairman to resign and named a cadre of young managers to stanch the firm's multibillion dollar losses. So bad that cash-strapped U.S. airlines scrambled to form alliances with foreign carriers to raise sorely needed funds. So bad that military contractors, faced with slackening defense orders, continued to shut plants and hunt for ways to diversify into civilian lines of business. And to make matters worse, a brutal combination of hurricanes, riots, floods and storms pounded insurers and local economies from Florida to Hawaii.

Not since the Great Depression had economic insecurity loomed so large in a presidential election year. And not since Franklin Roosevelt had a new President prepared to take office with so clear a mandate for economic change. THE ECONOMY, STUPID!—the celebrated slogan posted at Bill Clinton's campaign headquarters in Little Rock—became the watchword of the Arkansas Governor's march to victory.

Yet no sooner had the election ended than the economy showed signs of breaking out of its slump. The clearest signals were a surprisingly strong 3.4% surge in the Gross Domestic Product for the third quarter and a drop in the November unemployment rate to 7.2% from 7.4% the previous month. While some other indicators gave off mixed signals, widely watched gauges of consumer confidence rose sharply as the crucial Christmas shopping season arrived. With inflation hovering in the low 3% range and the Federal Reserve pursuing an easy money policy to hold down interest rates, some economists predicted a sustained rebound in 1993. But the recovery had shown signs of life several times before in recent years, only to falter each time beneath the weight of corporate layoffs and the failure of the economy to create new jobs.

Low interest rates helped account for much of whatever bounce business enjoyed in 1992. Securities firms thrived for the second straight year, with corporations issuing record amounts of new stocks and bonds to cash in on the low rates and vigorous trading. Mortgage interest dipped to levels not seen since the 1960s, giving the housing market a lift for much of the year. And while many banks remained burdened with sour real estate loans, the industry as a whole had healthy profits; lenders paid as little as 3% for customer deposits and invested the money in riskless government securities that earned about 6%.

The pace of job cuts accelerated at General Motors and other corporate giants as the year came to an end. After losing more than $7 million since 1990, GM dumped Robert Stempel as chairman and chief executive officer for, among other things, failing to move swiftly enough to phase out 74,000 North American jobs and shutter 21 plants. Then, with Christmas fast approaching, GM announced eight new plant closings and the elimination of nearly 14,000 jobs. Struggling IBM further darkened the holiday mood by announcing plans to trim 25,000 more workers from its payroll in 1993.

New turbulence shook the airline industry as the 14-year dogfight to control America's deregulated skies suddenly turned global. The big battle raged over British Airways' bid to acquire a 44% share of struggling U.S. Air and plug its flights into the British carrier's globe-spanning route map. British Airways dropped the plan after U.S. Transportation Secretary Andrew Card vowed to reject it. Card took that hard-line stance in retaliation for Britain's refusal to expand the access of U.S. carriers to Heathrow Airport, London's main international gateway.

With the cold war receding deeper into memory, U.S. defense contractors faced the prospect of closing down assembly lines for planes, tanks and ships and phasing out by 1997 fully one-third of their approximately 3 million remaining jobs. Some companies bailed out of defense work

altogether. In one 1992 megadeal, Martin Marietta agreed to pay $3 billion for General Electric's aerospace division, which makes satellites and radar and sonar systems.

Insurers weathered record payouts, the result of the fury directed at America's cities and countryside by both nature and man. The cleanup bill for Hurricane Andrew alone surpassed $15 billion in claims. While major firms had the financial muscle to withstand the storms, some small local companies were swept away.

The weak economy and heavy debts led TWA, Macy's and other household names to take refuge from creditors in the generous provisions of Chapter 11 of the U.S. Bankruptcy Code, which allows companies to stay in business while working out detailed repayment plans. That sparked a national debate in which critics charged that wily managers were using the code to stiff creditors and save their own jobs.

CRITICS AND SHAREHOLDERS VENTED THEIR WRATH against executives who paid themselves fat salaries and bonuses even as their companies stumbled. The frequently glaring gap between pay and performance stirred rebellions at annual meetings, where shareholders brought motions to cap executive compensation or tie it to a company's bottom line. In one battle, shareholders of Baltimore Gas & Electric asked the utility to limit the compensation of top officers to no more than 20 times the pay of the average company employee. The measure failed to carry, but such uprisings at least served notice on bosses and boards to be more accountable when setting salaries.

While American attitudes toward Japan remained stormy, U.S. companies scored some impressive gains against Japanese rivals. The year began with an ill omen when a suddenly sick George Bush collapsed in the lap of the Japanese Prime Minister and returned home from a trade trip without his promised "jobs, jobs, jobs." Behind the scenes, however, some U.S. high-tech companies were

succeeding nicely in head-to-head competition with Japan. Paced by new lines of powerful high-speed microchips, such firms as Intel and Motorola boosted America's share of the worldwide chip market from 37% in 1988 to 44%, surpassing Japan and giving the U.S. the global lead. U.S. companies also used technical breakthroughs to dominate sales of laptops and other portable computers, which Japan had pioneered.

The year brought landmark trade agreements that raised not only economic hopes but also political hackles in the U.S. and abroad. In one such deal, the Bush Administration completed talks with Canada and Mexico on the North American Free Trade Agreement, which would create the world's largest free-trade zone. But the pact, which requires congressional approval, stirred fears that U.S. firms would shift jobs to Mexico to take advantage of its low wages and lax environmental rules.

Only an eleventh-hour settlement headed off a major trade war between the U.S. and Europe. The flashpoint came when Washington threatened to slap punitive duties on French white wine to retaliate against subsidies that lowered the price of French soybeans and thus hurt U.S. exports. To prevent a protectionist free-for-all, the European Community agreed to reduce such subsidies despite the wrath of French farmers. The deal broke a six-year impasse that had stalled worldwide talks on lowering trade barriers for a wide range of goods.

All the 1992 upheavals left President-in-waiting Bill Clinton with something of an economic dilemma. On one hand, he needed to deliver on promises to get the economy rolling again. On the other, if the recovery really was gaining momentum on its own, any government effort to stimulate growth might simply rekindle inflation. But as dilemmas go, that one did not seem so bad. For many Americans, heartened by the change in the political order, prospects for the U.S. economy looked brighter at the end of 1992 than they had in years. ∎

THE LON

Forget the quick fix: rebuilding America's economy will take planning, patience and discipline

☒ DEFENSE BUILD-DOWN

In the short run, the end of the cold war removes a major support for industry. Until savings are redirected, it's a net loss to the economy.

1989: Military spending was rising at 3% annually.
1993: Expenditures will begin falling 5% a year.

☒ FALLING REAL WAGES

As global competition has increased and productivity has stalled, Americans have suffered a steady decline in their average income for nearly two decades.

1972: Hourly wage of private, nonfarm workers was $3.67.
1992: Adjusted for inflation, wages are down 13%.

☒ BUDGET DEFICIT

With a national debt of $4 trillion and huge interest payments to keep up, the U.S. has almost no room to stimulate the economy with a burst of spending.

1982: The federal deficit hit a record $128 billion.
1992: The total may reach a record $400 billion.

☒ AGING BOOMERS

The baby boomers have already bought their first homes and have started saving for retirement. The result: less demand for big-ticket items.

1986: Housing starts reached 1.8 million.
1992: This year's estimate is 1.2 million.

I F AMERICA'S ECONOMIC LANDSCAPE SEEMS SUDDENLY alien and hostile to many citizens, there is good reason: they have never seen anything like it. Nothing in memory has prepared consumers for such turbulent, epochal change, the sort of upheaval that happens once in 50 years. Even the economists do not have a name for the present condition, though one has called it "suspended animation" and "never-never land."

The outward sign of the change is an economy that stubbornly refused to recover from the 1990-91 recession. In a normal rebound, Americans would be witnessing a flurry of hiring, new investment and lending, and buoyant growth. But the U.S. economy remained almost comatose more than a full year and a half after the recession officially ended. Unemployment was still high, real wages declining. Some were heartened when the third-quarter growth rate rose to a surprisingly robust 3.9%, but both economists and President-elect Bill Clinton cautioned against premature optimism. The slump already ranks as the longest period of sustained weakness since the Great Depression.

That was the last time the economy staggered under so many "structural" burdens, as opposed to the familiar "cyclical" problems that create temporary recessions once or twice a decade. The structural faults, many of them lega-

cies of the 1980s, represent once-in-a-lifetime dislocations that will take years to work out. Among them: the job drought, the debt hangover, the defense-industry contraction, the savings and loan collapse, the real estate depression, the health-care cost explosion and the runaway federal deficit. The economy is likely to stand as Topic A for much of the 1990s. Quick fixes will not work, a point that many Americans seem to be accepting. In fact, that is the light at the end of the tunnel.

Until earlier in 1992, the U.S. seemed to be headed for a more normal rebound, thanks to the brisk tempo of export sales. But then the economy began to suffer from yet another new development: America's growing linkages to the slumping global economy. The world's economy did not grow at all in 1991, and is expected to expand only 1.1% in 1992. The currency crisis that swept Europe in September was a profound symptom of the West's stagnation. Germany's relatively high interest rates, run up by the cost of rapid unification, have prevented its major trading partners—including to some extent the U.S.—from lowering their own rates enough to boost their economies. Germany's high rates also put a damper on the primary U.S. export markets.

America's structural burdens have hit home most profoundly in terms of jobs. Official statistics fail to reveal the

G HAUL

CORPORATE CUTBACKS

To become more competitive and profitable, American companies have slashed jobs by the millions, most recently taking a heavy toll of white-collar positions.

1988: The U.S. work force increased by more than 200,000 a month.
1992: Monthly increases are running about 50,000.

REAL ESTATE CRASH

After a run-up in prices in the 1980s, the bubble burst, sending builders and bankers into a tailspin and leaving many homeowners with negative net worth.

1986: The office vacancy rate in midtown New York City was 9.7%.
1992: The rate is 17.7%, sending rents down.

DEBT HANGOVER

The borrowing binge of the 1980s leaves consumers with little leverage (or taste) for spending. It won't come back until the loans are substantially paid down.

1989: Non-government debt in the U.S. totaled $1.8 trillion.
1992: That figure stands at over $6 trillion.

BANKING BUST

After taking on too much risk under too little regulation, banks stumbled and S&Ls collapsed, leaving a costly cleanup and a shortage of solid lenders.

1989: Cost of the S&L bailout was estimated at $300 billion.
1992: The projected total has reached $500 billion.

GLOBAL SLUMP

The recession among industrial nations and uncertain prospects in Europe have thwarted U.S. exports, which until recently were thriving.

1989: The world's economy expanded 4.3%.
1992: A meager 1.1% growth is expected.

extent of the pain. Unemployment stood at 7.6% as 1992 drew to an end, far lower than the 1982 high of 10.8%, but more people are experiencing distress. A comprehensive tally would include workers who are employed well below their skill level, those who cannot find more than a part-time job, people earning poverty-level wages, workers who have been jobless for more than four weeks at a time and all those who have grown discouraged and quit looking. In 1991 those distressed workers totaled 36 million, or 40% of the American labor force, according to the Washington-based Economic Policy Institute.

PAY HAS COME UNDER ASSAULT AS WELL. THE much touted job gains of the 1980s were for the most part low-wage positions paying $250 a week or less. More than 25% of the U.S. work force now toils in this class of job, up from less than 19% in 1979. Laid-off workers who return to the market often must take huge pay cuts. After adjustment for inflation, the real income of U.S. workers has declined about 13% over the past two decades. White-collar employees have been particularly hard hit, in terms of both layoffs and slippage in their real wages.

What workers are experiencing is a momentous, tech-

nology-driven change akin to the industrial revolution in the 19th century. The displaced workers must now reintegrate themselves into an economy that increasingly rewards only highly skilled labor. The question then becomes, How do they make that leap? The answer is not being provided by either politicians or the economy, which leaves the unemployed to stare at the enormous gap between a job as a grocery clerk and some high-skill, high-wage position they cannot dream of getting.

The bogey behind much of the adverse change in the job market is global competition, the single most powerful economic fact of life in the 1990s. In the relatively sheltered era of the 1960s, a mere 7% of the U.S. economy was exposed to international competition. In the 1980s that number zoomed past 70%, and it will keep climbing. The first and most visible victim of the competition was the automobile industry, which suffered massive layoffs in the late 1970s and '80s. The latest point of impact is America's service sector, which includes everything from banks to airlines, publishers to insurance firms.

Part of the American competitive response has been technological, driven by the computer chip, which some analysts say has caused more industrial dislocation than any other advance in the history of capitalism. In the early

93

At a new Hilton in Chicago, more than 2,500 people applied for work

GLOOM: A fuller accounting of the unemployed includes workers who cannot find more than a part-time job and discouraged workers who have quit looking. Last year the total of people in such distress was 40% of the U.S. labor force.

A homeless family makes the best of it at a National Forest camp in Oregon

1980s it arrived in manufacturing in the form of robots and computerized machine tools; in the 1990s it is replacing back-room white-collar clerical workers in service industries. Like the shift from agriculture to heavy industry in the 19th century, the advent of a new technology ought to be creating a whole new class of jobs to replace the ones lost. That's not happening: the sudden transition has left too many workers in an economic twilight zone.

The good news is that some of America's industries have made huge progress toward becoming competitive. While General Motors is still struggling to become more efficient, Ford and Chrysler now rank as the world's lowest-cost producers of cars and trucks. Product-quality levels have kept pace, as has fuel economy. In service businesses, the waves of corporate cutbacks have sliced so deep that the worst may be over. Industries like retailing will have largely taken their lumps by the end of 1993, paving the way for a modest recovery.

One major obstacle to efficiency remains: a runaway U.S. health-care system, whose costs are rising more than 9% a year and today stand at $2,500 per capita, more than twice the level of most of the world's industrialized economies. Such costs add 15% to the price of every new motor vehicle, for example, threatening to eliminate the entire cost advantages achieved by Ford and Chrysler.

One legacy of the 1980s, the debt hangover, simply needs time to work itself out. The initial stages were painful, wiping out both borrowers and lenders. Bank regulators clamped down on lenders, while borrowers either swore off the credit habit or were deemed bad risks. The result was a credit crunch that has severely hurt businesses, especially small ones. In big business the load of $2 trillion in corporate debt is preventing the sort of capital investment the economy needs in the 1990s. But manufacturers are making some headway, having slashed business debt 12% in the past year alone. Consumers are finally beginning to swear off the habit as well, after running up the average credit-card balance to more than $1,600, in contrast to less than $500 in 1982. The debt-cutting trend is bad for retail sales in the short run but bodes well for the mid-1990s. Most committed to thrift are baby boomers, who want to save money for their children's education and for retirement.

The real estate bust has added to the insecurity, since many people who urgently bought homes during the run-up in the 1980s now find their equity shriveled. Low inflation has almost completely removed the pressure to dash out and buy a house before the price goes up.

The consumer-debt hangover will be far easier to solve than the government's. With the national debt estimated at $4 trillion and the 1992 budget deficit expected to reach nearly $334 billion, the government is limited in how much it can stimulate the downtrodden economy with the usual recession cure of a quick jolt of spending. While the national debt will hamper the economy over the long run, its net effects on growth over the short run are insignificant compared with such problems as unemployment, declining wages and worker dislocation.

The other primary slump-fighting tool, monetary easing, has just about been played out. The Federal Reserve Board has cut short-term interest rates 24 times since 1990, bringing them down from 9% to 3%, the easiest credit since the 1960s. But critics have complained that the Fed wasted its fuel by easing so gradually and slowly that the economy never got the swift kick it needed. Now rates are so low that the Fed has little room left to maneuver, and additional interest reductions have been hampered by the need to keep the U.S. dollar from dropping against the overmuscled deutsche mark. The crowning touch to America's economic woes is the end of the cold war, a wondrous development for the country's future but a bombshell in the short run. Besides letting huge clouds of steam out of the overall economy, the military build-down will take a huge personal toll on displaced workers.

That the American economy can withstand all this and not collapse is a testament to its resilience. Many economists are beginning to think the most valuable resource America can have in the first half of the decade is the willingness to tough it out. But the prospects for a rise in consumer confidence are linked directly to the rate at which the economy can manufacture jobs at decent wages. Those will be hard to find in the coming years, which will be spent curing these large and unwelcome burdens that America is suddenly forced to bear. Slow growth is the curse of the 1990s. But if it is managed correctly, there is no reason to believe American prospects in the long run are dim. They are not. What is required is a collective political will that has been conspicuously absent from the U.S. economic landscape for too long. ■

Banks are making solid profits again, thanks in part to credit-card business

GLIMMER: Slow growth is the curse of the 1990s. But if it is managed correctly, there is no reason to believe that American prospects in the long run are dim. What is required is a collective will that has been conspicuously absent.

In Vermont, jobless workers broaden their skills by learning how to weld

In For Repairs at

GENERA

The world's largest corporation takes on the world's largest problems. GM needs a fix-up, and the human cost will be brutal

THE END CAME WITH ALL THE BIT-terness of a military surrender. For weeks General Motors chairman Robert Stempel had tried to ignore the signals of discontent radiating from a hostile band of outside directors. When Stempel was hospitalized with an attack of high blood pressure, board members did not bother to phone him get-well wishes. When rumors flew that Stempel was about to be ousted, the board issued a statement that conspicuously lacked a denial. Finally, Stempel, 59, bowed to a point-blank demand from a third-generation GM board member who told him it was time to leave the post he had taken scarcely two years ago. Stempel finally stepped down on Oct. 26 from the helm of the world's largest company.

The resignation stunned employees who had heralded Stempel not long ago as an automotive redeemer who would bring out the best in GM. The ouster shook even Stempel's union adversaries, who feared what life would be like after the boardroom coup, which was led by John Smale, 65, the hard-charging retired chairman of Procter & Gamble. Smale emerged as the real power inside the embattled company. Employees braced for a take-no-prisoners conquest. Together with president Jack Smith, 54,

the former head of GM's profitable overseas operations, Smale and the board seemed poised to purge Stempel's top lieutenants and embark on a sweeping new round of layoffs to restructure the former flagship of American industry. The bloodletting promised to be deep and wide and painful. Impatient with Stempel's slowness in carrying out plans to close 21 of GM's 120 North American plants and cut 74,000 of its 370,000 employees over three years, directors planned to eliminate a total of 120,000 jobs during the decade. The first wave of cost cuts was announced on Dec. 3: seven parts plants and two assembly plants would be closed and 17,950 workers laid off. A major goal: to slash GM's labor costs of nearly $2,360 a car, which is almost $800 more than Ford's and $500 more than Chrysler's. "It's going to be brutal," warned a GM director. "We don't even have the luxury of thinking about a product strategy. We aren't going to be thinking great thoughts. GM has a three-year mission to restore its financial soundness."

That won't be easy for a company whose U.S. market share has plunged from a peak of 52% in the early 1960s to just 35% today. GM reported a $753 million loss for the third quarter and careened through a third straight year of deficits. Its North American division, the heart of its business, lost an astonishing $7.1 billion in 1991— or $1,700 for every car, truck and van it sold in the U.S., Canada and Mexico. The red ink was stanched somewhat by a $2.1 billion profit from abroad that helped cut the overall yearly loss to $4.5 billion—at the time,

GM's challenge: create more classics,

CLASSIC
1957 Chevrolet Bel Air: Snazz to burn
GM's gas-hogging V-8s and exuberant tail-finned sedans reflected the confidence of a nation newly-arrived at superpower status

the most dismal showing ever by an American company.

In more than just symbolic terms, GM's crisis ranks as the most dramatic culture shock in the transition of American industry from the fat years of the postwar era to the lean years of today. During the 1950s, GM's gas-hogging V-8s and exuberant tail-finned sedans reflected the confidence of a nation newly arrived at superpower status, with seemingly unlimited resources and skyrocketing productivity. Former chairman Charles ("Engine Charlie") Wilson immortalized GM's role when he told a congressional committee in 1953 that "what was good for the country was good for General Motors, and vice versa."

While Big Business has become far more circumspect since then, it has also become more global. The fate of GM (1991 revenues: $123 billion) has an impact on millions of people around the world. With more than 715,000 employees in 35 countries, GM meets $22.5 billion in payrolls from Prague to Kuala Lumpur and buys supplies from 28,000 companies. GM's U.S. auto business accounts for roughly 1.5% of the American economy, down from about 5% in the 1950s.

Its sheer size, however, is one of GM's greatest burdens. Because of arrogance and inertia, GM fell out of touch with its customers. Except for products of GM's Saturn and Pontiac divisions, young drivers increasingly spurn the company's cars for Japanese makes or other U.S. models. The median age for buyers of GM's bread-and-butter midsize lines is 45 for Chevrolet, 55 for Oldsmobile and 60 for Buick. By contrast, the age of U.S. buyers of Japanese cars ranges from 35 to 40. GM has foundered while the more nimble Ford and Chrysler cut costs and brought out popular models like the Ford Taurus and Chrysler's minivans. Moreover, GM has consistently ignored showroom signals about its cars. When buyers

CLUNKER
1966 Corvair Monza: Unsafe at any speed?
Designed to compete with small imports like VW's Beetle, the ill-fated Corvair was denounced by Ralph Nader in his muckraking book

yearned for minivans, GM simply slapped new plastic panels on a seven-year-old chassis and rolled out the Chevy Lumina All-Purpose Vehicle.

How did GM, whose charismatic leader Alfred Sloan pioneered modern corporate management, get into this fix? In large part, the company has been a victim of its past success and an insular culture that has refused to change. For 70 years, GM hewed to Sloan's vision of top-down control and decentralized execution, helping it build cars at lower cost than its rivals, while charging more for the quality and popularity of its models. But by the early 1960s GM was having trouble building small cars to compete with imports like the Volkswagen Beetle. Chevrolet's ill-fated Corvair, which Ralph Nader judged to be "unsafe at any speed," made few inroads against imports. Yet GM was lulled into complacency by the success of its Pontiac GTO and other trend-setting muscle cars. When buyers flocked to small cars during oil crises in the 1970s, GM's failure to produce a winning model

CLASSIC
1967 Pontiac GTO: Wide-body wonder
The success of its trend-setting '60s muscle cars lulled GM into a complacency ultimately shattered by the oil crises of the '70s

was ominous. The company's rush to downsize at the end of the decade led to the notoriously shabby quality of its X-car line.

GM moved boldly under Roger Smith in the 1980s, but often in the wrong direction. Smith's stated aim was to gear up the company for the 21st century, so he purchased Hughes Aircraft and Ross Perot's Electronic Data Systems. But despite the spending spree, GM's market share fell from 46% to 35% during the decade as consumers turned away from its unattractive products. Nor did GM have much success in transferring Hughes' electronic wizardry to auto assembly lines, or in using EDS to standardize its computer systems. Perhaps GM's crowning folly during the '80s was the reorganization of its North American operations into two clumsy megagroups, creating a new

fewer clunkers–and cut costs per car

level of bureaucracy sandwiched between the automaking divisions and GM's corporate headquarters. The results ranged from mass confusion to a proliferation of look-alike models.

Smith's failures put Stempel in an awkward position when the latter took over GM at the start of the '90s. As Smith's hand-picked heir apparent, Stempel had loyally seconded the chairman's plans. "Stempel always voted with Roger on everything," says a GM insider, "even though he used to tell me he knew things were wrong and disagreed." So even as Stempel went along with GM's wild ride through the Smith era, he learned the hazards of sweeping change.

That helped make Stempel wary of new directions when he became chairman, just as GM directors began calling for a major overhaul to fix the company. Stempel's defenders portray him as a scapegoat for errors that GM's now militant directors did nothing to stop. "He became captain after the *Titanic* had already hit the iceberg," says Harley Shaiken, a professor of work and technology at the University of California at San Diego. A 6-ft.-4-in. former college football tackle with a booming voice but a gentle nature, Stempel took a conciliatory approach toward downsizing the work force. He signed a U.A.W. contract that lets workers draw 95% of their wages for three years after being laid off as a result of technological change.

Stempel also had the misfortune of becoming chairman just as the U.S. was sliding into recession. That hindered sales of GM's 1991 fall line, one of its best in years. The redesigned models included the full-bodied Buick Park Avenue and the luxurious Cadillac Seville. With GM strapped for cash, its offerings for 1993 are limited mainly to a redesigned Cadillac Brougham and sporty Camaros and Firebirds.

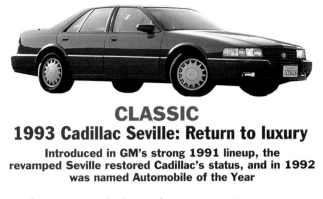

CLASSIC
1993 Cadillac Seville: Return to luxury

Introduced in GM's strong 1991 lineup, the revamped Seville restored Cadillac's status, and in 1992 was named Automobile of the Year

In the layoffs to come, brutality will have to be tempered. GM must now restructure its business without further alienating workers whose cooperation will be crucial to the company's success. While the U.A.W.'s relations with GM have generally been much stormier than with either Ford or Chrysler, the union seems willing to give the new management a chance. GM must also mollify suppliers outraged by the high-handed tactics of J. Ignacio López de Arriortua, a former European colleague of Jack Smith's who manages GM purchasing, and is reportedly under orders to cut the company's $500 million weekly supply bill at least 20%. To do that, López has been jeopardizing GM's long-term relations with its partners by demanding that they constantly re-

CLUNKER
1993 Chevrolet Caprice: Unsexy styling

While popular with police and taxi fleets, the Caprice, redesigned in 1991, was marked by a bulbous look and spotty performance that turned off many car buyers

submit their bids. At the same time, GM has been dragging its heels when paying bills. "GM's reputation as a gentleman in the industry is disappearing very quickly," says a leading supplier. "It's sad to see what's happening."

The laboratory for organizational change at GM is supposed to be its built-from-scratch Saturn division, but so far the results have been mixed. Saturn's costly gestation of seven years drained $5 billion from other car projects and stirred anger and envy within GM ranks.

The division has yet to make money for the company, in part because GM reportedly sells the car at a loss to build up its market share. But Saturn has in abundance what many of GM's other products so desperately need: prestige. The upstart division's high-quality products have proved so popular that customers have to put their names on waiting lists. If Saturn can translate its popularity into profit, the formula could help save the rest of the giant company. For, besides cutting costs, GM must now focus its attention on something the company has too often seemed to forget: how to build cars, trucks and vans that more people are happy to pay money to buy. ∎

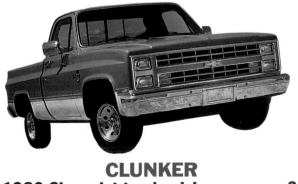

CLUNKER
1986 Chevrolet truck: pickup cover-up?

Company documents suggest GM had known since 1970 that fuel tanks were located unsafely, but neither rectified the problem nor recalled the trucks

FAT CATS AND FAIR TRADE

The U.S. and Japan square off on pay, perks and profits

T HE TRIP WAS BILLED AS A GLOBAL SHOWDOWN, AN expedition designed to "level the playing field," as American businessmen are wont to say. Yet even before George Bush's new 747 touched down in Tokyo on Jan. 7—bearing not only the President, but 18 U.S. corporate chiefs— the Japanese had deftly weakened the American campaign to win trade concessions by raising a touchy issue: large disparities in the pay of American CEOs and their Japanese counterparts.

Under particular scrutiny, naturally, were the salaries and perks of the three U.S. auto-company chiefs—Chrysler's Lee Iacocca, Ford's Harold Poling and GM's Robert Stempel—who accompanied the President. The three were paid a total of $7.3 million-plus in 1990, including more than $4 million in stock incentives.

By contrast, the heads of Japan's Big Three—Shoichiro Toyoda of Toyota, Nobuhiko Kawamoto of Honda and Yutaka Kume of Nissan—earned a total of $1.8 million, counting bonuses. Moreover, while the Japanese execs were presiding over thriving enterprises, the U.S. auto industry was just coming off one of its worst years ever. In 1991 sales of American-made cars plunged 12.6%, to 8.7 million; more than 40,000 autoworkers lost their jobs, and the Big Three rolled up losses of $7.5 billion.

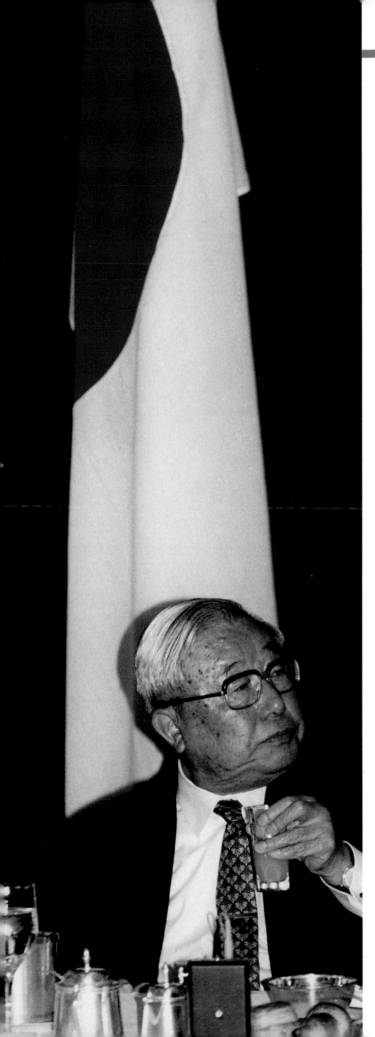

The public relations debacle for Detroit was only one of the problems on President Bush's star-crossed trade journey to Japan. First planned as a routine diplomatic swing through the Pacific, the trip was hastily converted by White House officials into a full-blown trade mission after growing public dissatisfaction with Bush's handling of the recession triggered a steep drop in his approval ratings. In an effort to counter criticism that he cared more about foreign policy than the woes of unemployed Americans, Bush proclaimed the trip was about generating "jobs, jobs, jobs."

He should have stayed home. Once he got to Japan, the President was forced to endure politely phrased, but nonetheless pointed, reminders from Prime Minister Kiichi Miyazawa about America's shortcomings, from homelessness and the AIDS epidemic to a decline in education. Miyazawa, fearful of adding to growing anti-Japanese sentiment in the U.S., did not want to send Bush home empty-handed. But the bargain struck in Tokyo would do little to cure the recession, create new jobs, or narrow the $41 billion U.S. trade deficit with Japan over the long term. Under pressure to open their markets, the Japanese agreed in the final hours of Bush's tour to find a way to buy more American cars, auto parts, computers, glass and paper. Some of these concessions were in the works long before Bush arrived; others sounded good, but were less than met the eye.

Fat cat got your tongue? The gulf dividing Chrysler's LEE IACOCCA and Toyota's chairman EIJI TOYODA is apparent at a Tokyo breakfast

For example, Bush claimed that Japanese automakers' pledge to double their purchase of U.S-made auto parts to $19 billion would create 200,000 U.S. jobs. But $15 billion worth of the components will be used in Japanese auto plants in the U.S, not exported to Japan. Even the $4 billion in parts that are shipped to Japan may eventually find their way back to America in Japanese-assembled cars headed for the U.S. market. Japanese manufacturers also agreed to assist American makers in marketing American cars in Japan. Bush paid a high political price in exchange for this thin gruel. By pressing Tokyo to commit itself to buy specific quantities of U.S. products, Bush abandoned his long-held free-trade principles for less competitive "managed trade," in which governments agree to pressure private industries to meet preset goals.

An outbreak of "Buy American" fever followed the trip, heightened by the perfectly timed publication of Michael Crichton's Japan-bashing potboiler *Rising Sun*. Yet public opinion surveys have consistently shown that voters blame American business practices more than Japanese unfairness for the trade imbalance. During a visit to Japan in November 1991, U.S. trade negotiator Carla Hills conceded that America's continued reliance on deficit spending hampers the nation's ability to save, invest and increase productivity. "We know the federal deficit is the problem," she said. "Too many people believe that the trade deficit is the result of closed markets. But closed markets are just the backdrop. Opening markets removes that backdrop and makes the problem less emotional." ∎

Seeking A New Future

Bill Clinton ran hard all the way to the White House, as America gambled on youth, luck, and change

FOR YEARS, AMERICANS HAVE BEEN IN A KIND OF vague mourning for something that they sensed they had lost somewhere—what was best in the country, a distinctive American endowment of youth and energy and ideals and luck: the sacred American stuff.

They had squandered it, Americans thought, had thrown it away in the messy interval between the assassination of John Kennedy and the wan custodial regime of George Bush. A wisp of song from years ago suggested the loss: "Where have you gone, Joe DiMaggio?"

Or perhaps the qualities were only hidden, sequestered in some internal exile, regenerating. Now Bill Clinton of Arkansas will ride into Washington brandishing them in a kind of boyish triumph. But are they the real thing? The authentic American treasures, recovered and restored to the seat of government? Do they still have transforming powers?

The full answers will come later. Everyone knows, for the moment, that Clinton's energy and luck are real. The world watched them. Clinton looked at very bad odds and gambled. He ran against an incumbent President whose re-election seemed, at the time, a mere technicality. And after an arduous, complex wooing, the American people responded to Clinton's gamble by taking an enormous risk of their own.

Americans deserted the predictable steward that they knew, the President who had managed Desert Storm steadfastly and precisely. At the end of the cold war, in a world growing more dangerous by the hour, they gave the future of the U.S., the world's one remaining superpower, into the hands of the young (46), relatively unknown Governor of a small Southern state, a man with no experience in foreign policy and virtually none in Washington either. They rejected the last President shaped by the moral universe of World War II in favor of a man formed by the sibling jostles and herdings of the baby boom and the vastly different historical pageant of the '60s.

Photographs for TIME by P.F. Bentley

Solitary Man

Jogging in Virginia. Always focused, Clinton earned the nation's respect with an earnest attention to issues and an impressive display of self-possession under fire.

The election of 1992 was a leap of faith in a sour and unpredictable year. American voters, angry and disgusted and often afraid of the future, began the campaign feeling something like contempt for the political process itself. Moreover, the White House of George Bush, impresario of Desert Storm, had deteriorated in some surreal, inexplicable way—had became feckless, confused, whining, rudderless. And discontent with politics was bottomed on a deep-

er anxiety. The famous sign in the Clinton headquarters in Little Rock, Arkansas, stated the essential problem briskly: THE ECONOMY, STUPID! The chronic recession had eaten deeply into the country's morale. Americans sensed that the problem was not a matter of the usual economic cycles but rather involved something deeper and scarier, a deterioration in what America was capable of doing. The nation's moral and economic pre-eminence in the years after World War II—the instinctive American assumption of superiority, the gaudy self-confidence—seemed to dim in the new world. The battleground ceased to be military and became economic, and Americans were not entirely prepared for this change in the game. Forty-six years after the Japanese surrendered on the deck of the battleship *Missouri*, the President of the U.S. went to Tokyo to plead for breaks for American cars and collapsed at the state dinner; that indelible vignette of American humiliation began the defeat of George Bush.

TIME's man—or woman—of the Year is traditionally defined as the person who has most influenced the course of the world's events—for good or ill—in the past year. Bill Clinton's successful campaign for the presidency of the U.S. makes him 1992's Man of the Year because of its threefold significance:

1) Improbably, abruptly, the election has made the Arkansan the most powerful man in the world—and therefore the most important—at a radically unstable moment in history, with the cold war ended, the world economy in trouble, and dangerous, heavily armed nationalisms rising around the globe.

2) Clinton's campaign, conducted with dignity, with earnest attention to issues and with an impressive display of self-possession under fire, served to rehabilitate and restore the legitimacy of American politics and thus, prospectively, of government itself. He has vindicated (at least for a little while) the honor of a system that has been sinking fast. A victory by George Bush would, among other things, have given a two-victory presidential validation (1988 and 1992) to hot-button, mad-dog politics—campaigning on irrelevant or inflammatory issues (Willie Horton, Murphy Brown's out-of-wedlock nonexistent child) or dirty tricks and innuendo (searching passport files). A win by Ross Perot would have left the two-party system upside down beside the road, wheels spinning.

3) Clinton's victory places him in position to preside over one of the periodic reinventions of the country—those moments when Americans dig out of their deepest problems by reimagining themselves. Such a reinvention is now indispensable. It is not inevitable. Clinton, carrying the distinctive values of his generation, represents a principle at home of broadened democracy and inclusion (of women in positions of equal power, of racial minorities, of homosexuals). The reinvention will have global meaning

New Tune
Practicing sax before appearing on Arsenio Hall. Clinton's election brought a much ballyhooed generation to the full harvest of power and responsibility.

as well. George Bush stated the winner's brief in Knoxville, Tennessee, last February: "We stand today at what I think most people would agree is a pivot point in history, at the end of one era and the beginning of another."

Bill Clinton's year was an untidy triumph of timing and temperament, both elements at work under the influence of a huge amount of luck. In the first place, George Bush's extravagant popularity in the wake of the war persuaded the supposed frontline Democratic possibilities—including New York Governor Mario Cuomo—to stay out of the race. That same aura of invulnerability clouded Bush's judgment and prevented him, until too late, from seeing the danger that he faced at home. It was Clinton's luck that Pat Buchanan behaved as if he were a mole and sapper in the employ of the Democratic National Committee.

But it was Clinton's best luck that the economy kept dragging along the bottom for the duration of the campaign. Brighter statistics were released after the election; if they had appeared before, Bush might now be preparing for a second term.

HISTORY MAY EVENtually decide that the key to Clinton's accomplishment (assuming he does well) lay in his temperament—in his buoyancy, optimism and readiness to act, in his enthusiasm for people and his curiosity about their lives. Clinton emerges from the sunnier, gregarious side of the American political character, home of F.D.R., Hubert Humphrey, Harry Truman—as opposed to the sterner, more punitive traditions distilled and preserved in their purest form in the mind of Richard Nixon.

He has a progressive agenda (family leave, worker retraining, for example) and believes it is the Federal Government's job to carry it out. But he knows—or has been warned within an inch of his life—that neither the lavish all-daddy government of Franklin Roosevelt's New Deal nor Lyndon Johnson's bountiful Great Society is a possible model in the '90s. The $290 billion deficit sits at the edge of American government like antimatter, like a black hole that devours revenues and social dreams. The better news is that the fiscal constraints Clinton faces will (as they say) empower his stronger side, his gift for improvisation—in giving poor people incentives to save money to start a business or buy a home, or in establishing a national-service program as a way for students to repay college loans.

Clinton's domestic ambitions, however, may be overtaken by the demands of international problems. In six months or a year, Americans may look back at their preoccupation with the domestic economy, with the question of whether it would be a good Christmas shopping season in American stores, and be amazed at their own insularity. "I might have to spend all my time on foreign policy," Clinton admitted three weeks ago. "And I don't want that to happen."

It will be quickly seen how the demands of an increasingly savage world may square with some of the gentler motifs that Clinton worked in the campaign—notably the themes of the recovery movement. Again and again in de-

President of the U.S. cannot invite a fanatic, murderous regime to come forward and speak of "the inner child that's hurting," the Inner Serb, the Inner Iraqi. The question is whether Clinton's impulse to act can, when necessary, override the more passive, tender protocols of therapy.

America periodically reinvents itself. That is the secret, the way that Americans dig out of their deepest problems. From the Civil War to the vast Ellis Island absorption to the New Deal, it is the way they save themselves from decline, stagnation and other dangers—including themselves. Every time, a melodrama of change (often raw and violent and, by definition, traumatic) has brought the country to a new stage of self-awareness and broadened democracy. It is miracu-

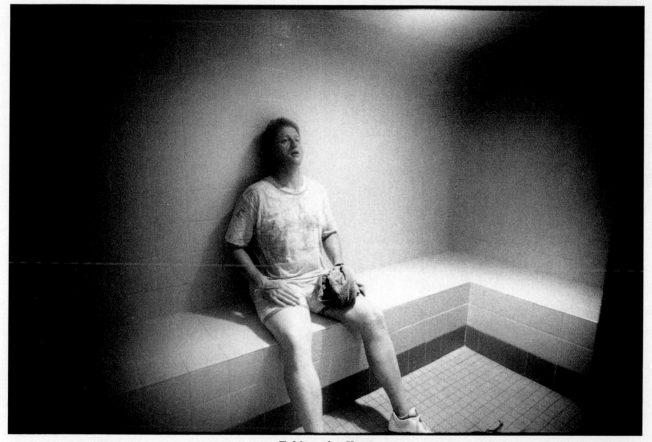

Taking the Heat

Clinton moisturizes his vocal cords before his acceptance speech. He gained 25 lbs. along the campaign trail from a junk-food diet.

bates and speeches, he talked about the need for Americans to find in themselves "the courage to change." The phrase comes from the Alcoholics Anonymous Serenity Prayer ("God, grant me the serenity to accept the things I cannot change, the courage to change the things I can, and the wisdom to know the difference"). Clinton, whose stepfather's violent alcoholism shaped his early life, and Al Gore, who often borrows recovery language and concepts, turned the Democratic Convention last summer into a national therapy session.

The subtext of the recovery-and-healing line is that America is a self-abusive binger that borrowed and spent recklessly in the 1980s while drinking too deeply of Reagan fantasies, and now needs "the courage to change" in a national atmosphere of recovery, repentance and confession.

There are obvious limits to the recovery approach. The

lous that the American transformations overall have been changes in the direction of generosity and inclusion.

The Clinton reinvention—if it succeeds—will bring his baby-boom generation (so insufferable in so many ways, and so unavoidable) to full harvest, to the power and responsibility that it clamored to overthrow in the streets a quarter of a century ago.

It is the boomers, born in the afterglow of American triumph in World War II and reared in the unprecedented and possibly unrepeatable postwar affluence, and now arrived at middle age, whose instruments most poignantly play the American note of mourning. For the moment, however, the note of loss will not be audible. In January 1993, Bill Clinton will come down Pennsylvania Avenue blaring, parading and bringing the American stuff—youth, energy, luck, ideals—like booty to his new house. ■

Power Couple

Buy one, get one free: How the Clintons turned their marriage into a political powerhouse

S HE MUST HAVE LOVED HIM SOMETHING AWFUL. That's what Hillary Rodham's friends concluded when she moved to Fayetteville, Arkansas, in 1974 to be with her law-school classmate Bill Clinton. There she was one moment, the hottest of young lawyers, recruited by a former Assistant Attorney General to serve as counsel on the House Judiciary Committee considering the impeachment of Richard Nixon, admired by aspiring officeholders for her work at the National Women's Education Fund. Yet the minute Nixon resigned, Hillary asked her roommate, Sara Ehrmann, if she would drive her, along with her 20 boxes of books and a 10-speed bike, to Arkansas in a '68 Buick.

Ehrmann agreed but spent the next 30 hours trying to talk her friend out of going. "You have the world at your feet," Ehrmann said. "Why are you throwing your life away for this guy?" When the two stopped at Monticello, a shrine to public service, Ehrmann tried one last time. "We haven't gone that far," she said. "You can still change your mind." But Hillary didn't change her mind.

Thus began a journey that would end in a remarkable and enduring partnership between two equals who somehow add up to more together than apart, a joint venture that would lead from the university to the Governor's mansion and finally, improbably, to the White House. The combination is so strong—their best friends acknowledge that they confide fully in no one but each other—and the personalities interlock so neatly that it may be safely said that neither one would be heading for 1600 Pennsylvania Avenue without the other. Sitting in the study of his official residence, the Arkansas Governor casually points to his wife in the easy chair next to him when asked who will be the Bobby Kennedy of his Administration. The morning af-

ter the election, the Governor says, he woke up, looked at his wife and just laughed.

Clinton first spotted Hillary in civil-liberties class at Yale Law School, where the intricacies of the Bill of Rights couldn't keep his mind—or eyes—from wandering over to the smart girl in the flannel shirt and thick glasses. She had already noticed him in the student lounge, bragging loudly about growing "the biggest watermelons in the world" back in his home state. Hillary had been president of the student government at Wellesley, the first student to speak at a commencement there and a minor celebrity for having been a multiple winner on the TV quiz show *College Bowl*.

Women were just beginning to come into their own, and Bill Clinton didn't see how she would ever allow herself to fall in love with a guy determined to spend the next 20 years working the pancake breakfasts in Pine Bluff.

But Clinton had something the analytic, disciplined Hillary admired: an effortless success, an ease about himself that drew people to him. Hillary recalls being in a dark-

Teamwork
The Clintons relax with a game of Ping-Pong at the Milwaukee convention center after a rally. Hillary was the real co-leader of his election effort.

ened classroom for a slide presentation of a brain-crunching legal problem. No one had a clue, and Bill had dozed off. But when it came time to propose a solution, he woke up, gave the answer and went back to sleep. The superconscientious Hillary—her mother Dorothy says she had organized a neighborhood Olympics, child care for migrant workers and a voter-registration project by the time she was 16—would never wing it like that.

But the mind has just so much control over matter. Says Clinton: "We just couldn't help ourselves." When his mother and brother came to watch the two in moot court, they cautioned Bill to go out with someone more like the girls back

home. Longtime friend Carolyn Staley says he set his mother straight, insisting he would never "marry a beauty queen."

When Hillary came to Fayetteville, she sublet a professor's house, taught law and ran the legal-aid clinic. Before making up her mind to stay, she went off to visit friends who had taken high-powered jobs in Washington, New York and Chicago "to see if I was missing something." She concluded she wasn't. They got married in 1975 in the new house that bride, groom and their families stayed up all night painting.

In some ways, the Clinton marriage is a carefully calibrated compensatory mechanism in which each fills in for the other's gaps, a right brain–left brain meshing of analysis and creativity, planning and spontaneity. He has the edge in coming up with ideas and selling them; she is better at separating the weak from the strong and making arguments airtight. She is the disciplined, duty-bound Methodist, carrying her favorite Scriptures around in her briefcase and holding herself and others to a high standard; he is a more emotional Baptist who sings in the choir. Hillary needs quiet time and has been known to excuse herself from her own parties at 11; as for Bill, the more people he has around him the more energy he has. She can cut short a long-winded aide with a crisp "Where are we here?," allowing her husband to leave the impression that he would have listened all day.

HILLARY WORKS TIRELESSLY—BUT OFTEN FRUITlessly—to counteract Bill's belief that tomorrow is at least another day away. During their four-day Thanksgiving visit to California, their first vacation in a year and a half, the frenetic President-elect played football, golf and volleyball, jogged twice, shook hands at a mall, went to a black-tie surprise party, ate at three restaurants unannounced and ordered room-service pizza at 3 a.m. Hillary asked Susan Thomases, a lawyer and an old friend, to become campaign scheduler in order to keep her husband "from working himself into a robotic trance." Still, at the end of a long campaign day, says press secretary Dee Dee Myers, "the Governor would rather stay up and putter instead of going to bed—channel surfing, calling friends, doing a crossword puzzle, reading a mystery."

Their minds are so attuned to each other's that, among Clinton's aides, the phrase "Hillary said" is equivalent to an Executive Order. Campaign staffer Skip Rutherford says that if you call the mansion with a question and get Hillary, you can ask your question and run with her answer. "She's never wrong about what he would want," he says. Aides had failed to persuade Clinton to appear on the Arsenio Hall show until Hillary was impressed by an interview with inner-city teenagers on the program during the Los Angeles riots. Hillary recommended that the theme of the convention not be the one that was famously proclaimed by the war-room sign THE ECONOMY, STUPID, but rather a positive, uplifting message about the future.

The secret of the Clintons' success, friends say, is that each thinks the other is the smartest person in the world. Nothing is really settled for Bill until Hillary thinks it's a good idea—and vice versa. During the campaign, after a tiring day, they

would climb back on the bus and collapse against each other in a heap. If the Governor's attention is flagging, says Betsey Wright, Clinton's chief of staff for a decade, the best way to get it back is to talk about something Hillary has done.

Clinton first won the governorship in 1978. It was a glorious period for the nation's youngest Governor, then 32, and his wife, who joined one of the city's most prestigious law firms. In 1980 Hillary gave birth to their daughter Chelsea in a difficult caesarean delivery. Until the campaign went into overdrive this year, one or the other, or both, has always managed to be home for dinner, and to take Chelsea to school, softball games and ballet performances. (One of the things that concerns the Clintons most is how to fence off a family life in the White House.)

In 1980 Clinton was stunned by an unexpected defeat in his re-election bid. But after figuratively sending the

Hillary works tirelessly—but often fruitlessly—to counteract Bill's belief that tomorrow is always at least another day away

Governor to his room for two years, voters welcomed him back for 10 more in 1982. Hillary started answering to Mrs. Clinton instead of keeping her maiden name. With the '60s ethic waning, a female attorney could wear silk and argue a case at the same time. Hillary still wastes as little energy as possible on such matters; during the convention, she left all decisions about her appearance to her Arkansas friend, Hollywood producer Linda Bloodworth-Thomason.

The Clinton blend of yin and yang brought about what may be the couple's most lasting legacy to the state that had long ranked last in most measures of school achievement. Both believed education was the key to the good life. Clinton remembers his grandmother Edith hanging flash cards by his high chair so that he knew all his numbers and letters by the time he was three years old. His teachers later got him through troubled times in a home with an alcoholic stepfather. For a woman of Hillary's generation, education was the way of liberation.

In 1983 the Governor appointed Hillary to chair an official commission on education standards. Night after night, she would hold meetings in school cafeterias; her husband, meanwhile, was softening up the legislature to raise taxes to

Road Warriors
After a long day of appearances, the couple shares a moment of downtime over cold pizza in a Chicago hotel. Friends say they confide fully in no one but each other.

upgrade the curriculum and eventually require competency tests of teachers. Irate teachers denounced Hillary as "lower than a snake's belly." But the bill got through.

THE ADMIRATION THAT HILLARY HAD EARNED OVER the years—as a lawyer with the Legal Services Corporation, chairman of the Children's Defense Fund, a member of numerous boards and a top-ranked litigator—made it all the harder for her to understand and deal with the harsh attacks on her during the campaign. The sight of her sitting defiantly in solidarity with her husband on *60 Minutes* fueled critics looking for evidence that she was pushy, arrogant and contemptuous of more conventional wives. In that January interview, which focused on Gennifer Flowers' claims that she had had a 12-year affair with Clinton, the two steadfastly refused to reveal more than that the Governor "had caused pain in his marriage." That their marriage held to-

gether in spite of those strains is probably the best testimony to their mutual belief in the partnership.

Hillary's public image improved as the year wore on and people got a fuller picture of her. The Republicans inadvertently guaranteed her more sympathy by bashing her from the podium at their Houston convention. According to polls taken since the election, the country seems to have softened on the "Hillary question." Perhaps a First Lady who consults lawbooks rather than astrologers doesn't look so frightening. And perhaps Bill Clinton has proved that it takes a solid, secure man to marry a strong woman.

The Clintons planned to begin their final journey to the Inauguration at Monticello—the very place where almost two decades ago Hillary had stopped on her way to Arkansas but finally chose not to turn back to Washington. Instead, she took a long detour through watermelon country. No one can ever know where the path not taken in 1974 might have led Hillary Rodham. But if her life continues to enrich Clinton's as much in the White House as it did in the Governor's mansion, then the country should be grateful that she drove on to Fayetteville, and will be headed up the Capitol steps once again, this time at Bill Clinton's side. ■

IMAGES '92
Unforgettable pictures of the year

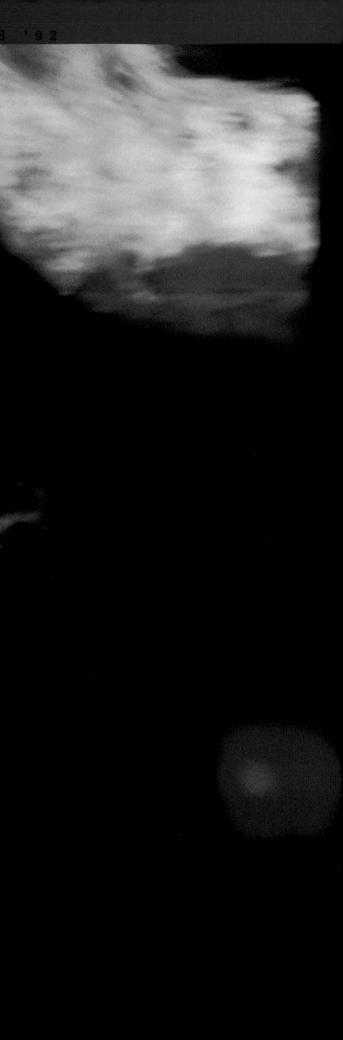

WE KNOW THAT IMAGES CAN HOLD history in place. We forget sometimes that they can also drive it forward. In 1992 Los Angeles exploded over the meaning of pictures of a black man being beaten by white police. And it was pictures—of spectral women and withered children—that launched the rescue mission in Somalia. It may have been awkward to have cameras meet the troops when they landed, but wasn't it also appropriate? In a sense it was cameras that had sent them there.

This was a year that disproved the truism that scenes of tragedy all blur together, that photographs of famine in Biafra and Ethiopia, Sudan and then Somalia just pile on in layers, forming a callus around the conscience. Brought face to face one more time with starvation, the world did not just shrug. And pictures gave other conflicts their own unforgettable faces. Some of the video-game visuals from last year's fighting in the Persian Gulf were strangely antiseptic, an invitation to forget that war is the mass production of individual suffering. The photographs from Bosnia-Herzegovina, where war has become serial killing under the guise of politics, made us remember.

Images are an imperfect route to knowledge. They crowd the senses; they can simplify; they can yell. But they make an impact that sets in motion the deeper operations of judgment. The secular faith of the 20th century insists that history is progress, that time's arrow points the human race toward an ever brighter future. Then the world dissolves again into tribal bloodletting, and we wonder whether history is cyclical, always orbiting through the same thickets of hope and misfortune. When we look at news photographs, we bring to them the questions that history forces upon us: What should we think of human affairs? What is to be done? Pictures don't tell us the answers. They tell us why the questions are important. *— By Richard Lacayo*

GROUND ZERO ON APRIL 29, the first night of the Los Angeles riots. Silhouetted against the flames of a liquor store, a looter flees at the approach of police. When it was all over, there were 53 dead, 2,383 injured and $775 million in property damage.

Ed Carreon / Orange County Register — SIPA

DADELAND, FLORIDA

HURRICANE ANDREW was the costliest natural disaster in U.S. history, leaving **61 dead and more than $22 billion** in property damage in Florida and Louisiana. An aerial view of flattened homes in a mobile-home park shows Andrew's power to destroy.

John Lopinot—Palm Beach Post/Sygma

NEAR CENTRALIA, ILLINOIS

HOPE. SOMETIMES IT'S something small on the horizon. After the Democratic Convention in July, Bill Clinton and Al Gore became a ticket to ride, touring eight states in six days in a caravan of buses. Along the route, one expectant family waved the candidates on.

Tomas Muscionico — Contact Press Images for TIME

NO HOPE. DURING a whistlestop tour three days before the election, Bush's campaign manager Jim Baker realizes that the race is lost. Moments earlier he had seen new figures showing that the President's last-minute surge in the polls had sputtered.

Dirck Halstead for TIME

SARAJEVO, BOSNIA

CHILDHOOD'S END. At a city morgue, sunlight falls across the body of a four-year-old boy killed at home by shellfire from Serbian guns. In April a Serb campaign of "ethnic cleansing" against Muslims and Croats began and was soon answered in kind.

Christopher Morris—Black Star for TIME

WASHINGTON

LIKE THE EPIDEMIC itself, the AIDS quilt has grown too large. More than 13 acres now, it is rarely laid out in its entirety. About 400,000 visitors saw it that way in October, when it had 20,064 panels, each made by the loved ones of someone claimed by the disease.

Jeffrey Markowitz—Sygma

Vaclav Havel

The play-wright/President on his life, his country —and the importance of good taste in public affairs

THE DEEPEST LAYER OF PRAGUE IS spiky, medieval, dark with coal dust. For years Vaclav Havel could look out from his dilapidated apartment building across the Vltava River and see the castle on the hill: Hradcany, the elaborate complex that dominates the city. On top of the medieval lies Prague's socialist layer, the residue of neglect and cynicism, the peeling paint, the shop shelves half empty from the day before yesterday when the Bohemians and Moravians and Slovaks were occupied—a nation land-bound and Lenin-bound.

Above all that, quickening the surfaces now, is a lively entrepreneurial city—Western glitz and electronics and hard money flowing in; McDonald's opening a second branch, this one on Wenceslas Square, where the "velvet revolution" transpired in November 1989 and near the spot where Jan Palach set himself on fire for Czechoslovak freedom in 1969, the spot where Havel laid flowers in 1989 and was arrested for the deed.

Peeping out everywhere is Franz Kafka's haunted, haunting face. Prague's presiding household god, he invented the castle as literature, his Prague castle the symbolic seat of mysterious, anonymous power, an effect the communists had a genius for. That Havel came to preside over the castle seemed the Czechoslovaks' graceful, transcendant leap out of the dark, an impish historical touch.

Havel, born in 1935 and raised in a well-to-do family, began as an absurdist playwright in the style of Ionesco or Beckett. An attitude of surrealist paranoia turned out to be the right optic through which to see the communist world clearly, and Havel had keen eyesight. Constricted as a playwright, he became a dissident. Imprisoned as a dissident, he became a symbol. Communism was brutal and stupid and corrupt. Havel was Czechoslovakia with brains, the country's better self, the visionary of "living in truth." When the communist state fell away in November 1989, it made some giddy, noble sense to install Havel as the first President of Czechosolovakia's new age.

When Havel resigned the mostly ceremonial office in July—the week before he spoke with TIME in the following interview—Czechoslovakia was splitting in two: the Slovaks in the eastern half of the country breaking off to form an independent state, the Bohemians and Moravians in the Czech lands to the west organizing a faster-moving, more entrepreneurial state. In November Havel announced he would run for President of the Czech republic. His moral leadership transcends Central European politics, for he asserts values not often advanced in world politics: courtesy, good taste, decency, and responsibility.

Q. *Are you relieved to have resigned?*

A. I am quite relieved, almost happy actually, because always when I accomplish something or make an important decision, it gives me a feeling of inner freedom and self-confirmation. It is one of the paradoxes of my life that I am experiencing such a creative feeling at the moment of my resignation.

Q. *You have had an unusual career, from playwright to dissident leader to President. Are you going to return to writing full time, or will you stay in politics?*

A. When I consider my life as a whole, it has been very adventurous. But it was not because I am an adventurer. I am a very calm and order-loving person, with a bourgeois background. I am even a little conservative. Despite these characteristics, fate and history and my almost chronic sense of inner responsibility have made my life full of paradoxes and absurdities. I was always active in public life as a citizen. This is something I will have to continue doing.

Q. *You use a vocabulary that is not heard very often in American politics. You talk of decency, good taste, intelligence.*

A. When I became President, I tried to bring a more personal dimension back to politics, because this world is endangered by "anonymization." We are becoming integral parts of mega-machineries, which move with their own uncontrollable inertia. I tried to accentuate the spiritual and ethical dimensions of political decision making. Certain changes of the

human mentality are necessary in order to deepen the feeling of global responsibility, which is not thinkable without a certain respect for a higher principle above my personal existence.

Q. *As we approach the year 2000, are you optimistic or pessimistic about the future?*

A. I cherish a certain hope in me, hope as a state of spirit—a state of spirit without which I cannot imagine living.

Q. *I have been fascinated by a phrase that you have used in your writings that translates into English as good taste. I wonder what you mean?*

A. I have found that good taste, oddly enough, plays an important role in politics. Why is it like that? The most probable reason is that good taste is a visible manifestation of human sensibility toward the world, environment, people. I came to this castle and to other governmental residences inherited from communism, and I was confronted with tasteless furni-ture and many tasteless pictures. Only then did I realize how closely the bad taste of former rulers was connected with their bad way of ruling. I also realized how important good taste was for politics. During political talks, the feeling of how long to speak, whether to interrupt or not, how to address the public, all these play a major role. All such political behavior relates to good taste in a broader sense.

Q. *Do people respond when you appeal to them on the basis of atmosphere, good manners, good taste?*

A. I feel that this appeal of mine is finding a positive echo, but an indirect one. Here we witness all the aspirations, battles and hunger for power. My position seems to be of one of a dreamer who mumbles about ideals, untouched by real life, whereas politics takes a different course. But this is a very banal view. In reality it seems to me that my constant repetition of certain things planted seeds, and the seeds I planted in the subconscious of the people are there acting indirectly. ■

Vaclav Havel's bizarre odyssey: from absurdist playwright to dissident, from dissident to symbol, from symbol to President of Czechoslovakia

Slobodan Milosevic

Sly, intelligent and ruthless, "The Butcher of the Balkans" turned Yugoslavia into a slaughter-house.

FROM A LEATHER CHAIR IN HIS SPAcious office in Belgrade, with a tin of his beloved cigarillos within reach, Serbian President Slobodan Milosevic strove to keep the war at arm's length. In a rare interview, he contended that Yugoslavia's bloody dissolution stemmed solely from the secessionist demands of the other republics. "All processes in the contemporary world tend toward integration," he said. "Nationalistic tendencies are against that general flow, that big river, that Mississippi." Confused? There is this clarifying coda: "In Serbia nationalists are not in power."

That is just double-talk. Of course nationalists are in power in Serbia, embodied in this pudgy-faced former communist bigwig with a belligerent jaw who has seized on generations of ethnic hatreds and resentments to turn what was Yugoslavia into a slaughterhouse. More than any other single person, Milosevic bears responsibility for the bloodshed through his unyielding determination to see Serbs united in one country carved from territory the communists left—fairly or unfairly—under the control of other nationalities. He is the power behind Radovan Karadzic, the militant leader of Bosnia's Serbs, and he has effective command of the old Yugoslav army; he could cool its operations if he were so disposed.

Milosevic is a throwback to the kind of violent nationalism that regularly rearranged Europe's borders in centuries past. But he is also a harbinger of what may happen elsewhere as the constraints of communism give way to long-suppressed emotions. His animating passion seems to be power, first and foremost, with national pride as a useful adjunct.

Until five years ago, his life read like a Bolshevik parable, though shadowed by personal tragedy. He was born in 1941 in the town of Pozarevac, near Belgrade, where he still keeps a modest weekend home. His father was a seminary-trained teacher of religion from Montenegro, his mother a fervent communist;

the two quarreled incessantly over ideological issues. Early on, his father abandoned the family, went back to Montenegro and later committed suicide. When Slobodan's mother killed herself in 1974, her devoted son was reportedly left distraught.

Milosevic spent many years as an ambitious communist apparatchik. His cleverest move was to hitch his star to Ivan Stambolic, a nephew of one of the most powerful Serbian communist leaders. For more than 20 years, Milosevic moved up the communist hierarchy in Stambolic's wake, succeeding him as Belgrade party chief and eventually as boss of the Serbian Communist Party. In late 1987 he sloughed off his mentor with ruthless precision. By 1989 he was the president of Serbia and today presides over Yugoslavia's remains: Serbia, Montenegro and the two provinces of Kosovo and Vojvodina.

Milosevic, says a European diplomat who knows him well, "is a brigand and a fanatic, but a sly, intelligent and sophisticated one." His arrival as head of the Belgrade party in 1984 ended a rudderless period of creeping liberalization, when the communists needed to solidify their grip on power after the death of Tito. Although Milosevic talked about economic reform, he slapped bans on writers and purged dissenters from TV and the press.

In 1987 he grabbed the opportunity to put his populism to work. He was dispatched to Kosovo, the southern province Serbs view as the cradle of their nationhood, where their complaints about mistreatment by the ethnic Albanian majority were on the boil. As angry Serbs tussled with police to enter a small meeting hall in Kosovo Polje, Milosevic emerged on a balcony to address the crowd with words that resounded throughout Yugoslavia: "No one has the right to beat the people!" In a show of personal courage, he strode out into the crowds to repeat the message, and the Serbs were galvanized.

"From that day, the balance changed," says economist Jurij Bajec, a former ally. "He knew how to touch the Serbs' national feelings . . . and he knew it would make millions come to hear him speak." Milosevic was a formidable presence at rallies throughout Serbia. "In less than a year," says Slavoljub Djukic, author of a critical biography of Milosevic, "he moved from being a second-rate politician to almost a god." In the process Milosevic purged the party of all opposition, turned television into an instrument of personal power and abolished the autonomy of Kosovo and Vojvodina.

The prospect of Serb domination under the intolerant Milosevic helped speed the secession of Slovenia and Croatia, whose own fa-

natically nationalist leader fueled fears among the Serb minority there. It was as the savior of the Serbs who live outside Serbia's borders—nearly one-third of the community—that Milosevic entered the fray. His strategy has been simple—and effective. He stirs up Serbs with talk of imminent genocide, then sets his proxies loose to "protect" them, with fatal consequences for Croats and Muslims. Yet he insists that his aim is not the creation of a Greater Serbia, only the preservation of Yugoslavia. "We don't want to be a puppet regime of any foreign force, unlike some others in Yugoslavia," he says, referring to Croatia's close ties with Germany. "Our people want to be independent and free, nothing else."

As Milosevic absolves himself of responsibility, how many more must die? Says a U.S. State Department official: "For him, the word compromise is a dirty word, meaning treason and surrender." Indeed, he appears to have hunkered down, convinced of his own righteousness. "We rejected the abolition of our country," he says. "If we have to be blamed for that, I am proud to be blamed for loyalty to my country." As hundreds die, thousands flee and Serbia faces international isolation, Milosevic's blame goes far beyond that. ■

Nothing interests Milosevic but Serb success, even if it means tens of thousands dead and dispossessed

127

Larry King

1992 was a career year for the man who turned talk shows into America's new political theater

WANT TO KNOW HOW AMBITIOUS Larry King, the top banana of talk-show hosts, is? When King, born Larry Zeiger, was growing up in Brooklyn, New York, and indifferent about school, his father went to the principal and suggested that Larry's teacher install him as eraser monitor. Most kids would have been horrified. Eraser monitors come in early, stay late, get all dusty with chalk, get razzed by classmates. But little Larry Zeiger thought the job was a promotion. Sitting out there on the playground, pounding erasers together and choking on chalk dust, he thought he was on his way at last.

Now, after a half-century of hustling and scratching, after no college and hard knocks, after working as everything from mail-room clerk to racetrack flack, after six marriages, one annulment and five divorces, after being arrested for grand larceny, after declaring bankruptcy, after suffering a heart attack, after all this and more, Larry King has finally arrived.

His weeknight shows on CNN and Mutual radio are watched and listened to by more than 4 million people. In the 1992 election, one King interview nudged Ross Perot into the presidential arena; another caused Dan Quayle to ruminate on what he might do if his daughter decided to have an abortion. George Bush and Bill Clinton dutifully trouped by to share King's electronic forum. Says King: "I'm 58 years old, and I'm having the best year of my life."

As he speaks, he is standing on the balcony of his posh eighth-floor apartment in Arlington, Virginia. He waves an arm through the air. "Some view, huh?" he says in his famed Brooklyn baritone. Some view: first the Potomac River, then a panorama of marble including the Lincoln Memorial, the Washington Monument, the Kennedy Center, the Jefferson Memorial. From his balcony King can also see the Watergate apartments, the home of his childhood friend Herbie Cohen. King used to tell a story about how he, Herbie and another Brooklyn teenager named Sandy Koufax (the Hall of Fame Dodger southpaw) once drove to Connecticut to settle an argument about how many scoops of ice cream you could get in New Haven for 15¢.

Good story. Funny, as King told it. He loves yarns and tells them all the time. His stories almost always feature some big-name celebrity. King's apartment walls are crammed with pictures of himself and famous stars. There are pictures of Ronald Reagan, Richard Nixon, George Bush. There's a story about every picture, about every name.

Some may even be true. The one about Cohen, Koufax and the ice cream, however, is not. Last year a Washington *Post* reporter checked with Koufax. The former Dodger said he'd never been to New Haven, and although he did grow up in the same neighborhood as King, they did not really become friends until they were adults.

So why did King make the story up? Part of the answer may lie in that Brooklyn playground where the little boy proudly pounded erasers. King, the son of Russian-immigrant Jewish parents, was one of those kids who, if they don't like the way things are, imagine them to be better. Ask him about the Koufax business, and he shrugs and looks away. "I tell a lot of stories that are part fact, part history, part imagination," he says quietly. "It was just a story. I guess I told it so often that even I thought it was true."

Every morning at 9, having worked the previous night until 2 a.m., King climbs out of his king-size bed, dons a running suit and a pair of Mephisto athletic shoes, then paces briskly on a treadmill for 30 minutes, a daily routine since his heart attack in 1987. He flips through six newspapers, eats a cardiologically correct breakfast, changes into his street clothes, descends to his black Lincoln Town Car and drives across the Key Bridge to Georgetown, where he gets his thinning hair done.

When the familiar swept-back hairdo has been built and lacquered, King often drives downtown for lunch at Duke Ziebert's, one of the capital's last old-fashioned, macho places to be seen. From his usual table, he can quickly scan and be scanned by, every patron who enters the restaurant. Between bites he waves to and chats with all the pols, power brokers and wannabes. In his first book, published in 1982, King wrote, "When I'm 58, I would like to have a newspaper column and be doing a one-hour radio interview show and a television talk show on a regular basis." Except that his radio show is three hours, those ambitions were fulfilled exactly.

It wasn't easy. His father died when Larry was only 10; his mother went on relief for a

year and then got a job in a sweatshop. After high school and a mail-room job, King caught a bus to Miami in 1957, determined to get on radio. He was finally hired as a disk jockey, changed his name, and by 1970 was a local hit. He had a radio talk show, a TV interview show and a newspaper column and was the color commentator for the Miami Dolphins. He played the horses a lot, drove Cadillacs and was married to a former Playboy Bunny named Alene while having affairs on the side — "I felt that Larry King deserved to be seen with beautiful women." He was generally behaving, as he put it, "as if I . . . didn't have to live by the same rules others live by."

To prove the point, he was running up huge debts and ripping off some of his wealthy acquaintances, notably Lou Wolfson, a Miami financier. Wolfson eventually filed a grand-larceny complaint against King, leading to his arrest by Miami police in late 1971. The charge was dropped three years later because the statute of limitations had expired.

Suddenly King was out of luck, out of money, out of work and out of his marriage. He moved to Louisiana, then fought his way back to Miami radio. Married by now for a fourth time and $350,000 in debt, he declared bankruptcy and moved to Washington and a chance at a national audience with a show for Mutual radio. But even as King was regaining his balance, a new crisis was looming. He was somewhat overweight, was working almost all night, every night, and was chain-smoking cigarettes. In February 1987 he felt the chest pains of a major heart attack that would force him to shape up and slow down.

Now, despite more bad marriages, he is at the top of his game. Having fulfilled one personal 10-year plan, King in the next decade would like to ease back gradually. He even dreams of taking a summer off to be a baseball announcer. But the man who was once a wide-eyed eraser monitor knows very well what got him where he is. "I never want to give up my TV show," he says. "If—God forbid—I ever became President, I'd keep right on doing *Larry King Live* from the White House." ■

Who's complaining? After a steep rise—and an even steeper fall—Larry King is the monarch of the TV talkers

Donna Karan

Talented, driven and willing to break the rules, the consummate career woman has built a formidable fashion empire

"L ET'S SPRAY THE MODELS! PATTI, could you get me some perfume?" Straight pins bristling from her mouth, Donna Karan is stalking the runway where she is about to present the spring collection to the fashion flock. She was up for most of the night coping with the usual crises. The jewelry, for instance. Karan decided she needed more gold. Fistfuls of silver pieces were hand-dipped in gold. All wrong. Back to silver.

As the models begin striding out for the show, Karan is in constant motion behind the curtain, tucking, smoothing, adjusting angles by an imperceptible (to anyone but her) fraction of an inch. Nothing escapes her eye. Everything has to be perfect. "Are you accessorized? . . . I told you I need a beret! . . . Lynn, move the belt!" From out on the runway comes the sound of Madonna singing her version of Peggy Lee's *Fever* as each model passes through Karan's last-minute scrutiny and touch-up. "Little black glasses! Who's next?"

Such painstaking, relentless attention to detail, fueled by an insatiable drive, defines everything Karan does. It has made her the darling of the fashion faithful, the quintessential stressed-out New York City career-woman-cum-celebrity. She is the only female interloper in the all-boys club of leading U.S. designers, whose longtime members are Ralph, Calvin, Bill, Geoffrey and Oscar. The future of American retailing, though, may belong to Donna.

In the rag trade, where rivals try to rip one another to shreds every season and a designer is only as good as his or her best collection, Karan's performance has been virtually seamless. At 44, in business for herself for just eight years, she has not only shaped a distinctively comfortable, sexy style as a designer but has also amassed a formidable empire as a businesswoman. Her 1992 revenues should reach $268 million, up from $119 million in 1989. By 1995, with ever increasing overseas sales, revenues might top the half-billion-dollar mark.

Karan has already become an established A-list name, a fixture at AIDS benefits and theater openings. Though older friends recall a time when she was "shy and introverted" at public functions, those days seemed long gone when Karan hobnobbed with Bill and Hillary Clinton at a pre-election Hollywood gathering. Still, Karan works too hard to spend much time on the social scene, or even at home in her sunny four-bedroom apartment on Manhattan's Upper East Side (lots of suede furniture and sweeping city views) or at her East Hampton beach house. When she travels to Italy several times a year, Karan spends more time looking at bolts of fabric than at Botticellis.

Some designers create beautiful fantasies hopelessly beyond the reach of ordinary mortals. Karan's gift is that she makes wearable, flattering clothes for real women. That sounds simple, but it is a rare talent on Seventh Avenue. "No one understands a woman's body better than Donna Karan," says Andrea Jung, executive vice president at Neiman Marcus.

If Karan seems right at home in the rough, insular world of New York's garment district, it may be because she was born into it. Her father Gabby Faske, who died when Donna was three, was a tailor; her mother Helen—famously imperious and demanding—worked as a sales representative and showroom model. After studying at New York City's Parsons School of Design, Karan went to work at 19 for Anne Klein, another lady who was notoriously hard to please. Burt Wayne, head of the Klein design studio and a good friend of both women, recalls meeting Karan for the first time at Klein's apartment. Donna was standing on the terrace, showing her various fabrics. "Her hair was blowing, the fabrics were flying. You could instantly see Donna's enthusiasm—and her tenacity." When Klein died in 1974, Karan took over the reins, just four years after arriving at the company. By this time she had married her first husband, Mark Karan, a clothing-boutique owner, and had given birth to their daughter Gabby. Donna later divorced Karan and married sculptor Stephan Weiss, whom she had known as a teenager.

Ever restless, Karan was eager to assert her creative identity beyond the Anne Klein line. In 1985 she mounted her first show, backed by Takiyho, the Japanese conglomerate that owned Klein. It was a hit: the eternally jaded fashion crowd gave her a standing ovation, whistling, wildly shouting her name. A month after that, she broke records at a special sale for customers of Bergdorf Goodman. Over the years, she has consistently demonstrated a golden commercial touch, but not by taking the predictable approach. Before Karan, for

example, most designers' second collections were watered-down versions of their high-priced lines. But when Karan opened her second line, DKNY, in 1989, she offered stylish, casual and affordable clothes, without cannibalizing her main collection.

No less contrarian was Karan's approach to hosiery. In 1987 she became convinced that women would spend more money if they could find heavier, more opaque pantyhose to cloak the sags that most female flesh is heir to. The product she came up with was nearly twice as expensive as usual hose. But the gamble paid off: customers recognized and paid for superior quality. This year the business is likely to gross $30 million wholesale.

Karan would be the first to admit that her professional success has come at a real personal cost. "Looking back, it was the most horrible pain of my life," she says. "When your child says, 'Don't go, stay home,' and the office is calling and screaming, it's brutal." Yet daughter Gabby describes her mother as "my best friend. I idolize her, and I want to be like her."

A lot of young women who work for Karan feel the same way, much as the young Donna felt about Anne Klein. Karan attracts talented people who are famously loyal and willing to put up with her constant demands. Sometimes, fighting the constant deadlines, she wonders what there is to envy. "I do love the ability I have to create something from nothing. What I hate is the pressure, the toll it takes on my physical being. Do I have to pay this price to do something I love?" The answer is yes, and she knows it. ∎

The designer's signature: relentless attention to detail and an intuitive commercial sense.

Woody Allen

On his love affair with Mia Farrow's stepdaughter: "The heart wants what it wants"

IN THE SUMMER OF 1992, WOODY ALLEN, America's most revered filmmaker, and Mia Farrow, his longtime companion and the waif who had matured into a madonna in reel and real life, were at war. What began as a skirmish over custody rights of three children escalated when Allen declared that he was in love with one of Farrow's adopted daughters, Soon-Yi Farrow Previn, and Connecticut police investigated a complaint of child molestation against Allen. Amid the turmoil, Allen spoke with TIME.

Q. *How could you get involved with someone who was almost a daughter?*
A. I am not Soon-Yi's father or stepfather. I've never even lived with Mia. I've never in my entire life slept at Mia's apartment, and I never even used to *go* over there until my children came along seven years ago. I never had any family dinners over there. I was not a father to her adopted kids in any sense of the word.

Q. *But wasn't it breaking many bonds of trust to become involved with your lover's daughter?*
A. There's no downside to it. The only thing unusual is that she's Mia's daughter. But she's an *adopted* daughter and a grown woman.

Q. *Were you still romantically involved with Mia when you became interested in Soon-Yi?*
A. My relationship with Mia was simply a cordial one in the past four years, a dinner maybe once a week together. Our romantic relationship tapered off after the birth of Satchel, tapered off quickly.

Q. *What was your relationship with Soon-Yi when you first started going over there to visit your children?*
A. I never had a single extended conversation with her. As a matter of fact, I don't even think she liked me too much. The last thing I was interested in was the whole parcel of Mia's children.

Q. *How did your relationship begin?*
A. One night, just fortuitously, I was over at Mia's, and I had no one to go to the basketball game with. And Soon-Yi said, I'll go. And so I took her, and I found her interested and delightful. This was a couple of years ago. Mia had encouraged me to get to know her. She would say, Take a walk with Soon-Yi, do something with her. Try and make friends with her, she's not really as hostile as you might think. Mia thought it was fine I took her to the game.

Q. *So then you started secretly dating her?*
A. No. I took her to a game again, maybe a month later. And we struck up a relationship.

Q. *How did your sexual relationship with Soon-Yi come about?*
A. We'd chat when I came over to Mia's house. It started to become hotter and heavier late last year, very late. We had a number of conversations, saw a couple of movies, and, you know, it just—well, I can't say there was any cataclysmic moment.

Q. *But you fell in love with her?*
A. Yes, yes. My flair for drama. What can I say?

Q. *She fell in love with you at the same time?*
A. That's hard to say. My guess is after. She returned my feelings.

Q. *You're a guy who can find moral dilemmas in a broken DON'T WALK sign. Didn't you see some here?*
A. I didn't see any moral dilemmas whatsoever. I didn't feel that just because she was Mia's daughter, there was any great moral dilemma. It was a fact, but not one with any great import. It wasn't like she was my daughter.

Q. *Did you ever discuss with her, "What is Mom going to think of this?"*
A. Mom would have thought more or less the same thing if it had been my secretary or an actress.

Q. *Come on!*
A. There is a different psychodynamic here, without any question, but the difference is one of small degree. If I had said to "Mom"—it was actually "Mia" that she called her—I'm in love with my secretary, there would have been some version of the same thing.

Q. *Did you really take nude pictures of Soon-Yi?*
A. Yes. Soon-Yi had talked about being a model and said to me would I take some pictures of

her without her clothes on. At this time we had an intimate relationship, so I said sure, and I did. It was just a lark of a moment.

Q. *What did Mia do when she found them?*

A. She hit the ceiling. I said, Look, our relationship has been over for some time. We should go our separate ways. The important thing is that we do what is right for our children. She was too angry. She instantly brought all the kids in on it, told all of them. This was Jan. 13. It was a dreadful thing to do. She phoned people saying I had molested her daughter, raped her daughter.

Q. *What did she do with Soon-Yi?*

A. She locked Soon-Yi in the bedroom in her apartment—there's a lot of corroboration of this—beat her on numerous occasions, smashed her with a chair, kicked her, raised black-and-blue marks.

Q. *Do you use your movies to work through dilemmas you're facing in life?*

A. No, people always confuse my movies and my life.

Q. *Inappropriate love with younger women seems to be a theme in your movies and your life, right?*

A. It's not a theme in my life. I've been married twice, both times to women practically my age. My two other relationships—Diane Keaton and Mia Farrow—they're not really much younger women.

Q. *Will your relationship with Soon-Yi continue?*

A. Yes. I'm in love with her. As soon as the reporters go away, we'll do the things we like to do. We'll walk and eat out and go to the movies and basketball games.

Q. *Do you consider it a healthy, equal relationship?*

A. Well, who knows? It's perfectly healthy. But I don't think equal is necessarily a desideratum. Sometimes equality in a relationship is great, sometimes inequality makes it work. But it's an equal-opportunity relationship. I mean, I'm not equal to her in certain ways.

The heart wants what it wants. There's no logic to these things. You meet someone and you fall in love and that's that. ■

Allen's storied love affair with Mia Farrow crashed into shards—and turned their motley postmodern family into a tabloid sensation

SOCIETY

"Bring back family values!" the combative
moralists cried. But at times the U.S. no longer felt
like a family, could not agree on
values and looked to be losing belief in its mission.

By LANCE MORROW

THE SYMBOLIC CRIME OF THE YEAR WAS CARJACKING. News of the incidents—cars suddenly seized at gunpoint as drivers waited at traffic lights or pumped gas—sent a small but unusual shock through American morale. The automobile has always been an important item of American myth, standing for mobility, convenience, speed, individual choice, independence. An American's home might or might not be his castle, but his car represented his true personal sanctum.

Carjacking seemed a kind of Third World touch. It suggested a new ratcheting-up in the direction of anarchy. It hinted of social menace that had burst out of the old holding tanks (the big-city ghettos) and entered the nation's broader life of orderly privilege. The number of carjacking incidents was small, disproportionate to the anxiety they stirred. But the mass of middle-class Americans have been accustomed to their immunities. The invasion of the car, their capsule of well-being, coincided with the onset of other kinds of vulnerability and intrusion.

The cold war was over: the fact had a telling effect on American social and moral psychology. Americans, who more than other people require some sense of national purpose, some coherent idea of themselves and their mission, were living in a new unfamiliar context. The struggle against communism, by which Americans had defined their purpose for more than 40 years, had ended in a decisive and even surreal fashion: the other side simply disintegrated. Now Americans felt disoriented. They told pollsters they had come to feel their own country had somehow gone off the track. The old stabilities of American life seemed unreliable. Something was wrong.

A sort of sociological wave theory might explain the sense of malaise, that toxic mood recycled from the last of the Jimmy Carter years. In the months leading up to the presidential election, depressive trends piled one on top of the other, like waves reinforcing one another to form a larger unified surge:

1) The recession seemed too chronic and corrosive to be a part of the usual economic cycles. The problems, Americans were told, lay deeper—in the enormous deficit, in the profligacies of the Reagan years, in the long-term overall decline of America. The word systemic recurred in the diagnosis. Jobs that went away to other lands or to new machines and microchips (and hundreds of thousands of them did) would not return, as they had after other recessions. America, which had grown sleek in the postwar years as the world's pre-eminent economic power (after all, the U.S. was the only big industrial country left standing in 1945), now faced a regenerated world of competition, from the Japanese, from Europe, from newer, livelier economies in the Asian Little Dragons (Singapore, Taiwan, South Korea, Hong Kong).

2) The baby boomers, who since they burst upon the '60s have always overemphasized every trend and turned it into a mass phenomenon—rock music, dissent, drugs, sex and so on—were now hitting the years of mid-life crisis. Their mood (a sense of bathos: Is that all there is? Am I now past the peak and in decline?) exaggerated the depressive feelings about the economy and other woes. But the election of a new President, the first from the generation, may have improved the disposition of many baby boomers. It gave them a sense that after so many years of what occasionally seemed like prolonged adolescence and the lengthening aftermath of the '60s, they had finally come into their own.

3) The sense of being in a new, alien world in the '90s distilled itself into this intuition in the mind of some Americans: We are not us anymore. The waves of new immigration so evident in American life in recent years became especially conspicuous as the recession went on. Black Americans hit with the usual severity by hard times came to feel once more cruelly bypassed as new immigrants, including many from Asia, leapfrogged past them into the American dream. America was acquiring so many new

genes and languages that it was losing some sense of its coherent self. Some Americans might censure that intuition, but the country is nothing if not an idea, a self-image that sometimes is blurred by the speed at which it is changing.

The year's great debate over multiculturalism centered on the 500th anniversary of Christopher Columbus' voyage to America. Was he the visionary explorer Americans had always thought, or a villainous colonializing genocidal slave master? The moral effort required to shift to a new perspective (leaving the decks of *Niña*, *Pinta* and *Santa María* and standing instead on the beach as these strange white-sailed, white-faced apparitions blew in from mysterious nowhere) was for some Americans an act of self-alienation. Among other things, Americans are not accustomed to thinking of themselves as immoral. To do so somehow invalidates the entire national exercise, which is supposed to be by definition virtuous.

The old American dilemma of race dramatically returned. The spectacle of the jury viewing the 1991 Rodney King videotape, then exonerating the police who beat King, then the terrible pageant of Los Angeles burning for several days—all these gave the country glimpses of itself that were ugly and difficult to square with the nation's traditional moral shine, that core of essential American goodness that Ronald Reagan, for one, had been a genius at evoking.

OUT OF SUCH DISQUIETS AROSE A COMBATIVE MORALism. It rose up in Pat Buchanan's campaign and in Vice President Dan Quayle's disquisitions on Murphy Brown. It had its moment in Houston at the Republican Convention, when Buchanan declared the nation to be in the midst of a religious war, a cultural war. The family values issue, however, did not ultimately play well for the Republicans. In part, such considerations were overshadowed in Americans' minds by the condition of the economy. In part, the Republican assault from the

right seemed to most people to be overdone. The scything, moralistic attacks on homosexuals sounded meanspirited and uncharitable in a year when the AIDS virus continued its devastations.

The family values issue may have failed as well because the majority of Americans sensed that the deeper aspects of American life that needed correcting could not be addressed with mere rhetoric, with angry preaching. The nation was manifestly in trouble, for example, in the way that it educates its young. Chris Whittle and his Edison Project offered an unusual, high-tech approach to overhauling the educational system, but Americans sensed that their difficulties were broad and deep.

The real problems of American women and mothers would not be solved by appeals to a domestic paradigm (father working, mother at home caring for the children) that actuality had left more and more behind. The debate about women's roles continued. Susan Faludi's book *Backlash: The Undeclared War Against American Women* argued that a counterrevolution in recent years has been subverting the earlier gains of feminism. Nor could Americans repress their anxiety, made clear throughout the presidential campaign, about the lack of health care they could afford. The country was intent on basics; economic danger had sharply focused the American mind.

It was the beset and vulnerable mood of the American middle class that defined the year, and that in many ways determined the outcome of the presidential election. The sense of vulnerability might have induced Americans to stay with George Bush, the President they knew, rather than leaping to an unsafe unknown. Instead they (or at least 43% of the electorate) voted to change leadership and try what Clinton promised would be a different road. A certain amount of light—or at least a sense of expectation—broke in upon the American mood after the election. But almost all Americans felt that the sunshine was provisional. ∎

Family Va

lues

Republicans said they're lacking. Democrats said they're changing. And Americans, the families behind the ruckus, said "Enough!"

FAMILY VALUES. THE PHRASE SOUNDS LIKE THE name of a discount center in the suburbs. In a sense, that is what it means: the concept is an American warehouse of moral images, of inherited assumptions and brand-name ideals, of traditional wisdom, of pseudo memories of a Golden Age, of old class habits. Here some of the culture's finest aspirations are on display, its handcrafted, polished virtues and a few handsome, valuable antiques. But also a lot of shoulder pads, Tic Tacs and mouthwash.

It is a telling peculiarity of the family-values issue that it is so often framed in visual memories of television shows. Many Americans conjuring images of an earlier family ideal think of *Ozzie and Harriet* or *Leave It to Beaver* or *The Donna Reed Show*. They may even think that family values are something enacted in black and white: the home returned to after school, the milk and cookies, a rustling of Mother in full stiff skirts.

In the 1992 election campaign, family values crept out of the nation's attics and kitchens and televisions to command center stage in the presidential campaign, as Republicans and Democrats fought to define what kind of country Americans want and what kind of lives they should lead. Yet the term family values is inherently subjective, and its use in the campaign blended a yearning idealism with a breathtaking cynicism.

DAN QUAYLE VS. MURPHY BROWN

The uproar began with a speech by Dan Quayle in San Francisco. Arguing that the recent Los Angeles riots were caused in part by a "poverty of values" that included the acceptance of unwed motherhood, Quayle scored the title character of the *Murphy Brown* TV show, a divorced television anchorwoman. In the series, the character portrayed by Candice Bergen got pregnant and chose to have the baby, a boy, who was delivered on the previous Monday's episode, watched by 38 million Americans. "It doesn't help matters," said the Vice President, when Brown, "a character who supposedly epitomizes today's intelligent, highly paid professional woman" is portrayed as "mocking the impor-

Then and now: left, the cover of the program for the Democratic Convention of 1956; above, Murphy Brown and family

tance of fathers by bearing a child alone and calling it just another 'life-style choice.' " Diane English, the executive producer of the television show, had a well-machined answer for Quayle: "If the Vice President thinks it's disgraceful for an unmarried woman to bear a child, and he believes that a woman cannot adequately raise a child without a father, then he'd better make sure abortion remains safe and legal."

Quayle, aides explained, meant to stir a debate over family values and Hollywood's treatment of them. He succeeded. A New York *Daily News* headline set the tone: QUAYLE TO MURPHY BROWN: YOU TRAMP! Switchboards at the White House and on TV and radio talk shows lighted up with callers, pro and con. The White House flipflopped on the issue, with press secretary Marlin Fitzwater at first criticizing Murphy Brown for the "glorification of life as an unwed mother," then later telling reporters that the TV character was "demonstrating pro-life values, which we think are good."

President Bush declined to criticize the show, but praised Quayle's speech in a private phone call. Before long the President followed Quayle onto the family-values bandwagon, claiming in a speech that "we need a nation closer to the Waltons than the Simpsons." Hollywood had the last word on that score, however, when Bart Simpson opened his show the following week by claiming, "We're just like the Waltons; we're praying for the end of the Depression too."

CONVENTIONAL VALUES

Convinced they had touched a nerve with the American public, the Republicans conjured up family values at their convention and turned the theme to powerful political effect. Their Houston show was gaudy—a hellfire tent meeting dissolving to a '50s television sitcom with flags and confetti and sometimes tinny modulations.

The family-values part of the Republican production was, as they kept saying of Bill Clinton, relentlessly slick. It depended on a sort of grieving, part-nostalgic assumption that Americans live amid unwholesome aliens (homosexual teachers who want to proselytize, condom distributors, abortion-mongers, she-devil lawyers named Hillary) in a postlapsarian age, after some immense moral fall (whenever or whatever that may have been), something that has gone hugely wrong in American life. As Marilyn Quayle said of the '60s (in a thinly veiled barb at Bill Clinton), "Not everyone demonstrated, dropped out, took drugs . . . or dodged the draft."

It is far from a new theme in U.S. history. In 1971 a young White House speechwriter, Patrick J. Buchanan, wrote a memo to President Richard Nixon suggesting that the theme be used as a weapon. His campaign strategy: cut the country and Democratic Party in half, and pick off "far the larger half." The Republicans told America that year that George McGovern meant "acid, abortion and amnesty." Nixon's "half" in the 1972 election was a landslide.

Now, 21 years later, Pat Buchanan rose before the delegates in Houston to declare what he called "a cultural war" and try to help tear off a fat half of America for George Bush. A '50s kind of week in several ways: Buchanan eerily reproduced the punitive, menacing quality of his boyhood hero, Senator Joseph R. McCarthy of Wisconsin. The role of threat to the American essence used to be played by communism. But moral squalor at home would do as well. Buchanan pounded at "the agenda that Clinton & Clinton [meaning Bill and Hillary] would impose on America: abortion on demand, a litmus test for the Supreme Court, homosexual rights, discrimination against religious schools, women in combat units . . ."

Buchanan glared like a Jesuit prefect of discipline and

stabbed the air. His rendition was family values in the bully's mode—an appeal to visceral prejudices, not to American ideals. Barbara Bush and the tableau of Bush children and grandchildren transmitted a softer version, a kind of Pepperidge Farm, white-bread appeal of handsome plenty.

RHETORIC AND REALITY

To approach the family-values question—which will outlast the 1992 election campaign and continue to inform America's political and social dialogue for years to come—it may be necessary to remember the formula of F. Scott Fitzgerald. He said the sign of a first-rate intelligence is the ability to retain two mutually contradictory ideas in the mind at the same time and still be able to function. The two mutually contradictory but simultaneously valid ideas involved here are these:

1) The issue of family values is the last refuge of a scoundrel—or of a threatened Republican incumbent. The issue is almost by definition a smoke screen, and a manipulation of closeted fears and prejudices. The Republicans were wary about emphasizing race in the campaign, sensitive to criticism of the way they used Willie Horton in 1988. And they had been making progress in attracting black middle-class supporters. So they switched their emphasis to family values with a sexual subtext: Murphy Brown, out-of-the-closet gay militancy, condom distribution in the schools, sexual flamboyance in publicly funded art projects, and so on. Dan Quayle and others working the values circuit liked to encourage the feeling that the American id was dangerously seeping up through the floorboards: Clamp down with the superego.

Further, family values, a flashy issue of opportunity, has about it a certain eloquent irrelevance, something like the old waving of the bloody shirt or the snake-oil vending that has always gone on in American politics. Another suspect side of family-values mongering: Why are so many conservatives, champions of individual freedom, so hellbent on coercing people to march in lockstep? Why does the authoritarian impulse win out over the libertarian?

And yet:

2) The subject on another level is profoundly relevant. It addresses cultural divides in American life that must be sorted out if the nation is to pro-

"We need a nation closer to the Waltons than the Simpsons."

—George Bush

"It doesn't help matters when prime-time TV has Murphy Brown . . . bearing a child alone and calling it 'just another life-style choice.'"

—Dan Quayle

"If [he] thinks it's disgraceful for an unmarried woman to bear a child . . . then he'd better make sure abortion remains safe and legal."

—Diane English, *Murphy Brown* creator

"We're just like the Waltons. We're praying for the end of the Depression too."

—Bart Simpson

ceed coherently. Although raised by opportunists seeking votes, the issue of family values goes to the soul of what kind of country Americans want and what kind of lives they live. The issue in the campaign represented more than mere partisan struggle. It was part of the nation's effort to assimilate—in the deepest sense to domesticate, to understand, to control—changes in American society over the past two generations: to deal with the consequences of sexual revolution, of women's liberation, of huge multicultural immigration from non-European sources; with the devastation caused by the drug trade; with the loss of America's long absolute postwar pre-eminence; with the fragmentation of the family. It was even a reflection of the baby boom generation's coming of age, having families and changing their moral perspective from individual self-gratification to a sobered emphasis on family.

In other words, it was not enough to dismiss the family-values issue as a political ploy in a tough Republican year.

In a TIME/CNN poll taken in mid-August, 71% agreed that "there is something morally wrong with the country at this time." Almost as many agreed that "television and other media . . . reflect a permissive and immoral set of values, which are bad for the country."

REPUBLICANS VS. DEMOCRATS

Republicans and Democrats often mean something quite different when they talk about family values. The Republicans point toward a cultural ideal (two-parent heterosexual households, hard work, no pornography, a minimal tolerance of the aberrant). Conservatives say Change the culture. Democrats think of family values as matters that might be addressed by government policy— which was precisely Dan Quayle's complaint. Conservatives uphold the private realm, Democrats the public realm. Conservatives stress individual responsibility and changing behavior to correct the problem; liberals are inclined to think first of programs to mitigate the bad effects of trends such as unwed motherhood.

During the Democratic Convention, Bill Clinton and Al Gore staged a sort of pre-emptive celebration of family values, claiming the issue for themselves. Clinton often sounded virtually Republican in his insistence on personal responsibility. "Our families have values," he said in his acceptance speech. "Our government doesn't."

Much Republican rhetoric posits a model of the family that is becoming rarer in reality. Almost all family values have to do with children, with how to make them happy and give them safe, decent lives. The real debate for Americans, says social historian Barbara Dafoe Whitehead, should concern "what all adults would give up to secure a childhood of innocence and freedom." Every expert and practically every citizen agree that children are better off being raised in a family with two parents. For various reasons, that is less and less the model of American child rearing.

Dan Quayle had a powerful point when he encouraged individual responsibility and morality. His argument ran aground here and there on free-market paradoxes: the unfettered market is unerring, but the free market in television produces two gay men in bed together in prime time (*thirtysomething* back in 1989).

Often the targets and emphases of the Republicans' family-values campaigns seem a bit off. What worries parents most is a sense that they have little control over the world in which their children are growing up, over its temptations, its drugs, its overheated sex, its atmosphere of astonishing casual violence. On the family-values dais in Houston, after Bush's acceptance speech, Arnold Schwarzenegger was a conspicuous honored guest. In the first few minutes of *Terminator 2*, Schwarzenegger, in order to steal someone's motorcycle, drives a long-bladed knife through a man's shoulder, pinning him to a pool table, and fries another man's hands and face on a restaurant griddle. Ten-year-olds watch Schwarzenegger's disgusting violence and absorb it as if it were normal, acceptable and heroic. The deeper energy in the values argument arises from parents' perspective upon the future. It makes them angry. And it ensures that this issue will continue to trouble Americans long after the Bush-Quayle and Clinton-Gore buttons have joined Ozzie and Harriet in the country's mental scrapbook. ∎

"Our families have values. Our government doesn't."

—Bill Clinton

"Not everyone demonstrated, dropped out, took drugs . . . or dodged the draft."

—Marilyn Quayle

NOT SINCE KING HENRY VIII BROKE WITH THE PAPACY 458 years ago had the normally decorous Church of England known such passion as it did on Nov. 11, when it swept away by a margin of two votes the rule that only men may serve as Anglican priests. Despite pleas for prayer and calm, the controversy will echo throughout the Anglican Communion, and reverberate through all of Christianity, for years to come. On one side are those who believe Christ's church is damaged when half its members are denied the chance to use their God-given gifts. On the other are those, including the leadership of the Roman Catholic Church, who believe that the male priesthood was instituted by Jesus Christ himself when he called 12 men as his Apostles, and thus cannot be altered. Activists consider the debate over the status of women to be one of Christendom's great and historic transformations.

As fate (or some other author) would have it, the American Catholic bishops were gathered in Washington at the time of the Anglican vote to approve an official letter on the role of women in the church, the product of nine years of attempts to straddle the demands of conservatives in Rome and feminists in the U.S. on such subjects as whether women can be priests and whether sexism is sin.

After agreeing to prepare the document in 1983, the bishops made an elaborate effort to hear out alienated women. The first draft in 1988 was filled with accounts of their distress and a call for women to be allowed to serve as deacons, performing ministerial functions. But the bishops soon faced a backlash from traditionalist women and antifeminist nuns. Three drafts later, the bishops emerged with a diluted version of the letter that satisfied no one. The angry left called it "almost laughable," and the angry right called it "an embarrassment." The bishops gave the letter only 55.5% support, far short of the 66% needed for approval; it will be issued as a "committee document."

The Vatican may consider feminism a faddish outside force that will dwindle one day, but in the U.S., and to a degree in Western Europe, it is an entrenched force in secular society and, increasingly, in Catholic parishes. The problem is that the women's-rights crusade is more and more enmeshed in projects of social, moral and theological reconstruction that have divided the churches. If the new Christian feminism is to succeed in the long term, many church people feel, it must not only claim power and authority for women but also demonstrate that gender equality enhances the church's spiritual and moral strength. ■

Face of the future? Anglican bishop Jane Dixon.

Feminism transforms religion as a second Reformation sweeps through Christianity

WOMEN
Challenge the Church

Reinventing America's Schools

Grand visions—and small societies—offer bold new paths for U.S. education

EDUCATION EXPERTS RARELY AGREE, BUT on one point they have reached consensus: America's public school system needs an overhaul. In 1992, two innovative visions of the schoolroom of the future captured their attention. The Edison Project was the brainchild of a wealthy media mogul, Microsociety schools of a frustrated former high school teacher.

THE EDISON PROJECT

Media millionaire Chris Whittle plans to create a new system of private schooling that he hopes will produce a smarter generation of American kids—and make him and his partners a profit as well. He also expects to inspire—indeed, compel—the existing public school system to change the way it instills knowledge. By year's end Whittle's enterprise was little more than an ambitious notion, yet it had already begun to attract some high-level talent: Yale University President Benno Schmidt resigned his post in May to head the venture.

The plan, called the Edison Project, envisions a nationwide chain of at least 100 for-profit grammar schools by 1996, serving 150,000 students. By the end of this decade, additional campuses would open, providing day care and primary and secondary education for 2 million students. Tuition would not exceed the $5,500 current average spent on each child now in public education.

A team of experts from the fields of education, business and journalism has been working out the details of the school system. They dismiss the notion that the only way to impart knowledge is to place a teacher in front of a small group. Each Whittle school would be linked by closed-circuit television to a central studio, which might result in a 1–to–1 million teacher-to-student ratio. Interactive electronic data banks would allow students to do comprehen-

THE EDISON PROJECT Media visionary Chris Whittle (standing) and former Yale president Benno Schmidt hope to create a nationwide system of affordable, effective private schools.

sive research on their own. Notebook computers would be as common as lunch boxes.

Over the next two years, the team will design an ambitious core curriculum, which will assume that today's high school education could be completed by a Whittle pupil by the age of 12. The first schools will initially accept children only from three months to six years of age. With each succeeding year, another class can be added, as the system grows along with its first generation of students. Whittle is leaning toward a "campus" approach for the schools, with all grades (including day-care facilities) located at the same site. Working parents are to be offered flexible class times to accommodate their schedules. Admission would be open to everyone; to broaden access, 20% of students would be given full scholarships. Whittle plans effectively to redistribute wealth from richer schools to districts populated mainly by the poor. Though he denies it, many observers

MICROSOCIETY SCHOOLS Students and staff assemble for a "town portrait" in Yonkers, New York. Mornings are devoted to traditional classes, afternoons to putting the lessons to work.

believe his schools cannot return a profit—while hitting the target annual tuition of $5,500—unless some future form of the Bush Administration School Choice plan, which would give parents tuition vouchers for both public and private schools, is adopted. Bill Clinton opposed vouchers for private schools in his campaign.

Some of the planned innovations seem driven by the need to cut costs. Teachers might make up only 30% of the total instructional force. The private schools would try to harness the talents of pupils in a variety of ways, including expecting students to tutor their peers as a way to develop leadership ability. Parents could be asked to work one day a month on a volunteer basis, helping out in the day-care center or study hall.

The teachers who join the new schools would be asked to exchange the security of tenure for a potentially lucrative equity stake in the company. Their base salary would be augmented by performance bonuses, a feature that could attract

"We [teachers] usually tell kids to sit down. Shut up. Get in line. But kids love to play. What Microsociety does is get them to role-play life."

the type of highly motivated, career-oriented men and women who today tend to shun teaching in favor of better-paying professions.

Whittle has already rankled many traditionalists with his profitable Channel One television network. That controversial venture provides a 12-minute morning newscast, complete with two minutes of commercials, to 7.8 million students each weekday. "I dread the thought of the profit motive infiltrating a noble area of public aspiration," says educator Jonathan Kozol. "Do we really want to give that power to Chris Whittle?"

"The motive of profit and the motive for public good are not mutually exclusive," says Whittle, a stylish 44-year-old who sports fancy bow ties and a shaggy hairstyle. "We are a private institution with a public mission." He is confident his new schools will benefit students, teachers and parents—and stay ahead of potential competitors. "Twenty years from now, there will be three or four major private providers of education," he says. "We will be just the first to get there."

MICROSOCIETY SCHOOLS

Imagine a school where children learn math by holding jobs, paying taxes and owning businesses that sell everything from pompom pencils to potpourri pillows. A school where students study logic and law by taking their peers to court and fining them in the school's own currency. A school where kids come to understand politics by drawing up their own constitution, drafting laws and deciding which days of the week baseball caps may be worn to class. Imagine, in short, a school where civics is not just a course but a continuous experience in playing with the building blocks of modern society. In five American elementary schools—two in Massachusetts and three in New York—such experiments already exist. Called "Microsociety," these programs bear as much resemblance to the standard neighborhood school—with its

traditional textbooks, work sheets and lesson plans—as fiber-optic communication does to sending smoke signals.

Microsociety is the dream child of George Richmond, a painter, teacher, author and acclaimed educator whose first job, at a Brooklyn elementary school in 1967, was a rookie teacher's nightmare. In the end, the young idealist from Yale threw up his hands and gave birth to his thesis: if discipline, willpower and the force of reason couldn't hook students, maybe freedom and responsibility would. Grades were a basic dilemma. Nowhere else, Richmond realized, were people expected to work without compensation. An A-plus could not be saved, or invested, or traded for something of value. That was how a teacher with a deep belief in the value of learning for its own sake began paying his students—in fake money—for completed assignments, good marks and perfect attendance. Students then used their profits to start up ventures: a postal system, a comic book, a loan agency. Disputes eventually led to the creation of laws, police, courts and a constitutional convention (democracy triumphed over a police state by a single vote). As they began to discover the relevance of reading and arithmetic through managing their miniature society, Richmond's students also discovered in themselves an enthusiasm for education—and a hunger for more.

Richmond wrote a book about his experience and eventually helped launch the first school based entirely on his Microsociety model in an empty library in Lowell, Massachusetts, in 1981. By 1987, the school's students were testing two years above the national norm in both reading and math. Then in 1990, 13 eighth-graders passed first-year college-level exams, again in reading and math. School attendance hovers around 96%, and during the past six years only five children have dropped out.

Under the Microsociety model, the schoolday is split in two. The morning is devoted to traditional classes in history, science, English and math. In the afternoon students put the lessons to work. They memorize multiplication tables not only to score well on problem sets but also so they can keep double-entry books, write checks, bill customers and complete financial audits. Skeptics have been worried that the Microsociety's heavy emphasis on grownup concerns like money, taxes and employment might shunt children onto a fast track to adulthood. Teachers rebut such claims by pointing out that the program taps one of childhood's most salient pleasures, the impulse to play, and harnesses it in the service of absorbing knowledge. "Think about what we usually tell kids when they come into school," says Fred Hernandez, a principal in Yonkers, New York. " 'Sit down. Shut up. Get in line.' That's counterproductive, because kids love to play. What Micro does is get them to role-play life." ∎

The War Against Feminism

Provocative new books by Susan Faludi and Gloria Steinem call the women's movement to arms

SUSAN FALUDI, 32, IS A SOFT-spoken, sharp-penned, Pulitzer-prizewinning reporter for the *Wall Street Journal* who spent four years writing *Backlash: The Undeclared War Against American Women*. In 552 crowded pages, Faludi constructed a thesis out of alarming though sometimes selective use of statistics bound together with ideological glue, designed to explain why many women turned against feminism in the 1980s. In 1992 her book not only became an unexpected best seller, it also became a staple of the op-ed pages, one of those landmark books that shape the opinions of America's opinion shapers.

Faludi made an unlikely polemicist. Smart, shy, with a self-deprecating manner, she claimed to be more comfortable in front of a terminal than a camera. An alumna of Harvard, the Miami *Herald* and the Atlanta *Constitution*, she left the *Wall Street Journal*, where she won a Pulitzer Prize in 1991, in order to handle the flood of speaking requests generated by her book.

More interesting still, Faludi's book topped out at No. 2 on the New York *Times* best-seller list, right behind a new book by Gloria Steinem. Many critics dismissed *Revolution from Within*, Steinem's treatise on the political implications of the self-esteem movement, as an exercise in squishy New Age thumb sucking. But as she toured shopping malls, Steinem was being mobbed by crowds. Something must have happened in the climate of relations between men and women for these books to have had such an impact.

What readers may have been looking for is an explanation of why, as reported by a TIME/CNN poll in February, 63% of American women do not consider themselves feminists. Faludi's answer: women reject feminism because of a backlash against it—a highly effective, often misleading campaign to discredit its goals, distort its message and make women question whether they really want equality after all.

Throughout history, Faludi argues, anytime women tried to loosen their corsets and breathe more freely, they were met with a suffocating counterattack. In the 1980s this

Two generations of feminists: Faludi and Steinem

backlash surfaced in the Reagan White House, the courts, Hollywood and, above all, the mass media, whose collective message to women went something like this: Feminism is your worst enemy. All this freedom is making you miserable, unmarriageable, infertile, unstable. Go home, bake a cake, quit pounding on the doors of public life and all your troubles will go away.

Faludi's book set off firecrackers across the political battlefield. Conservatives applauded her when she exposed the intellectual laziness of the mainstream press; liberals cheered when she exposed the hypocrisy of conservatives who put their own children in day care so they can travel around the country telling women to be homemakers. Columnist John McLaughlin, no special friend of the women's movement, called Faludi "the best thinker of the year," and the National Book Critics Circle handed her its prize for nonfiction.

The main reason for the book's success was the resonance of Faludi's questions. Were all the movies and television shows and advertisements that featured blissful mothers and frazzled career women intended, either consciously or subconsciously, to sow doubts in women's minds about their real goals? Or, as her critics countered, did the mass media merely pick up on concerns that already existed and touch a nerve that had been rubbed raw by a generation of out-of-touch feminist leaders?

The family-values agenda, Faludi says, was the rhetorical basis on which Reagan and Bush and scores of other Republicans swept into office in 1980, thanks to the votes of millions of women as well as men. Feminism, meanwhile, lost many of its government sponsors. Support for the Equal Rights Amendment reached 60% in 1981, only to be defeated the following year; the number of women seeking out battered-women's shelters soared, but federal funding shrank and the Office of Domestic Violence was shut down.

Faludi's chronicle of the backlash begins in 1986, after major magazines and newspapers trumpeted stories on an unpublished Harvard-Yale marriage study. The researchers claimed that a college-educated woman of 30 had only

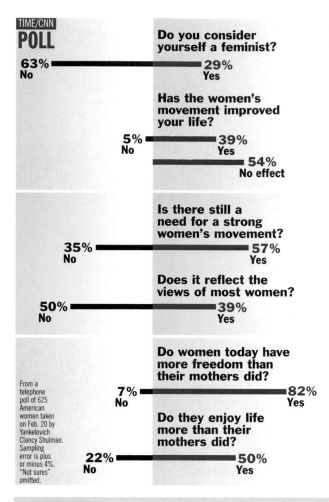

Do you consider yourself a feminist?

63%
No

29%
Yes

Has the women's movement improved your life?

5%
No

39%
Yes

54%
No effect

Is there still a need for a strong women's movement?

35%
No

57%
Yes

Does it reflect the views of most women?

50%
No

39%
Yes

Do women today have more freedom than their mothers did?

7%
No

82%
Yes

Do they enjoy life more than their mothers did?

22%
No

50%
Yes

From a telephone poll of 625 American women taken on Feb. 20 by Yankelovich Clancy Shulman. Sampling error is plus or minus 4%. "Not sures" omitted.

a 20% chance of finding a husband; by age 35 it was 5%; and by 40 she was "more likely to be killed by a terrorist" than make it to the altar, in *Newsweek's* memorable analogy. Faludi decided to write about "the marriage crunch," only to discover what demographers already knew: the figures were based on unorthodox calculations of unrepresentative samples. What bothered her was not just that the numbers were wrong; it was also that many of the stories read like morality tales, whispering threats about the cost of postponing marriage in favor of having a career. Fear of spinsterhood stormed into the popular culture, giving birth to a whole generation of desperate movie heroines, frantic sitcom spinsters, myriad self-help books.

Struck by the eagerness of the media to hype dubious scholarship, Faludi examined other trend stories to find their hidden message. She found fault with infertility studies, "toxic day-care stories," the notion of the Mommy Track and the *Good Housekeeping* ads of the New Traditionalist. To her, they all implied that the postfeminist woman was the one who had sampled having it all and preferred to give most of it up. In fact, the pattern of the '80s was dictated by economic reality: 69% of women 18 to 64 work today, in contrast to 33% in 1950. Although Faludi herself was occasionally guilty of the very trend she opposes—stretching data to support an argument—many readers agreed with Ann Jones, an author and professor at Mount Holyoke College in Massachusetts : "The big picture is there, and the big picture is accurate."

That big picture of the backlash, according to Faludi, has more to do with the messages that permeate everyday life, through television and movies, through fashions and advertising. It is on issues of symbol and representation that

Bucking the Backlash

Faludi and Steinem on mudslinging, labels, and "the death of feminism"

Q. *In dealing with the backlash against feminism, is it best to fight it head on or to repackage the feminist message, perhaps talking about "family" instead of "women's" issues?*

Steinem: That's a mistake. It renders women invisible. This is a revolution, not a public relations movement. You have to speak to the constituency. If you say "family issues" to most women, it's like going back to the past. To make changes, you need new language.

Faludi: All family issues should not be women's issues. They should be human issues. What bothers me is the implication that women have to prove they are good mothers before they can ask for anything else, and the only way they can ask for something else is through children.

Q. *Since most women today embrace the goals of the women's movement, why are so many of them reluctant to embrace the feminist label?*

Steinem: Women have two problems with the label. The first is that people don't know what it means. If they look it up in the dictionary and see that feminism just means the full economic, social and political equality of women, they'll agree. But the second is that people do know what it

means. If you say, "I'm for equal pay," that's a reform. But if you say, "I'm a feminist," that's equality for all females—a transformation of society.

Q. *Is that realization the result of countless headlines announcing the "death of feminism"?*

Steinem: That's always the way change is dealt with. The first big "death of feminism" headline was in 1969. Then the Equal Rights Amendment was either going to change Western civilization as we know it and destroy the family, or it was unnecessary because we already had equality.

Q. *Is anyone who criticizes your books necessarily an antifeminist?*

Faludi: No, as long as we're talking about responsible criticism. But so much of the criticism seems to be about a book I didn't write. I'm charged with saying there's a male

Faludi and the newly bred backlash theorists have the most fun and start the liveliest arguments over who really represented the Image of Woman in the 1980s.

This insidious new image, Faludi claims, was exemplified by Hope Steadman, the blissful, breast-feeding mother of *thirtysomething* who provided a postfeminist contrast to the "neurotic spinster [and] ball-busting single career woman." Or the Dress for Success models, who, in Faludi's lethal description, "trip down the runway in stiletto heels, hands snug in dainty white gloves. Their briefcases swing like Easter baskets, feather light; they are, after all, empty."

It makes an interesting parlor game for contrarian readers to provide the counterimages, women who successfully conveyed an image of strength and fulfillment, from Murphy Brown, Roseanne Arnold and Madonna to designer Donna Karan with her comfortable professional clothes. Feminist critics view Faludi's book as flawed and condescending because it treats women as victims, passively accepting what the culture imposes on them. Conservative critics charge that Faludi falsely conjured up a junta of antifeminists who conspired to force women to buy lacy underwear, watch reactionary movies, quit their jobs, mind the kids and do laundry.

Faludi, in fact, takes pains to make her targets more subtle. "The backlash is not a conspiracy, with a council dispatching agents from some central control room, nor are the people who serve its ends often aware of their role," she explains. "Some even consider themselves feminists."

Contrary to Faludi's backlash thesis, the signs that women are having second thoughts are not purely an invention of the media. In 1985, given the choice between having a job or staying home to care for the family, 51% of women preferred to work, according to the Roper Organization; by 1991 that number had fallen to 43%, and 53% said they would rather stay home.

Any social commentator who shatters myths and exposes hypocrisy has performed a useful service, and Faludi is no exception. She has inspired men and women to take a new look at the messages they absorb, messages that act as barriers to understanding or to justice. But it is also appropriate to argue, as founding feminist Betty Friedan does, that feminism also needs to "transcend sexual politics and anger against men to express a new vision of family and community. We must go from wallowing in the victim's state to mobilizing the new power of women and men for a larger political agenda on the priorities of life." Such conciliatory rhetoric is not backsliding. It too is a call to arms. ∎

VOICE OF THE BACKLASH: Phyllis Schlafly at a pro-life meeting at the Republican Convention. Steinem: "We've reached the point where the movement is powerful enough to make jobs for antifeminist women."

conspiracy out there to put women down. Anyone who says that can't possibly have read the book. I say about 14 times that I don't mean there's a conspiracy. This is not a book about hating men.

Q. *Does it matter that most of the mudslingers are women?*

Steinem: We've reached the point where the movement is powerful enough to make jobs for antifeminist women. I used to think that about Phyllis Schlafly. I thought, Well, at least she has a job.

Q. *You've been criticized for patronizing women by saying they were sheeplike in following orders and going back into the home, without understanding that many may have wanted to stay home.*

Faludi: I certainly don't regard women as sheep, and I believe I have far more respect for my own sex than the average TV programmer. To say that women and men have been manipulated by popular culture is not the same as portraying women as mindless victims. It's simply recognizing the power of the mass media.

Q. *What is the difference between the women's movement today and the one that existed a decade or so ago?*

Steinem: Throughout the 1970s, the movement was more consciousness raising in the classic sense. That still goes on, but now we're ready for institutional change. Women are beginning to connect our everyday lives to changing work patterns and even the government. It's a big leap to think that what happens to you every day—in the secretarial pool, in the shopping center—has anything to do with who's in the Senate or the White House. The connection is just beginning to be forged. We are only 25 years into what by all precedent is a century of feminism. But once you get a majority consciousness change, you also get a backlash. The future depends entirely on what each of us does every day. After all, a movement is only people moving.

SCIENCE

Searching to unlock nature's puzzles,
scientists explored the hidden birth of galaxies,
the bizarre life of giant organisms,
and the death of a single man 3,500 years ago

By J. MADELEINE NASH

SCIENTISTS DELIGHT IN IDENTIFYING HIDDEN PAT-
terns that link seemingly random events. But in
1992 even they were confounded by the variety of
puzzles nature managed to contrive. For starters,
there was all that weird weather. Torrential rains immobi-
lized places like Paris and Hong Kong and washed away
entire villages in Pakistan and India. The Middle East experienced the coldest, wettest winter in decades, while
southern Africa chalked up its worst drought in half a century. In the U.S., showers that normally moisten the Corn-
belt early in the growing season came instead at harvest
time. Hurricane Andrew left Florida in shambles. A howling nor'easter swept through New Jersey and New York,
swamping streets and stalling subways.

What forces conspired to produce so many freakish outbursts? Leading the list of likely culprits was El Niño, a
huge puddle of warm water that periodically forms in the
Pacific Ocean and alters weather patterns across half the
globe. Atmospheric scientists could not decide whether the
much anticipated greenhouse effect exerted any influence
or not. Perhaps, some speculated, the sun-blocking gas and
ash heaved into the stratosphere by Mount Pinatubo in the
Philippines countered the overall warming trend by tem-
porarily tugging the climate in an opposite direction. The
lingering legacy of Mount Pinatubo almost certainly contributed to an ominous increase in the size of the ozone
hole that appeared over Antarctica last year.

Equally unexpected, and just as alarming, was the underground jolt that nature delivered to Southern California, where a powerful earthquake centered near the small
town of Landers swiped a 70-km (45-mile) slash through
the Mojave Desert. In December, as aftershocks continued
to unnerve the region, seismologists warned residents of
the populous Los Angeles basin that they might as well get
ready for the long-feared Big One. By rearranging subterra-
nean stress fields, the Landers temblor had quadrupled the
odds of another large earthquake in the region, quite possi-

bly one that would rupture the mighty San Andreas, the
state's largest and most dangerous fault.

More challenges to scientific ingenuity came in the
form of disease-causing microbes. Legions of them have
quietly developed resistance to the miracle drugs known as
antibiotics. These superbugs, medical researchers warned,
are now powering a resurgence of old scourges, among
them tuberculosis, meningitis, streptococcal pneumonia
and a wide spectrum of staphylococcus infections.

The AIDS virus, pictured above, right, also extended its
reach in 1992, particularly in Asia, where heterosexual
transmission has emerged as the primary route of conta-
gion. By the year 2000, the World Health Organization
warned, 30 million men, women and children will be infected with AIDS, for which there is yet no vaccine, no cure.
Last year medical researchers began seriously considering
the possibility that the AIDS virus is not the sole villain, but
requires the assistance of some mysterious cofactor, perhaps a primitive bacterium known as a mycoplasma.

Although momentarily stymied in their battle against
AIDS, scientists have reason to hope they will ultimately
prove victorious. They know that through persistent and
clever interrogation, nature can frequently be persuaded to
reveal many of its deepest secrets. In the ethereal realm of
pure science, for example, 1992 delivered a rare and stunning glimpse of what the cosmos was like 15 billion years
ago, long before stars, let alone planets, had time to form.
NASA's Cosmic Background Explorer satellite snapped a
picture of giant clouds of gas on the very edge of the known
universe that were the progenitors of galaxies. Even the
most prosaic scientists were moved by the import of these
primordial concentrations of matter. Without them, it is
unlikely that the Milky Way and the humans who inhabit
it could ever have evolved. "If you're religious," exclaimed
astrophysicist George Smoot of the University of California, Berkeley, "it's like looking at God."

For astronomy in general, 1992 was filled with surprises,

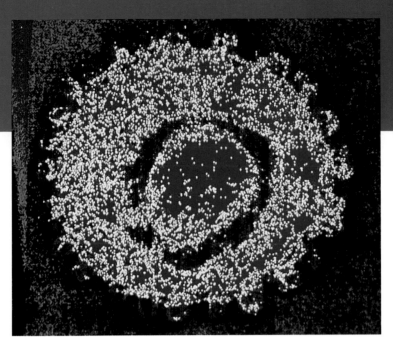

many of them delivered by the Hubble Space Telescope. Despite its blurred vision, the Hubble managed to glimpse a hint of planets surrounding newborn stars and bright spots of star formation that may represent the most distant galaxies yet. The Hubble also brought into fuzzy focus a likely black hole that sits like a whirlpool in the center of NGC 4261, a galaxy 45 million light-years from earth. On the ground, innovative techniques for making large telescope mirrors heralded another astounding era of astronomical discovery.

Medicine too had plenty to celebrate, especially remarkable progress in the treatment of depression and schizophrenia. At long last, new drugs have begun correcting the chemical imbalances that cause these afflictions and, in the process, are miraculously reclaiming lost lives. One poignant awakening occurred last spring when dozens of young adults, their schizophrenic delusions banished by the drug clozapin, donned suits and party dresses to celebrate the high school prom most of them had never been able to enjoy. New understanding of central-nervous-system biochemistry has also begun to revolutionize the treatment of spinal-cord injuries and stroke.

ON THE ENVIRONMENTAL FRONT, SCIENTIFIC STUDies continued to lend both urgency and legitimacy to a broad spectrum of concerns, including ozone depletion, global warming and a catastrophic extinction of plant and animal life around the globe. Last summer environmentalists and political leaders from 178 countries met in Rio de Janeiro to discuss the dispiriting ledger of threats to the natural world. Long on rhetoric and short on action, the Earth Summit appears to have been one of those rare failures that, paradoxically, may have succeeded—by laying the groundwork for future accord. In the U.S., consensus on environmental issues proved similarly elusive. Plans to protect the Chinook salmon and restore wolves to Yellowstone stirred up enormous controver-

sy, and environmentalists spent most of the year on the defensive. In the end, however, they succeeded in fighting off attempts to gut the Endangered Species Act and even managed to add 400 new species to the list.

Non-endangered species received their share of attention too. A Michigan fungus and a Utah aspen grove competed for the title of world's largest living organism. Fruits and vegetables in general got some long overdue respect. Simply by increasing daily intake of vitamin-rich foods, biochemists and nutritionists agreed, the aging U.S. population might be able to fight off cancer, heart disease and macular degeneration, a leading cause of blindness. For their part, allergy sufferers could rejoice that dust mites, pollen grains and all the other demons that torment them were brought to public attention. At the very least, greater understanding of the biological causes of wheezes and sneezes ensured a little more sympathy from relatives and friends. Scientists also gleaned fascinating insights into the biology of sexual identity, suggesting new answers to old questions: why, for example, it seems husbands never have to ask for directions and wives are always having to find their spouse's socks.

As always, the world of technology delivered some neat surprises, among them the electrifying comeback of the U.S. semiconductor industry and the very first broadcast of digital high-definition TV. Tiny video cameras and miniaturized instruments reduced the trauma associated with major surgery. New keyboard designs promised relief for computer users complaining of injured hands. And a copper ax 5,300 years old stirred appreciation for the technical sophistication of the celebrated Iceman and his Stone Age confederates. Last but not least, a molecular tool kit for delivering healthy genes to the diseased lung cells of cystic fibrosis patients was approved for experimental use. For the thousands who suffer from this inherited affliction, and for their families, 1992 can be said to have ended on an unusually felicitous note. ∎

CAN THE EARTH BE SAVED?

World leaders gathered at the Earth Summit in Rio to confront the planet's environmental ills, but a North-South clash thwarted the quest for meaningful action

FIRE Destruction of the environment is a global tragedy. In Brazil, rain forests are cleared and burned for farming; in Estonia, a cement plant spews pollutants into the atmosphere.

MORE THAN 100 HEADS OF STATE SHOWED up—including Prime Minister John Major, Chancellor Helmut Kohl, Prime Minister Kiichi Miyazawa and, once he finally made up his mind to go, President George Bush. The Dalai Lama joined a delegation of clerics, artists and green-minded parliamentarians. Hundreds of native leaders, from American Indians to Malaysian tribesmen, represented the interests of the world's indigenous peoples. All told, tens of thousands of diplomats, scientists, ecologists, theorists, feminists, journalists, tourists and assorted hangers-on gathered in dozens of auditoriums and outdoor sites for nearly 400 official and unofficial events, among them an environmental technology fair, a scientific symposium and a meeting of mayors. Peter Max's art appeared on special postage stamps. A Robert Rauschenberg poster was slapped up on walls. Placido Domingo

headlined a star-studded musical tribute to the planet. And a full-size replica of a 9th century Viking ship sailed in from Norway carrying messages of goodwill from children all over the world.

If size and ambition were the measures of success, the United Nations Conference on Environment and Development, held in Rio de Janeiro in June, would take all the prizes. The so-called Earth Summit, more than two years in the making, was the largest and most complex conference ever held—bigger than the momentous meetings at Yalta, Potsdam and Versailles. Those summits carved up empires, drew new borders and settled world wars. The agenda for the Earth Summit was more far-reaching: it set out to confront not only the world's most pressing environmental problems, from global warming to deforestation, but poverty and underdevelopment as well. Rather than creating common ground, the summit concluded with the

adoption of a series of watered-down resolutions to be voluntarily enforced. It thus only highlighted the widening political chasm between developed and developing nations.

The first Earth Summit, 20 years ago in Stockholm, launched thousands of grass-roots conservation groups around the world and spawned environmental agencies and ministries in more than 115 nations. It was held in the shadow of the cold war, when the planet was divided into rival East and West blocs and preoccupied with the perils of the nuclear arms race. With the collapse of the East bloc and the thawing of the cold war, a fundamental shift in the global axis of power has occurred. Today the more meaningful division, especially on environmental issues, is not between East and West but between the "North" (Europe, North America and Japan) and the "South" (most of Asia, Africa and Latin America).

While there has been some environmental progress in individual countries, the state of the world has mostly gone downhill. Air pollution, a major issue at the Stockholm conference, has grown significantly worse in most cities. Even more alarming, it is now overshadowed by broad atmospheric changes, such as ozone depletion and the buildup of greenhouse gases. According to the Washington-based Worldwatch Institute, one of the hundreds of environmental pressure groups that advised the Earth Summit negotiators, the world has lost 200 million hectares (500 million acres) of trees since 1972, an area roughly one-third the size of the continental U.S. The world's farmers, meanwhile, have lost nearly 500 million tons of top-soil, an amount equal to the tillable-soil coverage of India and France combined. Lakes, rivers, even whole seas have been turned into sewers and industrial sumps. Tens of thousands of plant and animal species that shared the planet with us in 1972 have disappeared. And, perhaps most distressing, the world's population growth rate has continued to soar—an issue so entangled with religion it was barely addressed at the meeting.

NORTH "The American life-style is not up for negotiation," said a U.S. delegate to the presummit negotiations at the United Nations in New York City. The North claims the developing nations of the South are consuming irreplaceable resources to provide for their developing populations.

Displaying a new feistiness on environmental matters, a coalition of developing countries, called the Group of 77, put up a remarkably united front at the talks. From their point of view, it is the rich world's profligate consumption patterns—its big cars, refrigerators and climate-controlled shopping malls—that are the problem. "You can't have an environmentally healthy planet in a world that is socially unjust," said then President of Brazil Fernando Collor de Mello. Countered a U.S. representative to a presummit negotiating session: "They [the developing nations] are trying to lay a collective guilt trip on us. The American life-style is not up for negotiation."

The tensions between North and South, and the financial conflicts that underlie them, were most clearly addressed in a 600-plus-page blueprint for action called Agenda 21, which set out to specify the problems that the world will face well into the 21st century and how to pay for the solutions. In presummit meetings, Agenda 21 became the main forum for North-South wrangling on every topic imaginable. Among the key areas of dispute:

WHO TURNED UP THE HEAT?

Most scientists agree that all the smoke and fumes and exhaust that humans generate will eventually alter the earth's climate. Those changes could be modest, or they could trigger coastal flooding, interior droughts, mass exoduses

and pockets of starvation. What irks some developing nations, in particular Brazil, is that many people who are worried about global warming point their fingers at the release of carbon dioxide from the burning of rain forests. The bigger threats are the CO_2 and other greenhouse gases produced in the industrial countries by the burning of fossil fuels. In per capita terms, individuals in the North generate nearly 10 times as much CO_2 from energy use as their counterparts in the South.

The problem for the long term is that people in developing countries want those consumer items that make life in the industrial world so comfortable, as well as environmentally costly—those private cars, refrigerators and air conditioners. A treaty to prevent climate change was to be the centerpiece of the Rio summit. But poor countries did not see why their plans for development should suffer in order to rectify a problem they did not create. Some rich nations did not want to sign on to anything that would threaten their life-styles or increase the cost of doing business. Trying to spur agreement, the European Community proposed cutting CO_2 emissions to 1990 levels by the year 2000, a relatively modest reduction. The U.S. steadfastly refused to consider any such rigid deadlines. The Bush Administration was worried that an arbitrary reduction in the output of CO_2 would mean a decline in industrial production and a further loss of jobs. The talks had just about reached an impasse when committee chairman Jean Ripert of France drew up a compromise text liberally sprinkled with what he called "constructive ambiguities." It requires nations to roll back greenhouse-gas emissions to "earlier levels" by the end of the decade and report periodically on their progress, but the target of reaching 1990 levels becomes merely a voluntary goal. That seemed to do the trick. Despite loud protests by environmentalists that the agreement was too weak, it was adopted.

WHO IS POISONING THE OCEANS?

Anyone who has been near the seashore lately—or listened to Jacques-Yves Cousteau on TV—knows that the oceans are a mess, littered with plastic and tar balls and rapidly losing fish. But the garbage dumps, the oil spills, the sewage discharges, the drift nets and the factory ships are only the most visible problems. The real threats to the oceans, accounting for 70% to 80% of all maritime pollution, are the sediment and contaminants that flow into the seas from land-based sources: topsoil, fertilizers, pesticides and all manner of industrial waste. Coral is particularly sensitive to sediment, and the reefs that fringe Asia, Australia and the Caribbean—and provide a home to many of the world's fish species—are already starting to die.

Every country contributes to the situation roughly in proportion to its size, although countries that are leveling their forests are making the runoff problem especially bad. Some ocean advocates called for a new global treaty that would deal specifically with land-based pollution. The U.S., on the other hand, favored strengthening international commitments to control land-based pollution, particularly at the national and regional levels. In the end, negotiators adopted the U.S. approach, agreeing that countries should commit themselves to cleaning up the seas but that it was premature to consider drafting a formal global treaty.

WHOSE WOODS ARE THESE?

Except for finances, no issue has divided North and South more sharply than the question of what to do about the world's remaining virgin forests. At the heart of the debate are the tropical rain forests—and a fundamental difference in how each side sees them. To industrial countries, they are a treasure trove of biodiversity and greenhouse-gas "sinks" that absorb CO_2 and thus help keep global warming in check. To developing nations, the forests are resources ripe for exploitation: potential farmland, a free source of fuel and a storehouse of exotic kinds of wood that command high prices overseas.

The Bush Administration had hoped to make deforestation a showcase issue going into Rio. The presummit discussions opened with a U.S.-inspired proposal for an outright ban on logging in tropical forests. But the developing countries retaliated by demanding that the language cover temperate and boreal (northern) forests as well. The move was clearly aimed at the U.S., which has strenuously resisted any scrutiny of the logging practices in publicly owned ancient forests in the Pacific Northwest.

The lines have been so sharply drawn on all the forest-protection issues that what was originally intended to be a legally binding forestry convention had been watered down months earlier to a nonbinding "statement of principles" that was adopted at Rio. Whether a full-fledged treaty will be negotiated later is still uncertain.

WHO NEEDS THESE SPECIES?

Not since the dinosaurs were killed off, say biologists, has the world experienced an extinction "spasm" like the man-made one that will wipe out 10% to 20% of the earth's estimated 10 million species of plants and animals by the year 2020. Since at least 50% of those species live in tropical rain forests, past efforts to save them have run into the usual lines of resistance from governments in the South, which resent any kind of meddling from the North. What makes the losses so unacceptable is that they are irreversible; once a species becomes extinct, it is gone forever.

Much of the debate in presum-

SOUTH "You can't have an environmentally healthy planet in a world that is socially unjust," insisted Fernando Collor de Mello, then President of Brazil. The South maintains it is the rich world's profligate consumption, from big cars to climate-controlled shopping malls, that is the problem.

TRASHED

Some of the 6.5 million tons of litter dumped in the oceans each year fouls the Peruvian shoreline, above. Growing population in coastal areas leads to more destruction of coastal habitats. The lemur from Madagascar, at left, is endangered; in the past 20 years, 1 million species have vanished from the world's tropical forests.

resource of the originating country. Nations would have control over who had access to their genetic resources, and if someone else found a way to make money from them, the originating country would collect royalties on each sale.

But in the most controversial event of the summit, President Bush refused to sign the biodiversity treaty, overruling his own appointee, Environmental Protection Agency head William Reilly. Bush was concerned that U.S. biotechnology companies, which want to fashion medicines and other products from genetic materials obtained in developing countries, might have to compensate those nations. The White House also did not approve of the mechanism proposed to distribute financial incentives to developing nations to protect endangered plants and animals.

Reilly, a true believer in the treaty, tried to help forge a compromise that would enable the U.S. to sign it, but the White House flatly refused to reconsider its position—a major embarrassment for Reilly in his dealings with fellow delegates in Rio.

In an effort to counter criticism on the biodiversity issue, Bush announced at Rio that the U.S. would contribute $150 million to programs that help developing countries preserve their forests. But the initiative rang hollow, given the Administration's encouragement of logging in ancient U.S. forests. Playing spoiler at the Earth Summit was a stunning role for the U.S., which after World War II was the driving force behind the creation of the United Nations and the World Bank. And the U.S. had a strong story to tell in such concrete measures as the Clean Air Act, transportation legislation, a pending energy bill and the ambitious Green Lights energy-conservation program. But instead of seizing leadership, the Bush Administration allowed European nations and Japan to be

mit meetings centered on the issue of who owns and controls the genetic information stored in those species. Traditionally, the benefits that came from genetic materials—seeds, specimens or drugs derived from plants and animals—went to whoever found a way to exploit them. Vanilla, for example, was a biological resource found only in Central America. It later became an important cash crop in Madagascar. Now a U.S. biotech company has developed a process to clone the vanilla flavor in a cell culture. If the firm sells the bioengineered version for less than natural vanilla and takes some of the market share, who will compensate the Madagascar farmers? Or the Central American Indians from whose lands the genetic material originated?

Before the meeting, it appeared likely that a legally binding treaty would be adopted that would include a provision making genetic materials of all kinds the sovereign

hailed as the summit's heroes for their willingness to support its agreements.

If any clear message came out of the meeting, it is that the 178 nations represented will all have to change if its agreements are to have any teeth. Most summit participants agree that the best hope for the future comes from changes in values prompted by grass-roots concerns. Maurice Strong, the summit's secretary-general, hopes that given the lack of leadership by governments, ordinary people will force politicians to live up to the obligations articulated at Rio. The more than 300,000 pledges by children to do something for the planet raise hopes that the next generation may mature with a deep awareness of the perils of waste and pollution. The question is whether they will learn that lesson in schools or whether it will be imposed upon them by a world run to ruin by their parents. ∎

The Real Power of Vitamins

New research shows they may help fight cancer, prevent heart disease and hold off the ravages of aging

I

T'S RAINING. FLOODING, TO BE PRECISE. BUT BUSI-ness is as brisk as ever at Mrs. Gooch's natural-foods market in West Los Angeles. As usual, traffic is backed up along Palms Boulevard as drivers wait for a spot in the store's parking lot. Inside, crowds jam the supplement section, which gleams with row upon row of small, white-capped vials. Here the pilgrims at the shrine of vitamins linger over labels, comparing brand names and dosages, trading health sermons and nutritional arcana. There are no fewer than 10 types and dosages of vitamin C to choose from, not to mention eight of vitamin E.

But for every true believer in the power of vitamins—and the U.S. has more devotees than any other country—there is an agnostic, a skeptic who insists that vitamins are the opiate of the people. Among the doubters are many doctors. They have been persuaded by decades of public health pronouncements, endorsed by the U.S. National Academy of Sciences and the National Institutes of Health, that claim people can get every nutrient they need from the food they eat. Popping vitamins "doesn't do you any good," sniffs Dr. Victor Herbert, a professor of medicine at New York City's Mount Sinai medical school. "We get all the vitamins we need in our diets. Taking supplements just gives you expensive urine."

Wavering in confusion between these two schools of thought are the vast majority of Americans, wondering whom to believe. But, thanks to new research, the haze is beginning to lift. And it unveils a surprise: more and more scien-tists are starting to suspect that traditional medical views of vitamins and minerals have been too limited. While researchers may not endorse the expansive claims of hard-core vitamin enthusiasts, evidence suggests that the nutrients play a much more complex role in assuring vitality and optimal health than was previously thought. Vitamins—often in doses much higher than usually recommended—may protect humans against a host of ills ranging from birth defects and cataracts to heart disease and cancer. Even more provocative are glimmerings that vitamins can stave off the normal ravages of aging.

Scientists have so far identified 13 organic substances that are commonly labeled vitamins. In the human body, they play a vital role in helping regulate the chemical reactions that protect cells and convert food into energy and living tissue. Some vitamins are produced within the body, but most must be ingested.

Mystique and faddish lore have long surrounded these essential biochemical compounds. Consider vitamins C and E. People have been gobbling vitamin C for 20 years in the certainty that it can cure the common cold, though evidence is still lacking. Vitamin E has been wildly popular for four decades because of its putative power to enhance sexual performance. In fact, studies indicate only that it is necessary for normal fertility in lab animals. More recently, B6 has won favor as a relief for premenstrual syndrome. Vitamin A is touted as a rejuvenator by people who mistakenly believe that it, like its synthetic relative Retin-A, can give wrinkled, mottled skin that youthful rosy glow.

It is just that hint of quackery that made vitamins a research backwater for years. Most reputable scientists steered clear, viewing the field as fringe medicine awash with kooks and fanatics. A researcher who showed interest could lose respect and funding. Certainly Linus Pauling

CAN YOU SURVIVE BY PILLS ALONE?

Can a "Jetson diet"–a futuristic feast of prefab pellets–supply all dietary needs? Vital nutrients like fiber and protein can be put into pills, but they would have to be taken in huge, impractical quantities. Food contains obscure nutrients that can't be put into safe pill form– and one more key ingredient–flavor!

ARE PILLS AS GOOD A SOURCE AS FOOD?

What about those who need a megadose of a particular vitamin? Pills made to digest easily–like gel caps–are as good as vegetables at delivering selected nutrients to the body, and may work better for those who refuse to eat their greens.

lost much of his Nobel-laureate luster when he began championing vitamin C back in 1970 as a panacea for everything from the common cold to cancer. Drug companies have been leery of committing substantial energy and money to studies, since the payoff is relatively small; vitamin chemical formulas are in the public domain and cannot be patented.

But attitudes have been shifting over the past few decades. Despite all the sneering, Pauling's speculations did get more scientists thinking about vitamins' impressive powers. As a class of compounds, they are known to produce hugely dramatic effects when missing from the diet: scurvy, pernicious anemia, rickets. What other exciting properties might they—or related compounds—have? Another driving force in the U.S. is the new "demographic imperative." With a rapidly aging population, America has moved its medical focus from treating acute illness to caring for chronic maladies like heart disease and cancer—a shift that has sent healthcare costs skyward.

Overriding all else, however, is the impact of scientific studies. Beginning in the 1970s, population surveys worldwide started to uncover a consistent link between diet and

health. A diet rich in fruits and vegetables, for instance, became associated with a lower incidence of cancer and heart disease. Researchers then turned to examining the data nutrient by nutrient, looking at minerals as well as vitamins, to see which are tied most closely with specific ailments. Low vitamin C intake appears to be associated with a higher risk of cancer, low levels of folic acid with a greater chance of birth defects, and high calcium consumption with a decreased danger of osteoporosis.

Intrigued by such clues, the National Institutes of Health, universities and other research organizations began funding laboratory and clinical investigations. By the late '80s, research exploring vitamins' potential in protecting against disease was on its way to respectability. Though the evidence is still preliminary, scientists are excited about several nutrients. Most of

DO OLDER PEOPLE HAVE DIFFERENT VITAMIN NEEDS?

Research suggests the elderly may need more of some vitamins than the young, including B6 and D. Medications can hinder vitamin absorption–and senior's flagging appetites can thwart vitamin intake.

DOES IT MATTER WHICH BRAND YOU BUY?

Most advertising claims are just hype, and pricing can seem as arbitrary as the pill color, but U.S. studies showed significant differences among brands in such areas as how fast a pill dissolves in the body. Stricter U.S. standards are due in 1993; even so, it's best to stick to brands sold by reputable stores.

the interest is being generated by a group of vitamins—C, E and beta carotene, the chemical parent of vitamin A—that are known as antioxidants. These nutrients appear to be able to defuse the volatile toxic molecules, known as oxygen free radicals, that are a byproduct of normal metabolism in cells. The molecules are also created in the body by exposure to sunlight, X rays, ozone, tobacco, smoke, car exhaust and other environmental pollutants.

Free radicals are cellular renegades; they wreak havoc by damaging DNA, altering biochemical compounds, corroding cell membranes and killing cells outright. Such molecular mayhem, scientists increasingly believe, plays a major role in the development of ailments like cancer, heart or lung disease and cataracts. Many researchers are convinced that the cumulative effects of free radicals also underlie the gradual deterioration that is the hallmark of aging in all individuals, healthy as well as sick. Antioxidants, studies suggest, might help stem the damage by neutralizing free radicals. In effect they perform as cellular sheriffs, collaring the radicals and hauling them away.

Supporters of this theory speculate that antioxidants may one day revolutionize health care. One

THE VITAMIN ALPHABET

	A/BETA CAROTENE	B₆	B₁₂	C	D	E	FOLIC ACID	K	NIACIN
Where found	A: liver, egg yolks, whole milk, butter BETA CAROTENE*: dark green leafy vegetables, yellow and orange vegetables and fruits *converts to A in the body	Meats, poultry, fish, fruits, nuts, vegetables	Meats, milk products, eggs, liver, fish	Citrus fruit, green peppers, strawberries, raw cabbage, green leafy vegetables	Liver, butter, fatty fish, egg yolks, fortified milk. Also produced when skin is exposed to sunlight.	Nuts, seeds, whole grains, vegetable and fish-liver oils	Green leafy vegetables, liver	Leafy vegetables, corn and soybean oils, liver, cereals, dairy products, meats, fruits	Grains, meats, nuts
Established benefit	Prevents night blindness and xerophthalmia (a common cause of blindness among children in poor countries)	Helps prevent anemia, skin lesions, nerve damage	Helps prevent pernicious anemia	Prevents scurvy, loose teeth; fights hemorrhage	Prevents rickets (bone malformation)	Helps prevent retrolental fibroplasia (an eye disorder in premature infants), anemia	Helps protect against cervical dysplasia (precancerous changes in cells of the uterine cervix)	Helps prevent hemorrhage	Prevents pellagra
Possible benefit	May reduce the risk of breast, lung, colon, prostate and cervical cancer, heart disease and stroke; may retard macular degeneration (a common cause of blindness among the elderly)	May protect against neural-tube defects in fetuses	May protect against heart disease and nerve damage. Possibly prevents neural-tube defects in fetuses during the first six weeks of pregnancy	May help reduce the risk of cancer and heart disease; retards macular degeneration in the eyes of the elderly	May help prevent osteoporosis and kidney disease	May reduce risk of angina and heart attack; may slow macular degeneration; may prevent spinal-cord damage in patients with cystic fibrosis	May help protect against heart disease, nerve damage, neural-tube defects	Possible role in cancer prevention	Possible cancer inhibitor

biochemist foresees screening people through a simple urine, blood or breath test to assess how much damage free radicals have done to tissue, much as patients today are screened for high cholesterol. Ultimately, says biochemist Bruce Ames of the University of California, Berkeley, "we're going to be able to get people to live a lot longer than anyone thinks."

Researchers are intrigued by evidence that Vitamin C may reduce the risk of cataracts in the eyes, and that Vitamin E may be helpful in preventing free radicals from injuring the heart. Holding center stage in antioxidant circles, however, is beta carotene, a complex deep orange compound that is naturally abundant in sweet potatoes, carrots and cantaloupes. Beta carotene is turned into vitamin A by the body as needed. That makes it impossible to overdose on beta carotene itself; however, taking too much vitamin A can lead to liver damage and other ill effects.

Doctors at Harvard Medical School, who have followed 22,000 male physicians as part of a 10-year health study, have made a stunning discovery about beta carotene. They found that men with a history of cardiac disease who were given beta carotene supplements of 50 mg every other day suffered half as many heart attacks, strokes, and death as those popping placebo pills. No heart attacks occurred among those in this group who received aspirin along with the beta carotene capsules. The Harvard researchers have begun a trial in 45,000 postmenopausal women to see if a similar effect occurs in women. Scientists speculate that the antioxidant helps prevent those nasty free radicals from transforming LDL, the bad form of cholesterol, into an even more menacing artery clogger.

Beta carotene may prove powerful in combating cancer as well. In countries such as Japan and Norway, where diets are rich in beta carotene, the populations have a low incidence of lung, colon, prostate, cervical and breast cancer. Pharmaceutical giant Hoffmann–La Roche is so enamored with beta carotene that it plans to open a Freeport, Texas, plant next year that will churn out 350 tons of the nutrient annually.

Vitamin complexes like beta carotene promise to continue to unfold as one of the great and hopeful health stories of our day. But for average Americans, the wisest strategy right now may be to redouble those efforts to eat more broccoli and carrots, spinach and squash, and to follow the familiar exhortations: get up and get moving, cut down fat and cut out smoking. No matter how powerful the antioxidants and the other nutrients turn out to be, they will never be a substitute for salutary habits. ∎

Invincible

EMERGING: Non-HIV cases
STALLED: The search for a cure
GROWING: Infection among women

WARS ARE USUALLY LAUNCHED WITH THE PROM-ise of a quick victory, with trumpets primed never to sound retreat. And the campaign against AIDS was no exception. Soon after researchers announced in the mid-1980s that they had discovered the virus that causes AIDS, U.S. health officials confidently crowed that a vaccine would be ready in two years. The most frightening scourge of the late 20th century would succumb to a swift counterattack of human ingenuity and high technology.

But no one was making victory speeches seven years later, when more than 11,000 scientists and other experts gathered in Amsterdam for the Eighth International AIDS Conference in July. The mood was somber, reflecting a decade of frustration, failure and mounting tragedy. After billions of dollars of scattershot albeit intensive research and halfhearted prevention efforts, humanity may not be any closer to conquering AIDS than when the quest began.

There is no vaccine, no cure and not even an indisputably effective treatment. While AIDS education has slowed the epidemic in developed countries, the disease continues to spread rapidly in many poorer nations. The World Health Organization says at least 30 million people around the world could be infected with the AIDS virus by the year 2000. Other experts think the number could reach 110 million.

Despite dogged detective work by the world's best researchers, AIDS (acquired immunodeficiency syndrome) remains one of the most mysterious maladies ever to confront medical science. The more researchers learn about the disease, the more questions they have. Human immunodeficiency virus (HIV), proclaimed to be the cause of AIDS, has proved to be a fiendishly fast-moving target, able to mutate its structure to elude detection, drugs and vaccines. No one knows for sure how HIV destroys the human immune system, and puzzled experts have debated whether the virus is the only culprit at work.

Bewilderment reached a new level in Amsterdam, where scientists reported cases of people who have an AIDS-like condition but have not been found to be infected with HIV. That frightening revelation raised the possibility that a new AIDS virus is emerging. Another theory, suggested by France's Dr. Luc Montagnier, who first discovered HIV, is that the strange cases were caused by one or more mutant forms of HIV that were altered too radically to be detected by standard blood tests.

Hardly any of the news at the conference was good. As groups of protesters staged daily demonstrations demanding more action against the epidemic, Dr. Jonas Salk suggested that vaccine researchers were on the wrong track. Delegates heard reports on the surging costs of treatment, warnings about the threat of AIDS-associated infections such as multidrug-resistant tuberculosis, and alarming projections that AIDS will become more of a heterosexual disease. The infection rate among women is rising, and will pass the rate in men by the year 2000. "We're dealing with something that's expanding out of control," said Dr. June Osborn, chair of America's National Commission on AIDS. Mark Harrington, a member of the New York City–based Treatment Action Group, summed up the situation more simply and grimly: "It's clear we're losing the battle. We have one class of drugs that slows AIDS down by two or three years, and then people go on and die."

THE MYSTERY OF NON-HIV CASES

The biggest surprise in Amsterdam was the talk about a new kind of AIDS. Dr. Jeffrey Laurence of the New York Hospital–Cornell Medical Center described five instances of people who suffered from an AIDS-like illness and yet bore no trace of HIV anywhere in their body. When a similar case was reported at the 1991 AIDS conference in Florence, it was dismissed as a fluke. In Amsterdam several scientists in the audience stood up to tell of other cases of non-HIV AIDS, bringing the total to about 30—a number that is small but impossible to ignore.

If a new virus does exist, AIDS will become even harder to prevent or cure. Pharmaceutical manufacturers have already been hampered by HIV's talent as a quick-change artist. In 1991 a group of promising anti-AIDS drugs had to be shelved because HIV adapted too easily to the medication. And drugs that prove effective against all forms of HIV will not necessarily knock out an entirely novel virus.

HIV is a formidable enough opponent, mainly because researchers still don't understand the method to its madness. Like all viruses, HIV is simply a strand of genetic mate-

AIDS

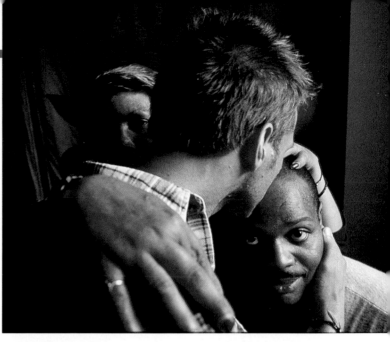

rial (in this case the nucleic acid RNA) surrounded by a protein coat. A virus lacks the tools to reproduce unless it invades a living cell and takes over the host's molecular machinery. The intruder can then produce many copies of itself, eventually killing the cell. One of HIV's favorite targets is the CD4 T-cell, an important player in the human immune system.

But there the understanding runs out. Why does HIV lie dormant in human cells, usually for years, before producing a full-blown case of AIDS? What triggers the deadly phase of the infection? How does the virus go about destroying the immune system? Even at the height of the disease, HIV particles are found in no more than 1 in 100 CD4 T-cells. And yet the cells that do not harbor the virus die off almost as fast as those that do. Some researchers think that HIV must somehow provoke immune-system cells to destroy themselves.

One prominent theory is that the virus needs an assistant assailant—a "cofactor," in scientific jargon. But the search for cofactors has been inconclusive. Although the presence of genital sores from syphilis or other venereal diseases makes transmission of the AIDS virus easier, neither the sores nor the microbes that cause them are necessary for HIV to spread. Researchers have also investigated the possibility that cytomegalovirus, a common form of herpes virus, might be the elusive cofactor, but eventually they ruled it out.

Montagnier believes the cofactor might be a mycoplasma, a primitive bacterium-like organism. The possible role played by this microbe may help explain one of the mysteries surrounding the origin of AIDS. Studies of blood samples preserved from decades ago show that HIV was present in Africa long before AIDS appeared. What caused the once harmless virus to turn deadly? Montagnier thinks it was a strain of mycoplasma that until recent years was confined to America. Somehow, somewhere, according to his theory, HIV and the mycoplasma got together in a group of humans, and that was the start of the AIDS epidemic.

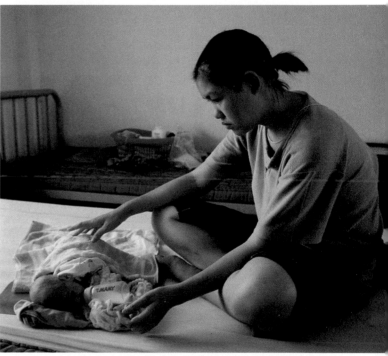

UNITED STATES: Stefan and Donald embrace at the Bialey House for homeless people with AIDS in New York City.

THAILAND: Infected by a client, this 19-year-old former prostitute passed the virus on to her six-month-old baby.

FRANCE: Hemophiliacs Laurent and Stephane got tainted blood in 1985. They contracted AIDS; Laurent died.

DR. LUC MONTAGNIER of Paris' Pasteur Institute was the first to isolate the AIDS virus, in 1983. At the Amsterdam meeting he reaffirmed his optimism that effective vaccines against AIDS will be found, probably before the year 2000. He, for one, claims he does not plan to be working on AIDS for the rest of his career. But then, who knows? "Dogmatism is a deadly sin in science," says Montagnier.

POWERLESS DRUGS, ELUSIVE VACCINES

If HIV were an ordinary virus, designing drugs to kill it might not seem like an impossible mission. "But it is a much more difficult virus than anyone anticipated," says Myron Essex, head of the Harvard AIDS Institute. "It has many more fancy genes to determine how it replicates. It has positive and negative controls that interact with cellular controls, which allows it to crank up rapidly or remain silent for a long time. It's a very, very unusual virus."

Most important, HIV can easily disguise itself by altering the proteins in its outer coat. When that happens, the job of finding and attacking the virus becomes harder. Even AZT, the most effective drug against HIV, is nowhere near as potent as doctors or patients hoped it would be.

First approved for use in the U.S. five years ago, AZT prevents one of the viral genes from making an enzyme, called reverse transcriptase, that is critical to HIV's reproduction. This action prolongs life by postponing some of the symptoms of AIDS. But in patient after patient, HIV eventually mutates into a form that is less vulnerable to AZT. As a result, its benefits often run out within 18 months.

The only other anti-HIV drugs approved in the U.S.—DDI and DDC—are variations on the AZT theme. Researchers have begun examining other types, however. One variety targets the gene that codes for another enzyme, protease, that is crucial to the manufacturing of viral proteins. The research looks promising, but a breakthrough is not expected anytime soon.

The same adaptability that makes HIV so troublesome to drug designers also threatens to stymie vaccine development. Researchers are not confident that they can devise a simple series of shots that would give a person lifetime protection against AIDS. To do that, a vaccine would have to ward off all of HIV's current strains as well as any future mutants.

Neutralizing HIV is especially tough because its coat is laced with sugar molecules that shield it from the human immune system. Some viruses, such as the one that causes polio, have no sugar in their protein coat. Others, like flu viruses, have only a little. It is no coincidence that the most effective vaccines have been made to fight these kinds of viruses. Never before have scientists tried to devise a vaccine against a pathogen as well protected as HIV.

Undaunted, researchers are testing about a dozen experimental vaccines. After the trials have been thoroughly evaluated, the most promising prototypes will be chosen—probably in the next two years—for testing to determine if they can stimulate the immune system to produce antibodies capable of blocking HIV infection. The trouble is that

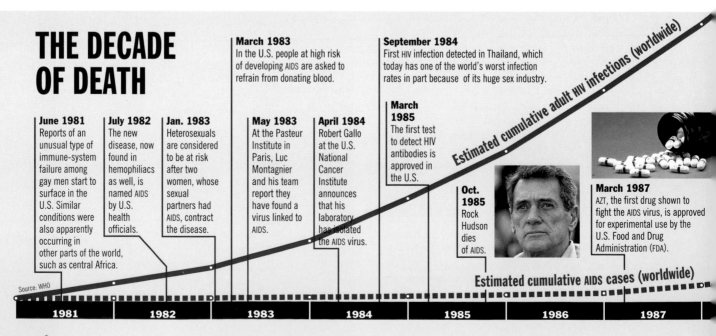

THE DECADE OF DEATH

June 1981
Reports of an unusual type of immune-system failure among gay men start to surface in the U.S. Similar conditions were also apparently occurring in other parts of the world, such as central Africa.

July 1982
The new disease, now found in hemophiliacs as well, is named AIDS by U.S. health officials.

Jan. 1983
Heterosexuals are considered to be at risk after two women, whose sexual partners had AIDS, contract the disease.

March 1983
In the U.S. people at high risk of developing AIDS are asked to refrain from donating blood.

May 1983
At the Pasteur Institute in Paris, Luc Montagnier and his team report they have found a virus linked to AIDS.

April 1984
Robert Gallo at the U.S. National Cancer Institute announces that his laboratory has isolated the AIDS virus.

September 1984
First HIV infection detected in Thailand, which today has one of the world's worst infection rates in part because of its huge sex industry.

March 1985
The first test to detect HIV antibodies is approved in the U.S.

Oct. 1985
Rock Hudson dies of AIDS.

March 1987
AZT, the first drug shown to fight the AIDS virus, is approved for experimental use by the U.S. Food and Drug Administration (FDA).

Estimated cumulative adult HIV infections (worldwide)

Estimated cumulative AIDS cases (worldwide)

Source: WHO

| 1981 | 1982 | 1983 | 1984 | 1985 | 1986 | 1987 |

scientists can only guess at what constitutes an effective collection of AIDS antibodies. No one has ever survived the disease to provide researchers with any clues. Even if the experiments go well, a preventive vaccine will probably not be available before the end of this century.

THE EVOLVING EPIDEMIC

One of the most baffling enigmas of AIDS is the fact that the disease spread primarily among homosexual and bisexual men in the U.S. and Europe but became a largely heterosexual infection in Africa. Researchers announced at the conference that they may have an answer. Based on a study of the newly emerging epidemic in Thailand, they concluded that HIV has shown predilections for different human host cells in different parts of the world.

Using biochemical tools that were not available at the beginning of the epidemics in Africa and the Americas, molecular biologist Chin-Yih Ou and his colleagues at the U.S. Centers for Disease Control found two distinct epidemics caused by somewhat different strains of HIV in the Thai city of Chiang Mai. Both epidemics started no more than four years ago, but one occurred mostly in intravenous drug abusers and the other started in female prostitutes. There was little overlap between the two groups.

The scientists discovered that the prostitutes were more often infected by a strain resembling those types found in Africa. Apparently, it preferred the moist mucosal tissue of the genital organs, making heterosexual transmission easier. The other variety, found in the drug abusers, appeared similar to strains detected in the U.S. and Europe. It thrived on immune cells in the bloodstream. As a result, transmission occurred through the exchange of contaminated blood, as might occur during the sharing of needles or in abrasive anal sex.

The rise of two or more dissimilar types of HIV could explain why AIDS did not explode among heterosexuals in the U.S. and Europe, yet spread rapidly among men and women in Africa and parts of Asia. HIV has still not evolved in the industrialized world into a form that is easily transmitted by heterosexual activity. But it probably will, given the virus' proven ability to mutate. "Over time, in the U.S., more and more strains will adapt to become more efficient at heterosexual transmission," Harvard's Essex says. " So far, there haven't been a critical number of people infected heterosexually. As that happens, you will get adaptation of the virus for transmission in that route. The heterosexual epidemic in the U.S. will expand."

1992 estimate: 10 million to 12 million

Already American physicians are seeing more women with HIV. In many AIDS clinics in San Francisco and New York City, women make up 30% to 50% of all new patients; about half became infected through heterosexual contact. They range from very well educated to barely literate, but most say they had no idea their sexual partners had engaged in high-risk behavior. In fact, because AIDS is still thought of as a gay man's disease in the U.S., many women discover they are infected only after they have passed the virus on to their children.

Tragically, even as AIDS goes in ever more dangerous demographic directions, government agencies throughout the world are failing to respond. Prevention programs are stalled or being abandoned. The World Health Organization's AIDS budget for 1992 was $90 million, down from $110 million in 1991. In the U.S. the National Institutes of Health requested $1.2 billion for AIDS in the 1993 budget, but President Bush trimmed that amount to $873 million, and Congress is likely to cut it even further.

By the year 2000 AIDS could become the largest epidemic of the century, eclipsing the influenza scourge of 1918. That disaster killed 20 million people, or 1% of the world's population—more than twice the number of soldiers who died in World War I. "This epidemic is of historic scale," says June Osborn of the U.S. AIDS commission, "but the response has been far short of historic." ■

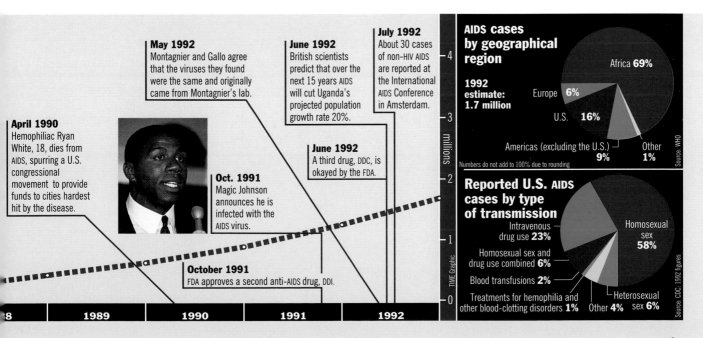

May 1992
Montagnier and Gallo agree that the viruses they found were the same and originally came from Montagnier's lab.

June 1992
British scientists predict that over the next 15 years AIDS will cut Uganda's projected population growth rate 20%.

July 1992
About 30 cases of non-HIV AIDS are reported at the International AIDS Conference in Amsterdam.

April 1990
Hemophiliac Ryan White, 18, dies from AIDS, spurring a U.S. congressional movement to provide funds to cities hardest hit by the disease.

June 1992
A third drug, DDC, is okayed by the FDA.

Oct. 1991
Magic Johnson announces he is infected with the AIDS virus.

October 1991
FDA approves a second anti-AIDS drug, DDI.

AIDS cases by geographical region

1992 estimate: 1.7 million

Africa 69%
Europe 6%
U.S. 16%
Americas (excluding the U.S.) 9%
Other 1%

Numbers do not add to 100% due to rounding

Source: WHO

TIME Graphic

Reported U.S. AIDS cases by type of transmission

Intravenous drug use 23%
Homosexual sex and drug use combined 6%
Blood transfusions 2%
Treatments for hemophilia and other blood-clotting disorders 1%
Homosexual sex 58%
Heterosexual sex 6%
Other 4%

Source: CDC, 1992 figures

1989 1990 1991 1992

HANG TIME
An aerial freestyle skier soars upside down in one of the four demonstration sports at the Savoie Games.

Thrill Ride

**Refreshingly free of squabbles
and scandals, Albertville
and Barcelona dazzle the world**

S orry, Mr. Barnum. From the opening parade of athletes to the lighting of the torch to the medal ceremonies of gold, silver and bronze, the Olympic Games are now the greatest show on earth. An Awesome Assemblage of Athletic Ability! A Brain-Boggling Baedeker of Brawn! And, of course, a Heavy-Handed Hubbub of Hype.

Yet somehow the Games of 1992 transcended the shouting, the sponsorships, the superlatives. Joyously staged in the Savoie region of the French Alps and in Spain's renascent Barcelona, these first Olympics after the cold war seemed cleansed of the partisan spirit that had marred earlier Games. With the focus on athletes—not politics—a simple sense of joy returned to the competition. Two billion viewers around the world found new pleasures in a ritual that is more ancient than most religions: men and women from every nation gathering in peace to surpass themselves.

▲ **CAN'T SEE THE FOREST**
In the Winter Games athletes face three adversaries: the competition, the clock—and the countryside.

▼ **SLIP SLIDIN' AWAY**
The men's single luge event in the village of La Plagne captivated visitors to the Winter Games—with an occasional exception

1992 OLYMPICS

F EBRUARY 1992—AND THE GREAT OLYMPIC CIRCUS pitched its tent in the Savoie region of the French Alps. In a soaring high-wire act, 57 events of the Winter Games were staged in 10 venues across seven valleys and 620 sq. mi. of the pine-serrated glaciers and peaks of the region.

The opening ceremonies in Albertville struck a note of Gallic assurance and zest, with balloon-topped stilt walkers and musicians suspended from cranes—Dr. Seuss meets the Olympics. But when the Games began, all eyes turned to the athletes: Italy's flamboyant skier Alberto Tomba took the downhill gold, making good on his promise to turn Albertville into "Albertoville." American Bonnie Blair won two gold medals in speed skating, and Kristi Yamaguchi of the U.S. outdueled Japan's Midori Ito to take the gold medal in women's figure skating.

▲ BLADE RUNNERS
More explosive and exciting than the traditional long-track events, short-track speed skating made its official Olympic debut in Albertville. Ki-Hoon Kim of Korea skated to the first Olympic gold medal in the men's 1,000-m race.

▶ SHALL WE DANCE?
Olympians from the former Soviet Union once again dominated the pairs event with their ballet on ice. Marina Klimova and Sergei Ponomarenko forced home-country favorites Isabelle and Paul Duchesnay into second place.

▲LET THE FLAMES BEGIN!
A fiery arrow ignites the Olympic torch in Barcelona's opening ceremony.

▼ HEP, HEP HOORAY!
Jackie Joyner-Kersee takes a victory lap after winning the heptathlon.

1992 OLYMPICS

THE SUMMER STOP FOR THE OLYMPIC CARAVAN: Barcelona, as Spain welcomed the modern Games for the first time. In the city where Picasso studied, where Salvador Dali grew up, where the fanciful buildings of Antonio Gaudí turn architecture into sculpted drama, the Games took on brilliance and grandeur. Buoyed by a wave of Catalan pride, Barcelona staged memorable ceremonies as a fiery arrow lit the Olympic torch.

Fittingly, Spain seemed to be the single all-around winner in the Summer Games; its athletes won 13 gold medals, after winning only four in the past 96 years. The Chinese team was a consistent surprise, and its women were everywhere—scoring all 10s in the uneven bars, winning an archery shoot with one bull's-eye after another, even striding off with the 10-km walk. The Unified Team forgot its differences long enough to enjoy one last triumph. And U.S. basketball superstar Magic Johnson defied his HIV-positive status to compete, sweeping Barcelona before him as Olympians from around the world vied for a picture, an autograph, a handshake. Tennis pro Jim Courier even found joy in living in a tiny room without air conditioning in the Olympic Village. "I wouldn't miss staying in the Village for anything," he said. "You get up in the morning and you see some of the best athletes in the world going for jogs or eating breakfast. It's indescribable."

166

▶ **WHOLE LOTTA SHAKIN'**
Disappointed American gymnast Kim Zmeskal got off to a shaky start on the balance beam, never regained her confidence, and did not win a medal. Tatiana Gutsu of the Unified Team took the gold in the women's all-around event; Shannon Miller of the U.S. was second. In the popular women's team competition, the Unified Team, representing republics of the former U.S.S.R., won the gold, the always tough Romanian women took the silver and the U.S. women the bronze. Li Lu won the women's uneven-bar event and finished second on the balance beam, as China served notice that it intended to be a gymnastic power in future Games.

▼ **KAYAK ATTACK**
Central Europeans dominated the exciting four-man kayak competition: Germany, Hungary and Austria placed one-two-three in the men's 1,000-m race.

167

OLYMPIC HIGH
Lift off! Chinese diver
Fu Mingxia floats above
the hills of Barcelona on
her way to the gold medal
in the women's 10-m
platform event.

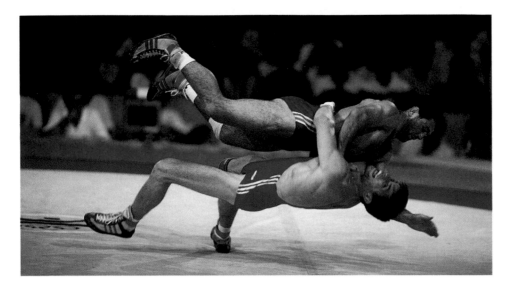

▲ BOWLED OVER
In a posture Praxiteles might recognize, wrestlers get horizontal in a sport that has changed little since the ancient Games.

◄ CUBA, SI!
"Buy me some plantain and Cracker Jack . . ." America's national pasttime went international when Cuba's tough team captured the gold in the first official year of Olympic baseball.

▲ WINGED VICTORY
Veteran Olympian Carl Lewis outdueled Mike Powell to win the long jump, then anchored the winning U.S. team in the 4 x 100-m relay.

▶ SUMMER SPLASH
Swimmer Summer Sanders (say that fast!) won the 200-m women's butterfly, was second in the 200-m individual medley and third in the 400-m medley.

◄ PEDAL TO THE MEDAL
Chris Boardman won the grueling 4,000-m individual pursuit event, finishing a full six minutes ahead of Germany's Jens Lehmann for Britain's only cycling gold.

Gold medalists
Winners of selected Olympic events

WINTER OLYMPICS

Bobsled

Two-man	**Weder/Acklin,** Switzerland
Four-man	**Austria**

Ice hockey **Unified Team**

Luge

Men's single	**Hackl,** Germany
Men's double	**Krausse/Behrendt,** Germany
Women's Single	**Neuner,** Austria

Figure Skating

Men's	**Petrenko,** Unified Team
Women's	**Yamaguchi,** USA
Pairs	**Michkouteniok/Dmitriev,** Unified Team
Ice Dancing	**Klimova/Ponomarenko,** Unified Team

Speed Skating	Men	Women
500	**Mey,** Germany	**Blair,** USA
1,000	**Zinke,** Germany	**Blair,** USA
1,500	**Koss,** Norway	**Boerner,** Germany
5,000 (3,000)	**Karlstad,** Norway	**Niemann,** Germany
10,000 (5,000)	**Veldkamp,** Nether.	**Niemann,** Germany

Skiing	Men	Women
Downhill	**Ortlieb,** Austria	**Lee-Gartner,** Canada
Combined	**Polig,** Italy	**Kronberger,** Austria
Giant slalom	**Tomba,** Italy	**Wiberg,** Sweden
Slalom	**Jagge,** Norway	**Kronberger,** Austria
Super G	**Aamodt,** Norway	**Compagnoni,** Italy
Moghuls	**Grospiron,** France	**Weinbrecht,** USA

Ski Jump

90k	**Vettori,** Austria
120k	**Nieminen,** Finland
Team 120k	**Finland**

SUMMER OLYMPICS

Baseball Cuba

Basketball USA

Gymnastics	Men	Women
Team	**Unified Team**	**Unified Team**
Individual	**Scherbo,** Unified	**Goutsou,** Unified
Floor	**Li,** China	**Milosovici,** Romania
Pommel hose	**Scherbo,** Unified	
Still rings	**Scherbo,** Unified	
Vault	**Scherbo,** Unified	**Onodi,** Hungary
Parallel bars	**Scherbo,** Unified	
Horizontal bars	**Dimas,** USA	
Uneven bars		**Lu,** China
Balance beam		**Lyssenko,** Unified

Swimming	Men	Women
100m Freestyle	**Popov,** Unified	**Zhaung,** China
100m Backstroke	**Tewksbury,** Canada	**Egerszegi,** Hungary
100m Breaststroke	**Diebel,** USA	**Roudkovskaia,** Unified
100m Butterfly	**Morales,** USA	**Qian,** China
400m Medly	**Darnyi,** Hungary	**Egerszegi,** Hungary

Track and Field	Men	Women
100m	**Christie,** Britain	**Devers,** USA
200m	**Marsh,** USA	**Torrence,** USA
400m	**Watts,** USA	**Perec,** France
800m	**Tanui,** Kenya	**Langen,** Neth.
1,500m	**Cacho,** Spain	**Boulmerka,** Algeria
5,000m (3,000)	**Baumann,** Germany	**Romanova,** Unified
10,000m	**Skah,** Morocco	**Tulu,** Ethiopia
110m hurdles (100)	**McKay,** Canada	**Patoulidou,** Greece
400m hurdles	**Young,** USA	**Gunnell,** Britain
4x100 relay	**USA**	**USA**
4x400 relay	**USA**	**Unified Team**
Marathon	**Hwang,** Korea	**Yegorova,** Unified
High jump	**Satomayor,** Cuba	**Henkel,** Germany
Long jump	**Lewis,** USA	**Drechsler,** Germany
Pole vault	**Tarassov,** Unified	
Shot put	**Stulce,** USA	**Kriveleva,** Unified
Discus	**Ubartas,** Lithuania	**Marten,** Cuba
Javelin	**Zelezny,** Czech	**Renk,** Germany
Decathlon	**Zmelik,** Czech	
Heptathlon		**Joyner-Kersee,** USA

ARTS

Step right up to the arts arcade! Watch
politics become show biz—and vice versa. See art
battle commerce! Hear moral inanities, gross ironies and
lung-busting angst. Thrill now—pay later.

By **RICHARD CORLISS**

WHAT CAN YOU SAY ABOUT AMERICAN POPULAR
culture in a year when the most prominent sax-
ophonist was Bill Clinton, the hottest TV personality is Ross Perot, the song title on everyone's lips is *Cop Killer* and the most seductive new movie
role model is Malcolm X? What can you say about social
politics in a year when Sinéad O'Connor is the most incen-
diary televangelist and Madonna the most controversial author, when Murphy Brown's single-motherhood is a roiling
campaign issue and Woody Allen's surrogate fatherhood
triggers the year's most rancorous court case?

What you must say is that 1992 proved the truth of the
modern maxim: in American politics everything is show
biz, and in modern show biz everything is political.

Typically, popular art coats the kernel of its message in
the chocolate candy of entertainment. You could watch
Clint Eastwood's hit western *Unforgiven* and hardly notice
that the Eastwood character is a metaphor for America's
self-appointed role as the world's top cop. You could hum
along with the year's crossover country music stars (Garth
Brooks singing *We Shall Be Free*, Mary-Chapin Carpenter
doing *He Thinks He'll Keep Her*) and hum right over the
songs' sermons about racial tolerance and domestic betrayal. You could be sufficiently dazzled by the grand sass of
the Broadway hit *Jelly's Last Jam* not to notice that the
show is essentially a denunciation of white America for its
exploitation of black American artists.

Mostly, though, the merger of politics and show biz was
right up front, where not even the electorate could miss it.
How apt that the presidential campaign was moderated by
Larry King, Katie Couric, Don Imus; and that Dan
Quayle's most memorable debate was with the fictitious
Murphy Brown. Ostensibly, the voters' challenge was to
decide which candidate could jump-start the economy,
but what they were really choosing was a host for the next
four years of America, the 24-hour talk show. So the contenders played roles that had as much cultural as political

heft. Clinton did Elvis. Perot was an infomercial huckster.
George Bush, when promoting "traditional family values"
(and implying that Clinton didn't have any), seemed to be
running for Pope.

On *Saturday Night Live*, Sinéad O'Connor ripped into
the Pontiff himself, tearing up a photograph of John Paul II
and proclaiming "Fight the real enemy!" The outraged
faithful responded to this gesture by crushing the Gaelic
gosling's CDs under a steamroller. Her anticlerical blasts
packed a wallop not just because she offended so many
Catholics but because she meant it, she really meant it. It
was one of the few statements in the year's pop culture that
could be taken at face value.

Nearly every other aural assault from belligerent pop
stars was either swathed in sarcasm or wrapped in First
Amendment parchment. When reggae singer Buju Banton
caught flak for his gay-bashing anthem *Boom Bye Bye*
("Faggots have to run/ Or get a bullet in the head/ . . . Get
an automatic or an Uzi instead"), a spokeswoman for Banton insisted that the odious lyrics were "a product of his environment, not a reflection of his personal convictions."
When Ice-T sang the body psychotic in *Cop Killer* ("I'm
'bout to bust some shots off/ I'm 'bout to dust some cops
off"), his spin doctors argued, correctly but disingenuously,
that the author of a work should not be mistaken for its subject. And the opinions expressed therein were not *at all* the
opinions of the media conglomerate that paid for the song.

Protests from police groups and others finally persuaded
Ice-T and Time Warner to remove the *Cop Killer* cut from
its album. (Not a good thing. The song should be available
and its sentiments should be reviled.) Usually, though, in
this age of debased social intercourse, the perps go free.
The sonic terrorists win the battle of art and commerce: every brutal slur supposedly testifies to our precious freedom
of speech, and every public act of moral inanity is a career
move. People do buy the stuff. In the ruckus over a Time
Warner label's rejection of his song *Bush Killa* (a fantasy

about shooting the President), the rap artist Paris saw orders for his album nearly triple. The entire cycle—outrageous act, outraged response, critical defense, press coverage, increased sales, general sheepishness—has become an elaborate and predictable species of performance art.

Madonna may not have invented this game, but she surely perfected it. As her very name suggests, the mode of her art is gross irony. Her career, with its evocations of Weimar-era decadence and '50s kitsch, is a virtual museum of bad taste. In her concerts, videos and films, the pop tart commits some cunning impropriety and then asks: "Have I shocked you? Good. But I was probably only kidding." Her latest rude giggle, a book called *Sex*, splayed and displayed her in what used to be called "provocative poses," many overlaid with the author's handwritten *pensées*. It was as if she had scrawled graffiti over her body. But the marketing was the message; *Sex* sold almost 500,000 copies in its first week. Once again, the public had bought Madonna—this time for $49.95.

POLITICAL INCORRECTNESS ALWAYS HAS A PRICE TAG. It rarely has a coherent ideology. If Sinéad O'Connor and Ice-T attack from the left flank and Madonna comes straight up the middle, then Rush Limbaugh advances from the right and Howard Stern from below. As much as anyone, these last two defined the culture of '92. Both use lethal doses of exaggeration—Limbaugh's *Hindenburg*-size ego, Stern's sexist misanthropy—to amuse and affront their audiences. Both have achieved nationwide celebrity through the lowly, local art of radio haranguing. Both are on their way to being one-man conglomerates: Stern with TV and movie deals, Limbaugh with a surprising hit TV show and a book, *The Way Things Ought to Be*, that topped the best-seller list before and after *Sex*. Finally, both have guy-next-door charisma with a dangerous edge. If you don't tune in, you might miss something—a mugging, say, dressed as caustic radio wit.

Did 1992 offer works of art or entertainment innocent of political implications? No, there never are such; every song or play, movie or TV show speaks in some way to the hopes or fears of the body politic. But art can also document the joy of being alive, the ache of surviving, the black hole of surrendering, the complicated business of being human. And should anyone wonder whether the lively arts can reach all these feelings with wit and skepticism and heart, we have proof in two words: *The Simpsons*. The adult cartoon show has shrugged off its early notoriety to reveal a middle-class family in all its caustic, befuddled humanity.

Away from the politico-aesthetic debates that raged at rock-concert decibel level, some people made good art. Films such as *Howards End* (from Britain), *Indochine* (from France) and *Raise the Red Lantern* (from China) proved there was room for passion and ambiguity in the genteel period drama. The craft and verve of *Guys and Dolls* and *Crazy for You* were so spectacular, you could almost forgive Broadway for not even trying to fill its 1992 theaters with 1992 music. For truly new musical theater, you had to go to the opera; John Corigliano's *The Ghosts of Versailles*, Philip Glass's *The Voyage* and William Bolcom's *McTeague* found sonorous signs of life in the fabulous invalid of serious dramatic music. The flood of CDs showcasing grand old musicians (Billie Holiday, Cole Porter, Bob Marley, Tammy Wynette, the real Elvis) remind the listener that a year's worth of new entertainment is the merest scrap from culture's banquet, spread out on a table that stretches past the horizon, past remembering.

"I can open your eyes/ Take you wonder by wonder," sings Aladdin to his princess in 1992's ravishing Disney cartoon. That's the artist's role too. And the audience's need? After all the lung-busting angst of a very political year, perhaps we all deserve a rest from thinking. "I feel stupid and contagious," sings Seattle band Nirvana in *Smells Like Teen Spirit*. "Here we are now, entertain us."

Note to the cultural élite: This year, lighten up! ∎

CINEMA

Snakes of Tinseltown

FASCINATION WITH THE BOX-OFFICE bull's-eye strikes fear into many directors' hearts. In every frame of their work you can smell the fear of failure. Robert Altman, director of the inside-Hollywood thriller **THE PLAYER,** is beyond all that. His view is Olympian. His camera, prowling like a house dick on roller skates, challenges you to find the crucial detail in each corner of an eight-minute opening shot. Delicate yet corrosive, *The Player* traces the career of studio big shot Griffin Mill (Tim Robbins) as he masters the Hollywood game. Michael Tolkin's script abounds in cynical wisdom without losing an appreciation for the grace with which the snakes of Tinseltown consume their victims. Altman, both favored and dismissed by Hollywood, is like St. Sebastian, plucking the arrows from his body and flinging them back, like gentle javelins, at the infidels.

Clintessence

TO YOUNG MOVIEGOERS TO-day, Clint Eastwood, at 62 long past his popular prime, may seem as old and irrelevant as Gary Cooper, Tom Mix, Methusaleh. Well, now . . . if the young won't respect a living legend, it seems a man has to tend to that problem himself. **UNFORGIVEN** is a dark, passionate drama, with good guys so twisted and bad guys so persuasive that virtue and villainy become two views of the same soul. It is also Eastwood's meditation on age, repute, courage, heroism—on Clintessence. His Will Munny is a gunfighter trying to escape the lure of notoriety. Ten years retired, he can't shoot straight or stay on a horse, and he's eager to dispel anyone's illusions of outlaw grandeur. A revisionist western, *Unforgiven* questions the rules of a macho genre, summing up and maybe atoning for the flinty violence that made

Eastwood famous. Yes, it is old-fashioned; but that's just another way of saying classic.

Skin Game

DESPITE THE HYPE OVER the high cost of its script (a record $3 million), its alleged antigay bias, and its original NC-17 rating (later changed to an R), the sexy thriller **BASIC INSTINCT** is just another entertainment gone wrong. The story premise isn't bad: femme fatale murder novelist Sharon Stone meets, makes love to, and maybe (or maybe not) threatens danger-loving cop Michael Douglas. Forget the standard objections: the tameness and sameness of most movie sex has become a bore, and the film cannot fairly be termed antigay. The film's real problems lie elsewhere: in the chilly, self-conscious sleekness of its production design, in the heartless and relentless thrill seeking of Paul

Beneath the glitz, *Basic Instinct* failed to thrill

Verhoeven's direction, in the too intricate, not entirely persuasive plotting. Its fundamental flaw is arrogance, the smug faith that its own speed, smartness and luxe will wow the yokels.

Stream of Dreams

DIRECTOR ROBERT REDFORD HAS FAITH-fully and entrancingly turned Norman Maclean's memoir-novella **A RIVER RUNS THROUGH IT** into a movie. The screenwriter, Richard Friedenberg, has gently expanded the original work, adding anecdotes and developing the boys' relationship with their father, a Presbyterian minister (Tom Skerritt), as well as young Norman's courtship of his wife (Emily Lloyd). Redford rigorously maintains the understated tone of a book that never plea-bargains, never asks outright for sympathy or understanding, yet ultimately, powerfully, elicits both. The movie is cool, quiet, and allusive, rich in unforced metaphors and feelings. Like Maclean's writing, the art of Redford's movie is all in the graceful casting of the line, not in the melodrama of the catch.

Glorious Visions

HOWARDS END, E.M. FORSTER'S richest novel, is the finest film yet by the great triumvirate of director James Ivory, producer Ismail Merchant and novelist-screenwriter Ruth Prawer Jhabvala. A delight of nearly any Ivory film is the ensemble of actresses. Here Emma Thompson has wit and magic, Helena Bonham Carter's fiercely pre-Rapaelite features have never been so

Howards End director James Ivory indulged his visual whims, yet honed each scene ruthlessly

fetching, and Vanessa Redgrave is her usual revelation, this time as a lady cocooned in elevated frailties. The 1907 story seems completely modern today, and its breadth allows Ivory to indulge his visual whims—the riot of landscape, the open-air intimacy of a punt on a sylvan stream—while forcing him and Prawer Jhabvala to hone every scene ruthlessly.

Men at Work

DAVID MAMET'S 1983 BROADWAY PLAY **GLENGARRY GLEN ROSS** dramatized his youthful experiences in a real estate office, where cold-blooded dinosaurs of capitalism worked their cold-blooded performance art on people too nice to say no. Now Mamet has filmed the Pulitzer-prizewinning play, intact and enhanced. Mamet's men talk for a living: they talk to keep from telling the truth. In their four-letter world, lying comes with the territory. A peerless ensemble—Ed Harris, Alan Arkin, Al Pacino, Jack Lemmon—fills the movie with audible glares and shudders. The play was zippy black comedy; the film is a photo-essay, shot in morgue close-up, about the difficulty most people have convincing themselves that what they do matters.

Battier and Better

THE 1989 MOVIE _BATMAN,_ DIRECTOR Tim Burton's first go at Bob Kane's comic-book character, was wan, jangled, lost in meandering murk. **BATMAN RETURNS,** though, is alive, not an effects showcase in a shroud. The script delights in elaborate wordplay and complex characters. Danny De Vito's Penguin is funny, lithe and daring: a vicious troll with a righteous grudge. But this brisk, buoyant movie gets its emotional weight from the tangle of opposites between two credible, beguiling outsiders. Michelle Pfeiffer's Catwoman turns a lonely secretary into a vengeful kitten with a whip. Michael Keaton's Bruce Wayne is a trussed-up do-gooder who cannot reveal his identity. Burton's pop entertainment soars into the realm of poetry.

Tepid Primer For Pride

THE MOVIE'S FIRST MINUTES PROMISE the fire this time. A Patton-size U.S. flag fills the screen and is set ablaze. Video clips of Los Angeles cops pummeling a helpless Rodney King are underlaid with the words of Malcolm X fulminating against the white devil. Flames of black rage gnaw at the flag until it is burned into a huge X. But

Pfeiffer as Catwoman

soon enough Spike Lee's much hyped **MALCOLM X** turns this complex militant's life into a tepid primer for black pride. A self-promoter, media manipulator and logomaker of genius (Levi's button-fly jeans, X hats), Lee is no filmmaker of genius. _Malcolm X_ is a lavish, linear, way-too-long storybook of Malcolm's career, the movie equivalent of an authorized biography. Denzel Washington embodies Malcolm with potent charm, but somehow his personality is blurred in Lee's stately, reverent biopic.

Magic Carpet

THE OLD WORLD—THE one of current Hollywood movies and TV shows—is in disrepair. In its tatty bazaar, peddlers hawk worn-out notions as if the items held their former glamour. Disney's animated comedy-adventure **ALADDIN** is an enthralling new world, where Boy meets, loses and gets Girl in an Arabian kingdom of cotton-candy palaces, tiger-mouthed pyramids, wicked viziers, larcenous monkeys, misanthropic parrots, a truly magic carpet and a genie who changes shape and personalities faster than you can say . . . Robin Williams! _Aladdin_ is a ravishing thrill ride pulsing at MTV-video tempo. Animator is a wonderful word. It means life giver. And, for the movies, life restorer. ■

Animated, indeed: Disney's _Aladdin_ brought fresh life to the movies

MUSIC

Country's Big Boom

GUESS WHO TOPPED THE CHARTS IN 1992? Well, how about a balding Oklahoma country singer whose idols include James Taylor and John Wayne, who prances across the stage like a cross between Mick Jagger and Ferris Bueller, swinging from rope ladders and smashing his guitar, and who brings 40-year-olds to tears with his existential hymns about accepting life's incidental malice? Outside of Seattle rock may have been moribund in 1992, but **GARTH BROOKS** sure was thriving.

By their sheer demographic weight, the nation's 76 million baby boomers continue to determine America's musical preferences. And what America preferred in 1992 was country. Brooks outsold Michael Jackson and Guns 'N Roses, country radio trumped Top 40, and Nashville churned out a posse of new stars: Alan Jackson, Clint Black, Trisha Yearwood, Vince Gill, Mary-Chapin Carpenter and Travis Tritt.

Significantly, country achieved its new luster without abandoning its heritage, stubbornly rooted in storytelling and simple melody. The new wave of country singers is dominated by artists who have succeeded largely on their own terms, consolidating an eclectic mix of contemporary sounds with old-fashioned catches in the throat, tinkles of the mandolin, sugary sobs and vertiginous swoops of pedal steel guitar.

This generation's performers are the first bred on both rock and country who are consciously choosing Nashville; Vince Gill turned down a chance to join the rock group Dire Straits to continue his country career. Today's hot country stars are more likely to be college graduates with IRAs than dropouts with prison records. The women sing about heartbreaks, but they also rejoice in their sexual independence and ponder their opportunities.

More than any other headliner, Garth Brooks encapsulates most of the complexities of the baby boomers. He was raised in an Oklahoma City suburb, where he listened to Kiss and Queen, and graduated from Oklahoma State, where he was a middling jock and an advertising major. He hides his receding hairline under his

Garth Brooks: under the Stetson, you'll find a bald spot

Stetson; he can be a pop nostalgist who croons old Billy Joel songs, a country nostalgist who traces his lineage to the backwoodsy George Jones, or a rock nostalgist who remembers what the back and forth between a jumping-jack-flash performer and his audience is supposed to be like.

Brooks has yet to prove he has the imagination of John Lennon, much less the death-defying charisma of Elvis, but he has broken all of Nashville's sales records. Until his 1991 *Roping the Wind*, no country album had ever entered *Billboard's* top chart at No. 1. Since his recording debut a short three years ago, Brooks has moved more albums with more velocity than anyone else in the history of Nashville: when the figures for *Roping* are added to

those for *Garth Brooks* and *No Fences*, his first and second records, and his two fall 1992 releases, he has sold more than 30 million records.

Country music seems right on time for the abstinent '90s. Marriage counseling is in, and so is staying sober. If rock is about feral impulses, country is about spiritual nourishment. Says Paul Shaefer, David Letterman's bandleader: "Country is soul music for white people, and people always return to soul music, because that's where the feeling is." For many of the nation's still growing ranks of country fans, the songs are precious musical absolutions, forgiving them for the vanities they cherished and lost, and gently nudging them through the undiscovered country of middle age.

The Puget Sound Rides a Wave

IN 1992, SEATTLE BECAME GROUND zero for American rockers. One band after another sprang up from the environs of the city's fast-lane bar scene onto the national charts. The lyrical band Queensrÿche sold more than 2 million copies of its album *Empire*. Alice in Chains, which lays down a kind of altered-consciousness heavy metal—the Doors, slamming—neared platinum-level sales with *Facelift*. *Nevermind*, by the Seattle-area trio **NIRVANA**, has sold 7 million, and the group's single *Smells Like Teen Spirit*, with its arch lyric ironies and crusher guitar chords, hit *Billboard's* Top 10 and helped get the band on *Saturday Night Live*.

Seattle boasted four thriving independent record labels; six key music clubs, like the Vogue, in the downtown area alone; and nearly that many recording studios. Representatives of rival record companies prowled the streets in major-label wolf packs, looking for the next bust-out band.

The Seattle sound is cussed, aggressive, incisively individualistic, and it comes, like matching tie and handkerchief, with its own attitude: cut down on flash, look regular, sound loud and sound off. Seattle rockers take almost as much pride in their ornery individuality as in their music.

More than any other group, Nirvana typified the new Seattle heat. "I feel stupid and contagious/Here we are now, entertain us" is one of *Teen Spirit's* more memorable lyric refrains, fully characteristic of the band's spiky style. The core members of Nirvana, lead singer-guitarist Kurt Cobain and bassist Chris Novoselic, teened together in Aberdeen, Wash., and teamed up to form Nirvana in 1987 (drummer David Grohl signed on later). Their first album, *Bleach*, recorded in three days at a cost of $600 and distributed by an enterprising local label called Sub Pop, made the band's members stars on the underground circuit.

Now, says Geoff Mayfield, *Billboard's* associate director of retail research, "what I'm hearing is that bands from L.A. or the Midwest are moving to Seattle and telling record companies, 'Yeah, we grew up here, and this is where we make our music.'"

American Operas Score

THESE ARE RICH TIMES for American opera. After years of prospecting in the wilderness of arid academic styles and played-out compositional veins, composers may finally have hit an operatic mother lode.

When New York City's Metropolitan Opera staged the world premiere of Philip Glass's **THE VOYAGE,** celebrating the 500th anniversary of the European discovery of America, Glass's long journey from obscure avant-gardist to mainstream cultural icon was complete. The opera strikes out for the noble horizon of all human striving; despite the technological resources at its disposal, it never quite gets there.

Glass's dreadnought manages to embrace not only Christoper Colum-

Nirvana: arch ironies, crusher guitar chords

bus' first trip to the New World but also the electric dreams of Stephen Hawking and the arrival of aliens on earth during the Ice Age. The sheer size of the production, however, often overwhelms David Henry Hwang's clliptical text. Glass's chug-chug style remains instantly recognizable, but his music has colored and deepened over the years. If in the end the opera, like its hero, doesn't land where it was headed, sometimes it is indeed better to travel than to arrive.

William Bolcom has given Frank Norris' 1989 novel **MC TEAGUE** a brash, distinctive voice. His score evokes turn-of-the-century America in a slick potpourri of retro modernism, long, loose-limbed melodies and irresistible ryhthmic invention. The libretto relates the story of an unlicensed dentist who falls in love with his best friend's girl, played by a marvelously sensual Catherine Malfitano. This new opera is eclectic, tuneful and frankly crowd pleasing. Americans want something with a beat they can virtually dance to. In *McTeague* they have it. ■

***McTeague*: American opera with a beat you can dance to**

THEATER

Off-Broadway's Bounty

EVEN WHEN BROADWAY GLITTERED ITS brightest, it would have been an exceptional week that brought the openings of fiercely funny and trenchantly topical plays by three of the nation's leading dramatists. That miraculous week occurred in late October 1992—but Broadway was not part of the buzz. For reasons ranging from finances to the tyranny of reviews, all three plays opened off-Broadway. Artistically, the week couldn't have been much richer. Economically, the theater still seemed to be passing the hat.

The showiest piece and ultimately the most moving was Larry Kramer's poignant gay Bildungsroman, **THE DESTINY OF ME.** Its main character, Ned Weeks, a stand-in for the author, was as hilariously self-congratulatory and self-critical as he was in the earlier Kramer play, *The Normal Heart*. More than a play about AIDS and death, *The Destiny of Me* was a play about homosexuality and life. It was irate, not about dying, but about having been unable to live and love.

At the other end of the scale of suffering was Wendy Wasserstein's drawing-room comedy with claws, **THE SISTERS ROSENSWEIG,** which centered on three sisters torn between compulsive overachieving and staying close to their ancestral Jewish roots in Brooklyn. Wasserstein was interested in serious issues, but in form and uproarious dialogue the play was a commercial comedy, a delight that was exquisitely performed, especially by Madeline Kahn as the ditsiest, daffiest and most devious of the sisters.

David Mamet's **OLEANNA** was a lapel-grabbing vision of political correctness cum intellectual terrorism, based on an innocent-looking encounter between a baffled and seemingly despondent college student and a haughty and fashionably iconoclastic professor whom she accuses of sexual harassment. The professor's ugly spiral downward was at once outlandish and entirely plausible—and ultimately very stirring. Mamet's play had the power to incense.

Broadway couldn't equal off-Broadway's brilliant trifecta, but it offered a number of memorable plays. Irish writer Frank McGuiness found a trove of snarky pub wit and schoolboy antics in **SOMEONE WHO'LL WATCH OVER ME,** about hostages held in a basement in Lebanon. Though well played by a deft British cast—Alec Mcowen as a prissy schoolteacher, Stephen Rea as a dissolute Irish journalist and James McDaniel as a tightly wound American doctor—the roles resembled the contrived ethnic jumble of old war movies.

At his lyrical best, former poet August Wilson can embed subtle and complex political commentary within the conversational riffs of fully realized characters. That is just what he did in **TWO TRAINS RUNNING,** his most delicate and mature work, if not his most dramatic. The subject was nothing less than the whole range of political, social and philosophical options by which black people have lived for the past couple of decades, yet the story remained, to all appearances, a glimpse of everyday existence circa 1969 in a run-down Pittsburgh luncheonette.

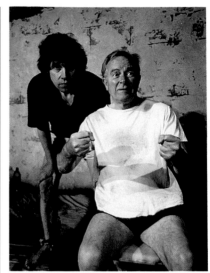
Someone: snarky pub humor

Musical Memories

1992 WAS THE YEAR WHEN LONG-BATTERED Broadway took heart again. And the show that crystallized its comeback was Frank Loesser's funny valentine to Gotham, **GUYS AND DOLLS.** For the first time in years, the most coveted ticket was not to one of the big British musi-

Guys and Dolls: Frank Loesser's funny valentine to Gotham

cals that disgruntled Yanks term "the chandelier show" (*Phantom of the Opera*); "the barricades show" (*Les Misérables*); "the helicopter show" (*Miss Saigon*); or "the felines show" (*Cats*).

As envisioned by director Jerry Zaks and set designer Tony Walton, the revival was a paean to urban zest. Faith Prince's over-the-top medley of mannerisms as Miss Adelaide was the evening's central delight and Nathan Lane as Nathan Detroit was supremely articulate in his comic songs.

A "new" Gershwin musical, **CRAZY FOR YOU,** was also greeted with cheers, less for what the show featured—a slow narrative, obvious jokes and completely undefined characters—than for its shameless retrospection, its bland assertion that Broadway's future lay in its past. More compelling was another Loesser revival, **THE MOST HAPPY FELLA.** Despite its irritating cuteness and insincerity, the show achieved emotional believability in Spiro Malas's performance in the title role.

Just when the Broadway musical seemed frozen in nostalgia, two new shows jolted it into the present. Playwright George C. Wolfe shook things up with **JELLY'S LAST JAM,** a biography of composer and performer Jelly Roll Morton that was as much a review of Morton's ethnic fealty as of his music. Although it failed as dramaturgy— it began slowly, ended abruptly, and was needlessly vulgar—the show succeeded as bouncy entertainment. As Morton, Gregory Hines vibrated with his glorious triple-threat talent as singer, dancer and actor.

William Finn's **FALSETTOS**—about a man who leaves his wife and son for another man, only to watch him die of AIDS—might not be most people's idea of entertainment. But *Falsettos'* three dozen musical numbers by the quirky and querulous Finn were Broadway's richest emotional experience.

A Streetcar Named Desire: a drawing card named stardom

Malibu on Broadway

IN THE SPRING SEASON OF 1992, A transfusion of new blood gave the theater a refreshing jolt of energy. Most surprising was the source of the elixir: Hollywood. An abundance of high-profile movie and TV stars returned to the risks and rigors of the live stage.

Alec Baldwin and Jessica Lange were sharing a sweaty embrace in a revival of **A STREETCAR NAMED DESIRE.** Alan Alda's wry wit and Judd Hirsch's in-your-face comic angst were on display in splendid tragicomedies by Neil Simon (*Jake's Women*) and Herb Gardner (*Conversations with My Father*). Those who preferred grandes dame could savor performances by Joan Collins in Noel Coward's *Private Lives,* Rosemary Harris in Simon's *Lost in Yonkers,* and Lynn Redgrave in Ibsen's *The Master Builder.* Elsewhere were Keith Carradine in *The Will Rogers Follies,* Cyd Charisse in *Grand Hotel,* Raul Julia and pop singer Sheena Easton in *Man of La Mancha,* and Al Pacino in Oscar Wilde's *Salome.* Martin Sheen and Rob Lowe joined Tony Randall in productions from Randall's new repertory company, the National Actors Theater.

Perhaps the most profligate display of star power came in Chilean writer Ariel Dorfman's thriller cum debate about South American politics, **DEATH AND THE MAIDEN,** which starred five-time Oscar nominee Glenn Close and Oscar winners Gene Hackman and Richard Dreyfuss. Another Hollywood veteran, Mike Nichols, directed.

How to account for the star stampede? First, producers loved their box-office magic. Dorfman's serious play opened to a musical-size advance sale of $3.4 million, and mixed notices had no effect at the box office. Yet for many actors, the move to Broadway was an artistic decision. They wanted to play classic roles, work with particular directors or co-stars, or demonstrate talent in a way films did not allow.

For other stars, recession cutbacks in Hollywood also played a part. Not that Broadway pay was exactly monastic. While Pacino worked for $1,000 a week, some stars commanded up to 10% of box-office gross, as much as $20,000 a week. ∎

The Open Window, 1905

ART

Matisse: The Color of Genius

SOMETIMES AN EXHIBITION WILL DEfine the work of a major artist for a whole generation. So with the Museum of Modern Art's Picasso retrospective in 1980. In 1992, New York City's MOMA did it again, with "Henri Matisse: A Retrospective," devoting most of its gallery space to an enormous survey of Matisse's paintings, drawings, collages and sculpture. The show was curated by art historian John Elderfield.

The last comparable Matisse show was staged in Paris in 1970, to mark the artist's centenary. It contained 250 works, and its catalog weighed 2 lbs. This one has rather more than 400 works, and its catalog tips the kitchen scales at 5 lbs. 7 oz., outweighing even MOMA's Picasso catalog by 11 oz. It wasn't an experience to approach casually, even if the box-office jam allowed it. But Elderfield's panorama of Matisse's achievement was so exhilarating, so full of rapturous encounters with one of the grandest pictorial sensibilities ever to pick up a brush, so steady in its narrative line and—not incidentally—so sensitively hung, that even those who went in with a certain foreboding came out walking on air and longing to start over again.

Matisse, paladin of modernism, is a long way from us now. Almost a generation older than Picasso, his counterpart, he was born in 1869, the year the Suez Canal opened. Everything that

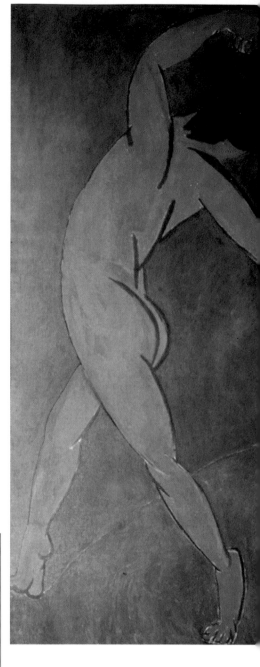

looked modern in Matisse's environment is now ancient, from the gas buggies that were just coming onto the streets of Paris when he was a student in Gustave Moreau's atelier to the Vichy politicians who ran France during the Nazi occupation as he painted in Vence.

As Elderfield pointed out in a catalog essay, Matisse's luck with the critics has always been peculiar. At the outset, part of the tiny modern-art public in Paris thought his work incoherent, ugly. Others, like Gauguin's friend Maurice Denis, praised its absolutist devotion to "painting in itself,

182

Dance (II), 1905

the pure act of painting." But there was never a shortage of critics who saw Matisse as a kind of magisterial lightweight. "[His] love of color equals the love of chiffon," said one.

This image of Matisse as a decorative, hence feminine, hence inferior painter tended to stick. Matisse's best-known remark about his art didn't help much either: he wanted "an art of balance, or purity and serenity, devoid of troubling or depressing subject matter," that would soothe the mind of "every mental worker . . . something like a good armchair which provides relaxation from physical fatigue."

The claim that Matisse was as avant-garde an artist as Picasso hardly took general hold in America until the 1960s, and came from his late work. For some years before his death in 1954, Matisse had been working to solve the split he had always experienced between drawing and painting. By cutting shapes out of precolored paper—cutting, as he saw it, directly into the color—and then pasting them on the surface, he closed the gap between outline drawing and color patch. As in *Memory of Oceania*, 1952-53, he gave the art of collage a brilliance, size and vivacity it had never had before.

Matisse was no more an abstract artist than Picasso. His paintings vividly communicate a tension between what he called "the sign" and the reality it pointed to. He had learned about this tension and its anxieties from Cézanne. For Matisse it was of prime importance, whereas in abstract art it tends to fall away, because one end of the cord is no longer anchored in the world and its objects.

Matisse had his leitmotivs, the full scope of whose recurrence only becomes clear in a show like this. One is the view through a door or window, from inside a room. One first sees it in

Conversation, 1908-12

Circus, 1908-12

atic as that of an Etruscan vase: blue sky, green billowing earth, red flesh inflicted with deeper, Indian-red drawing. It could not be more vivid or explicit, or better attuned to the fresco-like scale of the canvas.

And yet how provisional these dancers seem, compared with their ancestors; how deliberately imperfect, within the brusque signs for arched back, swollen belly, prancing, dragging, reaching. One clue to this is the complicated knot formed by the crossing legs of the second figure from the left, and the hands of the two dancers in front of her. There the circle of the dance breaks; the hands have come apart, they do not touch. Classical art would not show this. Choreographic "imperfection" matches those brusque details of visual depiction.

Matisse was the heir to an entire, and in his time still viable, tradition of European painting. *Conversation* is, on one level, an intimate interior—the painter in his pajamas chatting with Mme. Matisse in her chair. But its hieratic grandeur irresistibly puts you in mind of an Annunciation with angel (though wingless) and Madonna. In particular Matisse inherited the pastoral mode, replete with allegory. He refers to the poetry of his time—Baudelaire, Mallarmé—with the same sense of possession and community that Renaissance painters like Lotto, Giorgione and Titian alluded to Ovid's *Metamorphoses*.

One wonders what the long-term effect of this show will be. With luck, it will be at least equal in its impact on artists in the '90s to that of the Picasso show on artists in the '80s. We are at present surrounded with art of depressing triviality. On every side, the idea of quality is ritually attacked, so that many young artists have come to doubt the most basic experience involved in comparing one artwork with another—namely, that there are differences of intensity, articulateness, radiance, between works of art; that some speak more convincingly than others; and that this is not a political matter. Fifteen minutes in any room of this sublime exhibition was enough to blow such stale and peevish trivia away. Matisse did much, at the beginning of this century, to dispel the mustiness of academic art. At its end, he may still do the same to the mingy products of end-game academic modernism. ∎

1896, in a small, unremarkable study of an open door giving onto the sea in Brittany. From then on it appears whenever he is at full pitch: in *The Open Window*, 1905, as he is creating the speckled, radically colored world of Fauvism at Collioure in the south of France; in the great "decorative" paintings of 1908-12 like *Conversation*; in the astoundingly bare and mysterious *French Window at Collioure*, 1914; and so on to the palm tree, that, like a firework in the garden, fills the window of *Interior with an Egyptian Curtain*, 1948, its explosive light seeming to cast an inky black shadow under the bowl of fruit. The room is culture; the

window frames nature; it is a kind of picture-within-a-picture, another trope that Matisse was partial to.

It is a habit to speak of Matisse's "assurance," his Apollonian, almost inhuman, balance. Yet this simple idea does not survive the evidence of this show. The deeper one looked, the more doubt one found.

Matisse was less interested in "locked" and unified structures than one thinks. The ring of figures in *Dance (II)*, 1909-10, refers back to a long tradition of representations of bacchanalian dances, from the ancient Greeks through to Poussin. The color is almost as simple and emblem-

The Best of 1992

I N 1992 CONTROVERSY-MONGERS, COP-bashing rappers and pop-culture purvey-ors of belligerence and kinky sex all achieved fame—or its shady cousin, noto-riety. Yet behind the noise and glitz, some tal-ented, thoughtful people saved a decrepit park, encompassed American history in a seven-hour play cycle, brought new vigor to the opera.

Could it be that there is a more persistently wholesome and positive strain in American cul-ture than is dreamed of in Madonna's or even Dan Quayle's philosophy? How else explain the way *Aladdin* captivated the box office? The way *Murphy Brown* prevailed with its own ver-sion of family values? Or the way Garth Brooks sweetened the airwaves? In a year when the spotlight was reserved for those who provoked and outraged, there were many who illuminat-ed our times through craft, artistry and genius.

Movies

❶ ALADDIN Animation is pure moviemaking: not just the photographing of actors but the creation, frame by frame, of a whole new world. *Aladdin* paints that world in gor-geous colors, populates it with a menagerie of witty charac-ters and sets it spinning at Mach speed. **❷ UNFORGIVEN**

Eastwood in *Unforgiven*

Clint Eastwood's dark west-ern broods—laconically, ironically, tragically—on the morality of violence and the ambiguity of human motives. **❸ HOWARDS END** Handsome, of course, and of course handsomely acted. But the stately virtues of other Merchant Ivory movies are transcended in this collision of classes, tem-peraments and genteel ob-sessions. **❹ GAS FOOD LODGING** Addressing the topic of growing up poor and female in trailer-park America, director Allison Anders smartly skips the piety. A high-spirited low-budgeter. **❺ TOTO LE HEROS** An old man finds that memories of a magical childhood wilt in the heat of his passion for revenge. Belgian filmmaker Jaco Van Dormael's drama educates us to attend carefully to each of life's privileged moments. **❻ INDOCHINE** In Régis War-gnier's confident, delicate evocation of 1930s French colonial life, the politics of love offers both devastation and redemp-tion to a woman (Catherine Deneuve) and her adopted daughter, while the politics of revolution proposes the same for their soci-ety. **❼ RAISE THE RED LANTERN** In 1920s China, a lovely teenager is sold to a rich man as the fourth of his mistresses. Di-rector Zhang Yimou locates ripe melodra-ma and ravishing textural harmony in this bitter, seductive parable. **❽ A BRIEF HISTORY OF TIME** Errol Morris' documentary traces the evolution of physicist Stephen Hawking's theories and the devolution of his body after decades of assault from amyotrophic later-al sclerosis. **❾ BATMAN RETURNS** This gorgeous med-itation on mixed and masked identities turns a comic-

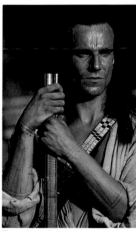
Day-Lewis as Hawkeye

book story into ghouly, ghostly comic art. **❿ THE LAST OF THE MOHICANS** Director Michael Mann's adaptation of a Great Ameri-can Chestnut has the sweep, scope, innocence and bustle of old-fashioned Hollywood historical dramas.

***Indochine* seascape**

Television

❶ JOHNNY CARSON'S FAREWELL (NBC) The *Tonight* show episode that best summed up the Carson era came the night before Johnny's final farewell, when Robin Williams made Johnny crack up and Bette Midler made him choke up. **❷ PRIME SUSPECT (PBS)** Helen Mirren as a London chief investigator faced with a baffling series of murders. Rare is the drama that works so well on two levels: as a crackling whodunit and as a finely tuned character study. **❸ THE WATER ENGINE (TNT)** This flight of paranoid fantasy—an adaptation of David Mamet's play about an inventor who runs afoul of sinister capitalist forces—was largely ignored or misunderstood. Too bad: director Steven Schachter and a terrific cast created the most stylish and haunting TV movie since *Twin Peaks.* **❹ ANDY KAUFMAN: I'M FROM HOLLYWOOD (SHANACHIE HOME VIDEO)** The stand-up comic and former *Taxi* star was TV's most daring put-on artist. This skillfully produced video is the startling account of a comic pushing the boundaries of satire and possibly of sanity. **❺ RODNEY KING'S APPEAL** The man at the center of the horrible Los Angeles riots nervously tried to restore calm: "Can we all get along?" Only one so totally unsophisticated in the ways of the media could produce the year's most emotional TV moment. **❻ THE BEN STILLER SHOW (FOX)** Fox's new sketch comedy series is the place to turn for savvy media satire. Ratings are low and the show is uneven, but at its best it's hilarious. **❼ BILL CLINTON ON MTV** Nowhere was this master of the Q&A format more engaging or quicker on his feet than in this lively studio encounter. **❽ SEINFELD (NBC)** Four New Yorkers sitting around griping: after a couple of seasons, this yuppie sitcom has finally established its idiosyncratic, laid-back tone. **❾ A DOLL'S HOUSE (PBS)** An impeccable British production of Ibsen's feminist classic. **❿ THE DONNER PARTY (PBS)** This harrowing account of the famous group of stranded settlers who resorted to cannibalism to survive was produced by Ric Burns. An artful mix of letters, diaries and archival photos.

Bette busses Johnny

Jerry Seinfeld

Macy in *The Water Engine*

Books

Ondaatje: stuff of dreams

FICTION ❶ THE ENGLISH PATIENT by *Michael Ondaatje.* Ondaatje's characters—a dying burn victim, a young nurse, a morphine thief and a Sikh defuser of unexploded Luftwaffe bombs—are spun of dreams and verbal magic. The quartet intersects at a critical moment in time: the last year of World War II, the beginning of the end of the British Empire and the start of the postimperial age. **❷ CLOCKERS** by *Richard Price.* Like a rock in a sock, this novel of drug deals and double-deals in a gritty New Jersey town squeezed between Newark and Jersey City packs a shattering wallop. Price spent time on the streets listening to the stories of pushers and police and getting the details and dialogue right. He puts his lowlifes on a high literary plane. **❸ ALL THE PRETTY HORSES** by *Cormac McCarthy.* This story of life in the borderlands of Texas and Mexico in 1949 evokes the coming of age of a young horseman who, with a sidekick, rides into Mexico in search of seasoning and adventure—and finds it in taming horses, loving a spirited young woman, and battling a corrupt policeman. In prose that echoes early Hemingway, McCarthy recalls a Southwest in the twilight of its legendary wildness. **❹ OUTERBRIDGE REACH** by *Robert Stone.* The characters in this tale about the dangers of the sea and the treacheries of media exposure live at the extremes. Stone's handsome couple risk comfort, security and their good marriage when the head of the house decides to sail in an around-the-world race and allows an untrustworthy documentary filmmaker to publicize the exploit. There are storms at sea and emotional whirlpools at home. Stone once again demonstrates he is our poet of doom. **❺ DREAMING IN CUBAN** by *Cristina Garcia.* This first novel by a Cuban American tells the poignant, often funny story of three generations of Cuban women and their varying responses to Fidel's revolution. Pro- and anti-Castro factions clash. Garcia's imagination ranges over the country's past, its heritage and—through the longings of a young American girl to reunite with her revolutionary grand mother in Havana—its future. **NONFICTION ❻ WHAT IT TAKES** by *Richard Ben Cramer.* In an election year supersaturated with tasteless sound bites and redundant punditry, who would

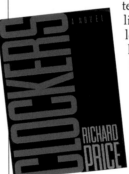

Ben Cramer: beyond cliché

pay $28 for 1,000 pages about the 1988 race for the White House? Enough readers to put this on 1992 best-seller lists. Cramer does for politics what Tom Wolfe did for the space program: get behind the clichés, public relations and media hype to reveal the ambitions, strengths and weaknesses of the candidates. **❼ UP IN THE OLD HOTEL** *by Joseph Mitchell.* This would be among the best books of any year. In fact it (they) was. The volume contains four previously published books by Mitchell, 84, the legendary reporter for the *New Yorker*; it is crammed with Mitchell's favorite subjects: visionaries, obsessives, impostors, fanatics, lost souls, street preachers and Gypsy kings and queens. Mitchell caught their cadences in pages of matchless American prose. **❽ KISSINGER: A BIOGRAPHY** *by Walter Isaacson.* Both admiring and critical of the former Secretary of State, Isaacson concludes that, despite his brilliance, Kissinger did not fully appreciate "the moral values that are the true sources of [America's] global influence." **❾ TRUMAN** *by David McCullough.* This hefty tome reminds readers that behind his image as the uncommon common man, Harry Truman was an old-fashioned back-room politician— and that the machine worked pretty well if it could produce such a decisive President. **❿ GENIUS: THE LIFE AND SCIENCE OF RICHARD FEYNMAN** *by James Gleick.* Nobel Prize-winner Feynman astonished his physicist peers with his penetrating intuition, skirt chasing and bongo playing; Gleick explains the paradoxes of Feynman's science and captures the life-force of a man who talked like a Brooklyn cab driver and thought like a god.

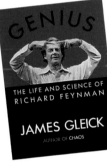

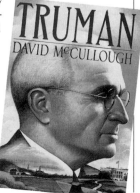

Music

Bartoli: Roman flair

❶ CECILIA BARTOLI ROSSINI HEROINES (LONDON) She's 26 and she's magic. This gem shows off the brilliant mezzo coloratura, sublime musicianship and infectious good humor of this Roman with a natural dramatic flair. **❷ BILLIE HOLIDAY THE COMPLETE BILLIE HOLIDAY ON VERVE 1945-1959 (VERVE)** A beautiful compilation of Holiday's waning years, great American music with frailty to spare but no hint of weakness. **❸ BOHUSLAV MARTINU COMPLETE SYMPHONIES (CHANDOS)** All six of the Czechoslovak-born Martinu's brilliant, idiosyncratic symphonies were composed in America. Performed with passion, this is the find of the year. **❹ MARY-CHAPIN CARPENTER COME ON COME ON (COLUMBIA)** Country meets the suburbs, and old careless love hooks up with genteel angst in this mature, play-it-till-it-wears-out album. **❺ ANTHONY DAVIS X, THE LIFE AND TIMES OF MALCOLM X (GRAMAVISION)** This penetrating musical portrait is at once a dazzling first opera and a powerful evocation of a man, his social milieu and, ultimately, his place in our history. **❻ CHARLIE HADEN HAUNTED HEART (VERVE)** Intrepid bassist Haden has fashioned an autobiographical musical journey that recreates in jazz the film-noir genre. **❼ TONY BENNETT PERFECTLY FRANK (COLUMBIA)** It takes a top talent to do so right by itself while paying homage to another. Moral: there are no definitive versions of great songs, only definitive singers. **❽ ARRESTED DEVELOPMENT 3 YEARS, 5 MONTHS AND 2 DAYS IN THE LIFE OF . . . (EMI/CHRYSALIS)** Refreshing life-affirming variations on rap's rage. The group's jazz-, funk- and reggae-laced tracks espouse such radical values as love and respect. **❾ HENRYK GORECKI SYMPHONY NO. 3 (NONESUCH)** One of the greatest works of our time, this crypto-Minimalist, radiantly spiritual essay on suffering and redemption could have come only from the deepest recesses of communist Poland. **❿ ERIC CLAPTON UNPLUGGED (REPRISE)** A lyrical heartbreaker. What makes this collection a triumph is the sense of strength and spiritual assurance that Clapton brings to his playing and singing.

Arrested Development

Haden: film-noir jazz

Theater

❶ THE KENTUCKY CYCLE Playwright Robert Schenkkan's nine plays span seven hours and two centuries. Mythic in scale but rooted in the evolving fate of the same few hundred acres of Kentucky, the cycle underscores the violence and unchecked injustice of our past. **❷ CONVERSATIONS WITH MY FATHER** Herb Gardner

Angels: farce and fantasy

digs deep in this story of a Jewish barkeep who is sure that success will come from assimilation, endless self-reinvention and faith in the American Dream. **❸ THE DESTINY OF ME** Gay activist Larry Kramer told his life story in *The Normal Heart* (1985) and resumed it in this off-Broadway stunner. Jonathan Hadary gave the performance of the year, balancing titanic rage, puckish mockery and suppressed

Mythic Kentuckians

self-pity. **❹ ANGELS IN AMERICA** Tony Kushner's 7½-hour epic about gay liberation, AIDS and the Reagan era. The appearance of an avenging angel was only one of the acts of theatrical and metaphysical daring in this brilliant if roughhewn jumble of politics, fantasy and farce. **❺ SPIC-O-RAMA** John Leguizamo gave himself an acting tour de force as all six members of a troubled Hispanic family in hilarious monologues that moved beyond performance art to become a true and deeply moving play. **❻ GUYS AND DOLLS** The greatest of Broadway musicals, exuberantly revived: a color-drenched tribute to big-city zest. Faith Prince's Miss Adelaide was the year's musical highlight. **❼ JAKE'S WOMEN** Alan Alda's unsinkable niceness tempered Neil Simon's unyielding self-criticism in this funny and engrossing play about a writer who prefers to deal with people as characters in his head. **❽ OLEANNA** Whether you think it's about sexual harassment or intellectual terrorism, David Mamet's zinger holds the mirror up to modern life. **❾ TWO SHAKESPEAREAN ACTORS** Richard Nelson's piece about competing 19th century acting troupes had three superb performers and an unjustly brief life on Broadway. **❿ INSPECTING CAROL** The Seattle Repertory Theater hilariously sends up censorship, the regional-theater movement's fear of the National Endowment for the Arts—and *A Christmas Carol.*

Oleanna: Mamet's maze

Design

❶ THE WORK OF FRANK GEHRY This year Gehry introduced a jaunty furniture line, springy bentwood shapes that look as if a team of Constructivist elves had decided to make chairs out of old picnic baskets. In Ohio his splendid copper-clad Cubist sculpture also doubles as a warren of classrooms and studios for the University of Toledo art department. **❷ SEATTLE MASTER PLAN** In Seattle city planners are looking for a way to shape the look and feel of the place for the long haul. The basic idea of their sensible master plan is to encourage a dense, old-fashioned city of well-defined neighborhoods and to discourage dispiriting, traffic-clogged sprawl of suburbia. **❸ LIED JUNGLE, HENRY DOORLY ZOO, OMAHA, NEBRASKA** The virtual-reality revolution in zoo design now has an impressive new

benchmark. The Lied Jungle at Omaha's zoo, designed by Stanley J. How & Associates, is both architecturally stupendous—a naturally lighted, eight-story-high dome containing 1½ acres—and zoologically thrilling. **❹ A/X ARMANI EXCHANGE PACKAGING** Designer Alex Isley has perfectly conjured the sexy utilitarianism and

Bryant Park, reborn

voguish grittiness of the '90s for the A/X Armani Exchange. The paper is pulpy and brownish, the handles are bits of clothesline. The niftiest A/X box is punched with an industrial-seeming grid of holes, and the inside slides open like a drawer. **❺ ORIOLE PARK AT CAMDEN YARDS, BALTIMORE, MARYLAND** If baseball is the last living vestige of a sweeter, more authentic America, the Orioles' new downtown stadium is a baseball kind of place. In addition to using good-old-days materials, the architects, HOK, put the (real grass) field 16 ft. below street level to reduce the stadium's bulk. **❻ 202 ISLAND INN, SAN DIEGO** Architect Rob Wellington Quigley has designed and built four low-rent, single-room-occu-

Virtual-reality revolution

pancy hotels. The latest is his best: 197 airy rooms that cost only about $20,000 apiece to build, landscaped courtyards and a reading room. The three-sided exterior is mag-

Gehry's University of Toledo art building

nificent, particularly its kooky Deconstructivist façade.
7 BCE PLACE GALLERIA, TORONTO In Toronto the
Spanish architect and sculptor Santiago Calatrava was
asked only to connect two new run-of-the-mill high-rise office towers called BCE Place with a pedestrian arcade. But

he produced a glori-
ous galleria, an extrav-
agant and exultant se-
ries of 90-ft.-high,
white steel-and-glass
arches enclosing a
granite expanse as big
as a football field.
8 BEEPERKID As
public life becomes
largely a matter of
wandering around
vast shopping malls,
keeping track of small
children is more anxi-

Jacket for *The Secret History*

ety provoking than ever. BeeperKid, conceived by Lev
Chapelsky, is a handsome, carefully designed solution.
One disk pins onto the kid, the parent carries the other, and
when they get more than 30 ft. apart the parent's unit issues
its beep. If the frantic parent decides to push a button, the
other unit also beeps, letting a relieved mom or dad zero in
on the misplaced offspring. **9 BRYANT PARK
RENOVATION, NEW YORK CITY** The backyard to New
York City's grand Beaux Arts public library, Bryant Park
had become urbanistically wretched. By opening a new entrance, broadening others and adding Neoclassical features, the architects (Hanna/Olin Ltd., Hardy Holzman
Pfeiffer) have achieved a small miracle. **10 BOOK
JACKET FOR *THE SECRET HISTORY*** For Donna Tartt's
best-selling *The Secret History*, designer and mixed-media
virtuoso Chip Kidd and fellow designer Barbara De Wilde
put type on a transparent acetate dust jacket and wrapped
that around a hard cover printed with a photograph—a
smart, craftsman-like, viscerally compelling package.

Sports

Barry Bonds: big numbers

1 Sport is a story of
numbers, on or off the
field. Baseball's best
player, Pittsburgh out-
fielder Barry Bonds, got
the biggest ones: $43.75
million for six years in
San Francisco. Base-
ball owners cried pover-
ty—and demanded to
reopen their contract
with the players' un-
ion. **2 32** The digits
on the jerseys of Magic
Johnson and Shaquille
O'Neal. The N.B.A.'s dazzling '80s era of Magic and Larry
Bird has ended; O'Neal will take over. **3 64 AND
172** Number of nations competing
at Albertville and Barcelona. The
Olympics delivered thrills aplenty.
And—in figure skating—a few
spills. **4 117-85** Score of the
Olympic men's basketball finals. The
Dream Team was a brutal, pointless
spectacle, akin to the Harlem Globe-
trotters' humiliating a flat-footed
pickup team. **5 3** Joe Montana's
ranking on the San Francisco 49ers'

Tyson: guilty

quarterback chart. While Montana's elbow healed, his replacement, Steve Young, had an MVP season, while another ace, Steve Bono, occasionally spelled Young. **6 100,
4x100, 400** Three Olympic highs. Gail Devers won the
women's 100-m race 16 months after nearly having her feet
amputated. Carl Lewis anchored the U.S. men's 4x100-m
relay team, which set a world record. And in an inspiring
400-m semifinal, Briton Derek Redmond collapsed with
a hamstring pull, then rose and, aided by his weeping father, staggered to the finish. **7 1** Number of women who
have played a game in a major-league team sport. For one
period of a preseason skirmish, Manon Rheaume, 20, was
in goal for the N.H.L.'s Tampa Bay Lightning.
8 922335 Mike Tyson wears that number now as a
guest of the Indiana penal system, after being convicted of
rape; the ex-champ forever damaged the genial stud image
of star athletes. **9 0** As in *O Canada*! With the "national

**Benchwarmer
Montana**

pastime" in chaos, it was apt baseball
looked elsewhere for its "world champions." Canada's team, the Toronto Blue
Jays, defeated the Braves in a six-
game palpitator of a World Series.
10 40 One estimate of top-level
male figure skaters in North America who have died of AIDS-
related diseases. Sport, once
a refuge from matters of life
and death, is now a win-
dow into them.   ■

TONY (BIG TUNA) ACCARDO, 86, reputed Mafia leader and successor to Al Capone. Selected by Capone as one of his personal bodyguards, Accardo was believed to have set up the bloody St. Valentine's Day Massacre in Chicago in 1929.

ROY ACUFF, 89, country-music singer who in the 1930s became the first to bring the traditional music of the Tennessee hills to a national audience.

STELLA ADLER, 90, acting teacher who influenced a generation of actors. Adler, who learned the Stanislavski method from its source, stressed the creation of a role through imagination, eschewing the psychological emphasis of Lee Strasberg.

PETER ALLEN, 48, flamboyant, show-stopping Australian-born entertainer. Allen was discovered by Judy Garland and was married for seven years to her daughter Liza Minnelli.

NESTOR ALMENDROS, 61, magician with a movie camera, whose cinematography illuminated films including *My Night at Maud's, The Story of Adèle H., Days of Heaven* and *Sophie's Choice.* The son of a Loyalist who fled Spain after Franco took power, Almendros studied film in Rome, taught Spanish at Vassar, and made documentaries in the early days of the Castro revolution, until he lost his film-critic job for publishing subversive opinions. In the 1980s he directed two scalding films, *Improper Conduct* and *Nobody Listened,* that itemized the torture of homosexuals and other renegades in Cuba.

LYLE ALZADO, 43, former N.F.L. defensive lineman whose strength and exuberance made him an All-Pro twice in 14 seasons. After retiring from football, Alzado became a spokesman against the use of body-building steroids, which, he said, triggered the brain cancer that killed him.

ARLETTY, 94, legendary French actress who starred in *Hotel du Nord* and *Les Enfants du Paradis.*

ELLIS ARNALL, 85, reformist Georgia Governor. In a single term he shattered prison chain gangs, repealed the poll tax and led Georgia into the 20th century.

ISAAC ASIMOV, 72, hyperprolific writer of science fiction and popular science. A compulsive writer, Asimov produced nearly 500 books on subjects from physics to Shakespeare. At 21 he wrote the short story *Nightfall,* which many regard as the best science-fiction work of all time.

FRANCIS BACON, 82, master painter of the soul in torment. Born in Dublin, Bacon created an emblem for the postwar mood of dissatisfaction with his smeared and twisted figures who writhe in brightly colored confinements. Although he was regarded as one of the great modern artists, his unyielding gloom was not to every critic's taste.

WALTER LANIER ("RED") BARBER, 84, sportscaster who for more than three decades served up a stream of play-by-play palaver for the Cincinnati Reds, the Brooklyn Dodgers and the New York Yankees with a down-home eloquence that painted pictures for his listeners in the days before television.

FREDDIE BARTHOLOMEW, 69, curly-haired Dublin-born child actor of 1930s Hollywood movies. While visiting the U.S. with his aunt, Bartholomew was offered the title role in the 1935 film *David Copperfield,* which made him an overnight star. Roles in such classics as *Little Lord Fauntleroy* (1936) and *Captains Courageous* (1937) followed, but by the early '40s his acting career was in decline; after a stint as a daytime-TV-show host, he eventually became an advertising executive.

MENACHEM BEGIN, 78, abrasive,  driven and seemingly uncompromising leader of Israel who signed a peace treaty with Egypt and concluded the Camp David accords with U.S. President Jimmy Carter and Egyptian President Anwar Sadat. Born in Poland, he earned a law degree at the University of Warsaw, then became national commander of Betar, a right-wing paramilitary group that advocated the violent ouster of the British from Palestine. When the Germans invaded Poland in 1939, he fled to Lithuania. A year later he joined the anti-German Free Polish Army and served with the British forces in Palestine. There in 1943 he took command of the Jewish terrorist organization Irgun; the British put a $30,000 price tag on his head.

Not until 1967, when he joined the government as a Minister Without Portfolio, did Begin acquire a measure of respectability. In May 1977, on his ninth try to become Prime Minister, he scored a stunning upset, leading the right-wing Likud bloc to victory. He talked incessantly of Israel's claim to Judea and Samaria, that part of Israel along the West Bank of the Jordan River that was taken from Jordan in 1967. Yet after Sadat made his decision to go to Jerusalem in 1977, Begin found it a gesture so bold and imaginative that he signed a peace treaty with Egypt. The gamble earned both men a share of the Nobel Peace Prize in 1978.

Yet Begin's government pursued a policy of aggressive expansion. He presided over the annexation of the Arab sector of Jerusalem and Syria's Golan Heights. When his wife of 43 years died in 1982, he resigned and went into seclusion. More than three decades ago, he wrote that the struggle to create the state of Israel could be summed up in a single sentence: "We fight, therefore we are."

JOSEPH BLOCK, 90, folksy, independent steel executive. A grandson of the founder of Inland Steel, Block started as a mill hand in 1922, and held nearly every position in the company before becoming chairman himself in 1959. His civic conscience and common touch led him to throw the weight of his company behind securing a fair-employment law in Illinois and redeveloping East Chicago.

ALLAN BLOOM, 62, conservative critic of higher education whose 1987 book *The Closing of the American Mind,* a defense of traditional academic standards that sold more than a million copies, made him a darling of the Reagan era.

SHIRLEY BOOTH, 94, actress whose gift for gabby characters peaked with a Tony-winning performance on Broadway as the embattled wife of an alcoholic in *Come Back, Little Sheba* and in a 1961-66 run on television as the maid Hazel.

WILLY BRANDT, 78, visionary European statesman and Chancellor of the former West Germany. By the time of his death from cancer, he had achieved the great goals of his life: the end of the cold war and the restoration of a unified Germany to the family of nations.

It was an achievement symbolized by the somber drama of a man on his knees: Brandt, on a freezing December day in Warsaw in 1970, before Poland's memorial to the heroes of the ghetto. Here was a German Chancellor making an act of atonement for his country's wrongs, a gesture that electrified the world. Brandt was awarded the Nobel Peace Prize for 1971; he had been named TIME's Man of the Year a year earlier.

Brandt came from humble beginnings. He was born Herbert Frahm in Lubeck in 1913 and was reared largely by his maternal grandfather, an ardent socialist. In 1930, not yet 17, he joined the party. He took the nom de guerre Willy Brandt when Hitler outlawed leftist parties in 1933. Later that year, he fled to Norway on a fishing boat just as the Nazis were about to arrest him.

In 1940 German troops occupied Norway, and Brandt fled again, this time to Sweden. He returned to Norway after the war and began a career in the Norwegian foreign service; in 1947 he reapplied for the German citizenship the Nazis had stripped from him. When it was restored in 1948, he went to work as an aide to Ernst Reuter, the colorful mayor of West Berlin, witnessing the Soviet blockade of the city and the Berlin airlift that saved it.

Brandt's political career began in 1949 with his election to West Germany's first Bundestag. In 1957 he became mayor of West Berlin. He ran in 1961 and '65 as the Social Democrats' candidate for Chancellor, but lost both times after brutal campaigns. With the formation in 1966 of a grand coalition between Christian Democrats and Social Democrats, Brandt came back as West Germany's Vice Chancellor and Foreign Minister; he won the chancellorship three years later. He came to believe the fate of the two Germanys should be decided by Germans and that the key lay in improving relations with the East, particularly the U.S.S.R.

Under his bold policy—*Ostpolitik*—Brandt signed nonaggression pacts with the Soviet Union and Poland in 1970 and renounced claims to 40,000 sq. mi. of former German territory incorporated into Poland. He also signed a treaty in 1972 to normalize relations between West and East Germany, reversing the Bonn government's isolation of its communist rival. But his successes in diplomacy contrasted with disarray in domestic policies. When a close aide was arrested on charges of spying for East Germany, Brandt resigned under pressure, a move he later regretted. He did not withdraw into bitterness, but in his later years evolved into an honored, even beloved, elder statesman.

JOHN CAGE, 79, idiosyncratic American composer. Cage was an indifferent musician, but one of the century's seminal theoreticians. He wrote music for radios, blenders, flowerpots, whistles, cowbells, tape recorders and prepared pianos. His free-ranging eclecticism influenced three generations of American composers, including Morton Feldman, Frederic Rzewski and Philip Glass. "There is no noise," he once said, "only sound."

MORRIS CARNOVSKY, 94, actor who triumphed in Shakespearean roles after being blacklisted during the 1950s.

G. HARROLD CARSWELL, 72, former federal appeals court judge nominated to the Supreme Court by Richard Nixon but rejected by the Senate.

CHARLES ("HONI") COLES, 81, dapper, light-footed actor and tap-dancing virtuoso, whose masterly footwork went generally unrecognized until he went on Broadway in 1949 to join *Gentlemen Prefer Blondes.* With his partner, dancer Cholly Atkins, he created one of Broadway's most memorable soft-shoe teams.

CHUCK CONNORS, 71, television actor whose glinting, gunfighter eyes and rugged persona symbolized the rectitude and independent spirit of the American frontiersman.

RALPH COOPER, late 80s, creator and master of ceremonies of amateur night at the Apollo Theater in Harlem. Cooper introduced a number of performers who later became superstars, including Billie Holiday, Ella Fitzgerald, Sarah Vaughan and Michael Jackson.

ROBERTO D'AUBUISSON, 48, ultrarightist strongman linked to death squads during El Salvador's 12-year civil war. As founder of the Nationalist Republican Alliance, or ARENA, D'Aubuisson emerged as a hero to wealthy landowners resisting demands for land redistribution and political reforms. His large legion of foes, however, viewed his machismo and ruthlessness as a significant cause of his country's violence, which cost 75,000 lives.

SANDY DENNIS, 54, actress who turned nervous mannerisms into a trademark style. Dennis, who took a bohemian but disciplined approach to her work, won a 1966 supporting-actress Oscar for her performance as a frightened young faculty wife in the film *Who's Afraid of Virginia Woolf?* She also won Tony Awards for her roles in *A Thousand Clowns* and *Any Wednesday.*

MILESTONES

MARLENE DIETRICH, 90, legendary German-born actress and singer whose elusive glamour made her an international star for more than a half-century.

Dietrich was born bourgeois in Berlin; her father died when she was a child, and her stepfather was killed in World War I. By 1929 she was making a career on the German stage and screen. It was then that Josef von Sternberg noticed her and cast her in *The Blue Angel*, the story of a sadomasochistic relationship between a nightclub singer and a middle-aged high school teacher who becomes obsessed with her. On its enormous success, Sternberg went to Hollywood, and Dietrich followed. They were teamed for six more pictures before the studio finally separated them.

Dietrich went on to make herself into a more flexible, enduring and ultimately more appealing figure, demonstrating a gift for raucous invulnerability and bold self-parody. Her fierce anti-Nazism before World War II and her heroic exertions to entertain Allied troops during it endeared her to people as no movie role ever did. And as a "glamorous grandmother," sewed into her astonishing costumes for her fabled cabaret and concert appearances, she confirmed for a final time the remarkably tenacious—if still distant—terms of the public's devotion.

HELEN DEUTSCH, 85, prolific screenwriter whose first major success was in 1944 as co-writer of *National Velvet*, a tale of training a horse for the Grand National Steeplechase. The hit film, named one of that year's 10 best, catapulted a young Elizabeth Taylor to stardom.

WILLIE DIXON, 76, Chicago blues great whose songs were inspirations for dozens of rock musicians. An accomplished singer and guitarist, Dixon was also the writer of *Little Red Rooster* and *I'm Your Hoochie Coochie Man*. His songs were sung by Elvis Presley, Jimi Hendrix and the Rolling Stones.

ALEXANDER DUBCEK, 70, reformist leader of Czechoslovakia whose brave attempt to introduce "socialism with a human face" during the Prague Spring of 1968 was crushed by Warsaw Pact tanks. Stripped of his party membership after the crackdown, Dubcek reemerged in November 1989 to join Vaclav Havel in proclaiming a democratic Czechoslovakia.

MILLICENT FENWICK, 82, pipe-smoking former Republican Representative from New Jersey who was the inspiration for the character Lacey Davenport in the *Doonesbury* comic strip.

JOSE FERRER, 80, suave stage, screen and television actor whose career spanned a half-century. Ferrer, who was born in Puerto Rico, passed the entrance exam for Princeton University at 14. He went on to win an Academy Award for Best Actor for his role as the long-nosed romantic poet in 1950's *Cyrano de Bergerac*. His later films include *Moulin Rouge, The Caine Mutiny, Lawrence of Arabia, Ship of Fools, A Midsummer Night's Sex Comedy* and *Dune*.

M.F.K. FISHER, 83, eloquent doyen of food writers. In hundreds of pieces for the *New Yorker* and in 15 books, Fisher elevated the subject of food to a cultural metaphor. Noting that for many years critics dismissed her subject as a "trifle," Fisher riposted, "It seems to me that our three most basic needs, for food and security and love, are so mixed and mingled and entwined that we cannot straightly think of one without the others. So it happens that when I write of hunger, I am really writing about love."

LISA FONSSAGRIVES-PENN, 80, elegant fashion model who led her profession during the 1940s and '50s. Born in Sweden, Fonssagrives posed for some of the most famous photographers of the

age, including Irving Penn, whom she married in 1950. About modeling, she said, "It is always the dress; it is never, never the girl. I'm just a good clothes hanger."

EMERSON FOOTE, 85, who, as president of the Foote, Cone & Belding advertising firm, in 1948 dropped the $12 million American Tobacco account, and as chairman of McCann-Erickson in 1964 quit because he was opposed to handling cigarette clients.

PAUL FREUND, 83, a leading authority on constitutional law. Freund, who taught at Harvard Law School for 37 years, helped sensitize generations of lawyers to the Constitution's protection of individual liberties. When Freund passed up the opportunity to become the U.S. Solicitor General in favor of scholarship, President John F. Kennedy replied, "I'm sorry, I hoped you would prefer making history to writing it."

WILLIAM GAINES, 70, who built *Mad* magazine into a satirical empire, making a national icon of its gap-toothed cover boy, Alfred E. Neuman, with his "What—me worry?" mantra. Gaines was the anti-Luce; *Mad* was the only place for children to get an uncensored glimpse behind the perky facade of '50s life, and he bore paternal responsibility for a large swath of pop culture from the past 25 years.

VINCENT GARDENIA, 70, actor who blended the passion of Italian opera with the patois of the Brooklyn streets in a 50-year career, including a Tony-winning turn in Neil Simon's *The Prisoner of Second Avenue* (1971) and Oscar-nominated roles as the hard-edged baseball manager in *Bang the Drum Slowly* (1973) and the softhearted philanderer in *Moonstruck* (1987)

JIM GARRISON, 70, New Orleans judge and district attorney who was the most relentless proponent of the theory that President Kennedy was murdered by a conspiracy of government officials and right-wing extremists.

DOTTIE GREEN, 71, baseball player for the Rockford Peaches, champions of the All-American Girls Professional Baseball League, which thrived during World War II.

PHILIP HABIB, 72, career diplomat who influenced U.S. policy for three decades. Habib was head of the peace talks in Paris that ended the Vietnam War. He helped arrange the cease-fire in Lebanon and the P.L.O.'s withdrawal from that country in 1982. He was also instrumental in persuading Philippine President Ferdinand Marcos to go into exile in 1986.

CLARA HALE, 87, self-taught social worker. Harlem's legendary Mother Hale cared for drug addicts' babies and other forlorn infants at her Hale House.

ALEX HALEY, 70, author of *Roots: The Saga of an American Family* and co-author of *The Autobiography of Malcolm X. Roots,* published during America's Bicentennial in 1976, was Haley's fictionalization of the tracing of his ancestry back to its West African roots. The next year it became the basis for an eight-part television mini-series that provided a rude reminder that the birth of the nation was not without severe moral complications. Haley's Pulitzer-prizewinning account of the slave trade and plantation life—always gripping, not always accurate—made white America confront its own dark roots. For millions of African Americans, however, Haley's publishing and video sensation was a cause for celebration. His "faction," as he called it, provided them with both a history and an identity. The book was ultimately translated into 30 languages.

S.I. HAYAKAWA, 85, outspoken semantics professor who, while acting president of San Francisco State College in 1968, faced down rioting students and became a hero to conservatives. In 1941 Hayakawa published *Language in Action,* a best-selling introduction to semantics. Although sympathetic to demands for a black-studies department at San Francisco State in 1968, Hayakawa defeated protesters' attempts to close the campus. Sporting his trademark tam-o'-shanter, he climbed atop the demonstrators' sound truck and ripped out the wiring of their loudspeaker. As Republican Senator from California from 1977 to 1983, Hayakawa advocated a lower entry-level wage for teenagers but was known mostly for dozing through briefings. He later led the movement to establish English as the official language of the U.S.

FRIEDRICH HAYEK, 92, economist whose 1944 book *The Road to Serfdom,* a critique of socialism, made him a hero to conservatives. Hayek influenced American economists with his seminars at the University of Chicago in the 1950s and '60s. He argued that governments that intervene in the marketplace with price controls and income-redistribution schemes inevitably become tyrannical. The collapse of the command economies in the Soviet Union and Eastern Europe was vindication of Hayek's views. He shared the 1974 Nobel Prize for Economics with Gunnar Myrdal.

BENNY HILL, 67, zany British comedian whose appearances on American television in the 1980s created a cult following. For 30 years Hill's slapstick humor, pop-eyed leer and knowing wink won him fans in more than 100 countries. Responding to criticism that his skits, replete with skimpily-clad women, were sexist, Hill declared, "If my sketches teach anything, it is that for the male, sex is a snare and a delusion. What's so corrupting about that?"

GRACE HOPPER, 85, retired Navy rear admiral and computer-science pioneer. After receiving a doctorate in mathematics from Yale in 1934, Hopper taught at her alma mater, Vassar. In 1943 she joined the Navy and used the forerunner of modern computers to do ordnance calculations. Hopper helped develop UNIVAC, the first large commercial computer. At 60 she was recalled to active duty to help standardize the Navy's computer languages. She retired in 1986 as the nation's oldest active-duty officer. A blunt woman who smoked unfiltered cigarettes, she once called the women's movement "tommyrot and nonsense," declaring, "Being a woman won't hold you back if you have the desire, the courage and the skills."

IRVING KAUFMAN, 81, federal judge who sentenced Julius and Ethel Rosenberg to the electric chair in 1951. The Rosenbergs were convicted of conspiring to deliver atom-bomb secrets to the Soviet Union. Although the judge wrote a number of landmark decisions during his career, he was plagued by the controversial case throughout his life.

EDDIE KENDRICKS, 52, pop and soul singer. Kendricks' polished, passionate tenor topped off the soulful chords of the Temptations for Motown in the '60s, in such hits as *The Way You Do the Things You Do, My Girl* and *Just My Imagination.*

ALBERT KING, 69, blues guitarist. A black musical virtuoso, he influenced younger white superstars such as Stevie Ray Vaughan and Eric Clapton.

OTTO KLINEBERG, 92, social psycologist whose studies on the intelligence scores of black students helped win the Supreme Court's landmark school desegregation case in 1954, of Parkinson's disease. Lawyers in *Brown v. Board of Education* cited Klineberg's findings to prove that segregated schools provided unequal education.

RALPH LAZO, 67, American voluntarily interned in a World War II relocation center. When the internment of people of Japanese ancestry began in California in 1942, Lazo, who was of Mexican and Irish descent, decided to go with his Japanese-American friends to the Manzanar Relocation Center. Lazo was subsequently drafted by the Army and was awarded a Bronze Star for heroism in combat.

VICTOR LOUIS, 64, shadowy Russian journalist who served as a conduit to the West for the Communist Party and the KGB during the cold war. As a correspondent for the London *Evening News* for 29 years, he used his Kremlin ties to scoop the rest of the world; he knew before Western reporters that Nikita Khrushchev had been ousted as the Soviet leader. Though Louis denied spreading KGB disinformation abroad, some Western journalists were convinced otherwise.

SIR KENNETH MACMILLAN, 62, principal choreographer and ex-director of London's Royal Ballet, credited with reviving the tradition of full-length ballet in Britain.

MILESTONES

BARBARA MC CLINTOCK, 90, pioneering geneticist whose discoveries about "jumping genes"—the movement of small segments of DNA around chromosomes, causing unexpected patterns in heredity—won her a 1983 Nobel Prize and revolutionized her field.

WILLIAM MC GOWAN, 64, founder and chairman of MCI Communications Corp., America's second largest long-distance phone company. Under McGowan, MCI challenged AT&T's monopoly in a landmark antitrust suit that led to the breakup of AT&T in 1984.

OLIVER MESSIAEN, 83, pre-eminent French composer. A devout Roman Catholic, Messiaen reflected in his music his mystical faith, love of nature and complex sense of color and rhythm.

WILBUR MILLS, 82, powerful former chairman of the House Ways and Means Committee. After gaining a seat on the prestigious committee in 1943, the young Arkansas Democrat became its pre-eminent authority on taxation and longtime chairman. His career declined abruptly after he was involved in a 1974 drunken-driving incident that landed Fanne Fox, a stripper, in Washington's Tidal Basin. In his later years he was an active advocate of alcoholism treatment.

GEORGE MURPHY, 89, Hollywood song-and-dance man turned politician. Murphy appeared in 55 films with such stars as Gene Kelly, Shirley Temple and his longtime friend Ronald Reagan. He served two terms as president of the Screen Actors Guild, and after retiring from acting was elected Senator from California in 1964.

CHRISTIAN NELSON, 98, pioneering confectioner who created the Eskimo Pie. Running an ice-cream shop in Onawa, Iowa, in 1919, he placated a boy struggling to choose between chocolate and ice cream by combining the two. The result proved a sensation.

JAN OORT, 92, Dutch astronomer, who established that the Milky Way rotates and that the earth's solar system lies on its outskirts. He did pioneering work on the "dark matter" that pervades the universe, and in the 1950s proposed the existence of the Oort Cloud, a vast collection of ice chunks lying far beyond Pluto, now thought to be the birthplace of comets.

BERT PARKS, 77, perennial master of ceremonies of the Miss America Pageant and game-show host. Parks, whose rendition of *There She Is* serenaded winners in Atlantic City for 25 years, was unceremoniously booted from the pageant in 1979 because of his age. In 1990 Parks got the last laugh when he appeared in a much lauded cameo in the film *The Freshman,* singing a satirical version of *There She Is* to a lizard.

MOLLY PARNIS, ninetyish, fashion designer whose versatile dresses were worn by First Ladies from Mamie Eisenhower to Betty Ford.

ANTHONY PERKINS, 60, actor who starred as the motelkeeper Norman Bates in the Alfred Hitchcock thriller *Psycho.*

MOLLY PICON, 93, star of Yiddish theater and vaudeville since the century was young.

ALBERT PIERREPOINT, 87, Britain's best-known hangman, who dispatched 433 men and 17 women in a 25-year career. Pierrepoint, who defended the noose as humane and quick, became a foe of capital punishment after he retired in 1956.

MIKE PLANT, 42, solo transoceanic yachtsman and adventurer who was presumed dead after his 60-ft. racing sloop *Coyote* vanished in the North Atlantic en route from New York to Les Sables-d'Olonne, France.

SAMMY PRICE, 83, "King of Boogie Woogie", a Texas-born pianist who teamed up with such jazz greats as Sidney Bechet and Lester Young during a seven-decade career, influenced generations of younger players with his hard-driving style.

EMILIO PUCCI DE BARSENTO, 78, fashion designer, whose use of bright colors and bold geometric shapes won the favor of Jacqueline Kennedy, Grace Kelly and Elizabeth Taylor.

SATYAJIT RAY, 70, evocative Indian filmmaker whose first and most celebrated films (*Pather Panchali, Aparajito* and *Apur Sansar*) constituted a trilogy that was epic in everything but physical scale. Ranging over three decades, embracing both village and city life in modern India as well as the most basic human emotions, the works traced the growth of their protagonist, Apu, from childhood to young manhood. Financed on the scrounge and shot on weekends by an amateur cast and crew, the trilogy brought its director worldwide acclaim. He went on to create a superb body of work that eloquently portrayed a society devastated first by colonial oppression, then by postcolonial cultural confusions.

STEVE ROSS, 65, visionary company builder and chairman and co-CEO of Time Warner Inc. who had an unerring instinct for the art of the deal and projected an aura that was larger than life. Born Steven Rechnitz in Brooklyn, he was the son of a struggling oil-burner salesman who changed the family name to Ross when his son was in kindergarten. Ross's first jobs were in Manhattan's garment district as stockboy and later salesman. In 1954, after marrying Carol Rosenthal, he went to work for his new father-in-law's funeral parlors, where he first began to build his empire. It was a catchall conglomerate named Kinney Services, whose businesses included parking garages, cleaning services, limousine rentals and magazine distribution.

In 1969 Ross purchased Warner Bros.-Seven Arts, a fading shadow of the great Hollywood studio it had once been. He soon sold off Kinney's unglamorous sidelines to concentrate on movies, pop music and television. Ross reacted to Hollywood glitz as if born under klieg lights, becoming a confidant of stars and sharing with them his lavish life-style. His enterprise flourished, though his reputation was tarnished twice: first when close aides were convicted in a racketeering scheme involving a theater in which he had invested, and then when Warner nearly went under because of the crash of its previously profitable Atari video-games division.

Warner's 1990 acquisition by Time Inc. paid off handsomely for Ross; his compensation package exceeded $78 million in 1990, the cost to Time Inc. of buying out the stake he had accrued in Warner over 30 years. Ross had his critics, but even they would concede that he was unrivaled as a salesman—and a merchant of dreams.

ANTHONY (FAT TONY) SALERNO, 80, cigar-chomping former boss of New York City's Genovese crime family. In 1986 FORTUNE rated Salerno the most powerful and wealthiest gangster in America. He died in a federal prison in Masssachusetts.

LEE SALK, 65, child psychologist and author who wrote eight books on family relationships. In his 1973 book, *What Every Child Would Like His Parents to Know*, he cautioned against the abandonment of full-time motherhood. "The attention you withhold from a young child," Salk wrote, "will be demanded doubly when he is older." He knew about sibling rivalry from his own family: his brother Jonas invented a polio vaccine.

ERIC SEVAREID, 79, versatile journalist whose career spanned five decades. He first found fame as one of "Murrow's boys," a group of crack newsmen assembled by Edward R. Murrow for CBS radio in Europe before World War II. Sevareid scored a coup when he became the first newsman to report that France was about to surrender to the Germans. For nearly three decades he contributed eloquent, carefully crafted political commentaries.

WILLIAM SHAWN, 85, editor of the *New Yorker* from 1952 to '87. A quiet tyrant of talent and taste, Shawn presided over the magazine that was the arbiter of all things literary and social. During his 35-year reign, he published such writers as John Updike and Ann Beattie; such landmarks of advocacy journalism as Rachel Carson's environmental salvo *Silent Spring* and James Baldwin's racial-justice manifesto *Letter from a Region in My Mind*; and some of the most unrelenting criticism of U.S. policy in Vietnam.

SYLVIA SYMS, 73, cabaret singer whose intimate, expressive voice led Frank Sinatra to call her "the best saloon singer in the world."

JOHN SIRICA, 89, the federal judge  whose insistence on learning the truth in the Watergate scandal was central in bringing down Richard Nixon's presidency. Sirica presided over Watergate cases for five years. Impatient at times with the evasiveness of the defendants, some of the most powerful men in the government, Sirica frequently took over the questioning himself, acting like a dogged prosecutor. His decision to require Nixon to turn over incriminating tapes led to the President's resignation. But Sirica, who was TIME's Man of the Year in 1973, felt that justice was ill served by that result. "He should have stood trial," Sirica wrote in his memoirs. "No matter how great his personal loss, Nixon did manage to keep himself above the law."

JAMES ALWARD VAN FLEET, 100,  four-star general who led combat campaigns on D-day, at the Battle of the Bulge and in the Korean War. President Harry S Truman called Van Fleet "the greatest general we have ever had."

SAM WALTON, 74, founder of Wal-Mart Stores. When he died after a long battle with cancer, he was eulogized as a man whose chain of discount stores had transformed American merchandising. Walton perfected a hands-on management style that instilled a sense of team enthusiasm among the 380,000 employees he liked to refer to as "associates." In the process, he became America's richest person, his family's wealth estimated at $23 billion. But he also became the patron saint of a down-home style of megawealth; es-

chewing the fancy trappings of power, "Mr. Sam" drove a Ford pickup truck and hopped around the country to visit stores, take the pulse of consumers and inspire his workers. Walton's brilliantly simple concept of "everyday low price" retailing became such a pervasive force that it redesigned the social structure of rural and small-town America. But critics said the vigor of his suburban stores drained the vitality and individuality from the downtowns of smaller communities.

WANG HONGWEN, 57, youngest member of China's Gang of Four during the 1966-76 Cultural Revolution. He and three other Gang members were responsible for purging tens of thousands of party members and intellectuals and launching ultraleftist ideological and political campaigns. In 1981 he was sentenced to life in prison for wrongful persecution and plotting to overthrow the government.

JAMES WEBB, 85, pioneering leader of the National Aeronautics and Space Administration who is credited with guiding the space agency from its fledgling beginning to to landing a man on the moon.

LAWRENCE WELK, 89, bandleader whose wholesome charm and "champagne music" made him a TV phenomenon. Born in a sod farmhouse in North Dakota, Welk learned the accordion from his father and began performing professionally at 21. His weekly show on ABC was derided by some as schmaltzy, but its easy-listening quality charmed millions from 1955 to '71. Said Welk of his style of music: "You have to play what the people understand."

CORNELIUS VANDERBILT WHITNEY, 93, descendant of Eli Whitney and Cornelius Vanderbilt who co-founded Pan Am with a $3,150 stake.

C.V. WOOD, 71, master planner who pioneered the development of major theme parks from Disneyland to Six Flags over Texas. As Disneyland's first employee, Wood oversaw the site selection and construction of the park. After leaving Disney, he supervised the creation of the first Six Flags theme park, in Arlington, Texas, and the moving of London Bridge to Arizona. ∎

INDEX

MacMillan, Sir Kenneth, 193
Mcowen, Alex, 180
McTeague, 175, 179
Macy, R.H. (retailer), 5
Madonna, 23, 33, 175
Mahdi Mohammed, Ali, 60
Major, John, 10, 84, 86, 89, 150
Mala, Spiro, 181
Malcolm X, 177
Malfitano, Catherine, 179
Mamet, David, 177, 180
Mammography, 13
Mardi Gras, New Orleans, 7
Marriage, feminism and, 145-146
Martin Marietta, 91
Martinu, Bohuslav, 187
Matisse, Henri, retrospective, 182-184
Mayfield, Geoff, 179
Meinhold, Keith, 24
Merchant, Ismail, 176
Messiaen, Oliver, 194
Metropolitan Opera (New York), 179
Mexico, 19
MIAS, 22
Michelangelo computer virus, 9
Microsociety schools, 143
Milk, health effects, 23
Miller, Shannon, 167
Mills, Wilbur, 194
Milosevic, Slobodan, 27, 76, 126-127
Mitchell, Joseph, 187
Miyazawa, Kiichi, 4, 101, 150
Moldova, 70
Monetary easing, 95
Montagnier, Luc, 158, 159, 160
Montana, Joe, 189
Montenegro, 72, 76
Morton, Andrew, 15, 85
Morton, Jelly Roll, 181
Mount Pinatubo, 31, 148
Mount Spurr, 30
MTV, national elections and, 43, 186
Mulroney, Brian, 19, 23
Multiculturalism, 134-135
Murphy Brown, 12, 17, 135, 137, 174
Murphy, George, 194
Musawi, Sheik Abbas, 6
Museum of Modern Art, 182-184
Music, 178-179, 187
Musical theater, 180-181
Muslims, 3, 27, 72-74
Myers, Dee Dee, 108

N

Nagorno-Karabakh, 70
Narasimha Rao, P.V., 27
NASA, 19, 148
National debt, 95
National Endowment for the Arts, 7
Nelson, Christian, 194
New Jersey, 61
New Orleans, Mardi Gras, 7
Nicaragua, 30
Nicholas, Nicholas J., 7
Nirvana, 5, 175, 179
Niyazov, Saparmurad, 82
Nobel prizes, 28-29

Noriega, Manuel, 11
North American Free Trade Agreement
    (NAFTA), 19, 70
Novoselic, Chris, 179
Nunavut, 12
Nunn, Sam, 38
Nutrition, 149, 156

O

Oakley, Robert, 60
Obituaries, 190-194
Oceans, pollution, 153
O'Connor, Sandra Day, 16
O'Connor, Sinéad, 21, 22, 32, 174, 175
Off-Broadway theater, 180-181
Oleanna, 180, 188
Olympia & York, 12
Olympics, 162-173
    basketball, 189
    gold medal winners, 173
    Summer Games, 17, 166-173, 189
    Winter Games, 7, 162-165, 173
Ondaatje, Michael, 186
O'Neal, Shaquille, 189
Oort, Jan, 194
Opera, American, 179
Operation Rescue, 64
Operation Restore Hope, 2, 51, 58-61
Oriole Park, Baltimore, Md., 188
Osborn, June, 158, 161
Ozone hole, 148

P/Q

Pacino, Al, 177, 181
Pandas, giant, 27
Panic, Milan, 27, 76
Paris (rap artist), 175
Parker-Bowles, Camilla, 33, 85
Parks, Bert, 194
Parnis, Molly, 194
Patten, Chris, 23
Pauling, Linus, 155-156
Perkins, Anthony, 194
Perot, Ross
    800 number, 43
    appeal of, 35, 174
    campaign, 6, 14, 50
    charges against Bush, 14, 46
    debates, 22, 32, 48
    election polls, 12, 41, 43, 44
    election results, 24, 37-38, 104
    election timeline, 40-41
    infomercials, 43
    profile, 42-43
    reentrance into race, 20, 22, 46-47
    talk shows and, 6, 43, 128
    withdrawal from race, 16, 44
Peru, 10, 20-21
Pfeiffer, Michelle, 177
Phar-Mor, 19
Philippines, 24, 31
Picon, Molly, 194
Pierrepont, Albert, 194
Planned Parenthood, 64
Plant, Mike, 194
Player, The, 176
Poindexter, John, 27

Poling, Harold, 100
Pollution, of oceans, 153
Ponomarenko, Sergei, 165
Post Office, 19
Powell, Charles, 89
Powell, Mike, 170
POWS, 22
Presley, Elvis, stamp, 14
Previn, Soon-Yi Farrow, 132-133
Price, Richard, 186
Price, Sammy, 194
Primaries, 6, 8, 10, 12, 14, 37-41
Primerica, 21
Prime Suspect, 186
Prince, Faith, 181
Procter & Gamble, 23
Pucci de Barsento, Emilio, 194
Quayle, Dan, 33, 128
    debates, 48
    family values (*Murphy Brown*), 12, 17,
        39, 135, 137, 139, 174
Quayle, Marilyn, 138
Quebec, 22-23
Queensrÿche, 179
Quigley, Robert Wellington, 188-189

R

Rabin, Yitzhak, 18
Race, 134-135
Radice, Anee-Imelda, 7
Rain forests, 152, 153
Raise the Red Lantern, 175, 185
Ray, Satyajit, 194
Reagan, Ronald, 18, 46
Rea, Stephen, 180
Redford, Robert, 176
Redgrave, Vanessa, 177
Redmond, Derek, 189
Reggie, Anne, 17
Reilly, William, 154
Religion, 25, 140
Republican Convention, 18, 46, 135, 137-
    138
Revolution from Within, 145
Rheaume, Manon, 21, 189
Richmond, George, 143
Riots, Los Angeles, 2, 10, 50, 112-113, 135
Ripert, Jean, 152-153
River Runs Through It, A, 176
Robbins, Tim, 176
Robertson, Pat, 32
Roe v. Wade, 10, 16, 51, 63-65
Ronstadt, Linda, 21
Roping the Wind, 178
Ross, Steve, 7, 194-195
RU 486, 23
Runyon, Marvin T., 19
Russia, 4, 6, 14, 27, 70, 78-82
Rutherford, Skip, 108

S

Salerno, Anthony (Fat Tony), 195
Salinas de Gortari, Carlos, 19
Salk, Jonas, 158
Salk, Lee, 195
Sanders, Summer, 170
Sargent, Claire, 32

INDEX

CREDITS

Note: When two pictures appear on a single page, they are credited from top to bottom or left to right. If more than two appear, credits run clockwise from top left of page.